TED PHILIPAKOS

ON LEVEL TERMS

10 Legal Battles That Tested and Shaped Soccer in the Modern Era

Cover and interior design by Monica Alejo/Ankerwycke.

In 1215, the Magna Carta was signed underneath the ancient Ankerwycke Yew tree, starting the process that led to rule by constitutional law—in effect, giving rights and the law to the people. Today, the ABA's Ankerwycke line of books continues to bring the law to the people. With legal fiction, true crime books, popular legal histories, public policy handbooks, and prescriptive guides to current legal and business issues, Ankerwycke is a contemporary and innovative line of books for everyone from a trusted and vested authority.

Printed in the United States of America.

18 17 16 15   5 4 3 2 1

Library of Congress Cataloging-in-Publication Data

Philipakos, Ted, author.
  On level terms : 10 legal battles that tested and shaped soccer in the modern era / Ted Philipakos.
    pages cm
  Includes bibliographical references and index.
  ISBN 978-1-62722-286-0 (alk. paper)
  1. Sports--Law and legislation--United States. 2. Soccer--Law and legislation--United States. 3. Soccer--Law and legislation. 4. Soccer--Law and legislation--Cases. I. Title.
  KF3989.P45 2015
  344'.099--dc23
                    2014041314

Discounts are available for books ordered in bulk. Special consideration is given to state bars, CLE programs, and other bar-related organizations. Inquire at Book Publishing, ABA Publishing, American Bar Association, 321 N. Clark Street, Chicago, Illinois 60654-7598.

www.ShopABA.org]

ON LEVEL TERMS

10 Legal Battles That Tested and Shaped
Soccer in the Modern Era

ACKNOWLEDGMENTS

TO MY FRIENDS AND COLLEAGUES in the soccer business in the States and in Greece, from players to agents to club staff to journalists, I am ever grateful for your continuing respect and support. Without you, I would have no place in the game that I love.

To everyone at New York University's Tisch Institute for Sports Management, Media and Business, thank you for making me a part of this amazing school. To four of my colleagues in particular—Bob Boland, Dave Hollander, Lee Igel, and Wayne McDonnell, all former professors of mine—the examples you've set and the knowledge and passion you've shared has had a tremendous impact on me. And to my students—our work makes me better all the time and our relationships have truly enriched my life.

To my editor, Jon Malysiak, I'm forever indebted to you for giving me the opportunity to take on this passion project. And without your positivity and encouragement, I may not have been able to get through it. I also want to thank my research assistants, Kaveh Akbari and Rocco Totino, for making important contributions when I really needed them. Others invaluable to the writing process include Miles Davis, John Coltrane, Lee Morgan, Wayne Shorter, Art Blakey, Dexter Gordon, Charles Mingus, Herbie Hancock, Bill Evans and more.

And to my family—my parents, and Peter and Natasha—simply put, absolutely nothing is possible without you.

FOREWORD

By Garth Lagerwey

General Manager of Major League Soccer's Seattle Sounders

I FIRST MET TED AT A RESTAURANT in Salt Lake City a few years ago. He was representing a Greek player who had been on trial with us. After watching him for a week, we knew this player was a good person, but not a great player. Over dinner, Ted nearly convinced me that was enough to sign the player. While we eventually passed on that opportunity, Ted did get the player signed with another team and I left with a profound respect for his thought process and acumen. We kept in touch, and Ted pursued a kind of career I would want to follow if I didn't have my current job. In addition to his work as an international player agent, he became a professor teaching sports management, which just sounds cool and is the type of class that I would have clamored to attend as an undergrad. Even a brief conversation with my academic advisor would lend some perspective as to how high a compliment that is. I didn't believe in attempting to think before noon and soccer practice started at 3:30pm, so that didn't leave a wide window for classes, but I would have gone to a Philipakos lecture at the crack of dawn.

In some respects it is strange to think of Ted now as an accomplished author. This is not a result of any doubt regarding his writing credentials, but rather my obsession with the movie *Ted*. I have a tendency to chuckle to myself as I picture Mr. Philipakos as a literary incarnation of that irascible teddy bear waxing poetic upon legal issues of the day. It is with a certain relief that I read entire chapters without stumbling upon any vulgarities. Of course, anyone named after the former king of Macedonia, the man who fathered and laid the groundwork for the greatest empire of its age, deserves more serious consideration.

To that end, I enjoyed perusing Ted's book. Having personally lived through the first chapter on *Fraser v. MLS* as the union spokesperson for the case, it was both grueling and gripping to recall those events. Ted gives a lucid and balanced account that makes both the events of the case and the caselaw understandable and accessible. That pattern repeats itself as he ranges across the U.S. and Europe examining how modern soccer became what it is today. When you work in the trenches of player contracts and transfers as Ted and I do, it is easy to forget how some of the madness involved in those deals comes into being. The legal foundation for one of a handful of the world's few functioning truly global systems is both intricate and interesting, and I enjoyed Ted's account and the detail he provides.

Whether taken from a king's perspective or that of Seth MacFarlane, I think Ted has done a service to a broad audience in providing a new avenue for all readers who obsess over every kick of the ball on the weekend to better understand the foundations of this beautiful game. And for that, I thank him.

INTRODUCTION

PROFESSIONAL FOOTBALL OR SOCCER HAS for decades been and continues to be conditioned by the law in countless ways. As such, an understanding of the evolution and operation of the game is not complete without an understanding of certain landmark court decisions and fundamental legal principles. Your favorite European club's transfer market dealings? They can be traced directly back to *Bosman*. Are you a fan of Major League Soccer? It might be a completely different league if not for *Fraser*. And the list goes on.

On Level Terms sets out to explain and put into context a selection of key cases and concepts, and to do so in an accessible style. Altogether, this book explores several aspects of the game—including the organization and regulations of leagues and governing bodies; the finances of clubs; the market for players; racism; violence; concussions; and broadcasting—and several areas of law—including antitrust or competition law; labor law; contract law; bankruptcy law; tort law; and media and intellectual property law.

On Level Terms opens in the United States (Chapters 1–5) and then shifts over to Europe (Chapters 6–10). This division was made because of important differences between American law and European law and between American soccer and European football. Having said that, skipping around is encouraged, if it suits your interest.

In Chapter 1, *Fraser* establishes the foundation of Major League Soccer, which is now entering its 20th season. Chapters 2 and 3 delve into the tumultuous history of Major League Soccer's predecessor, the North American Soccer League, which existed from 1968 to 1984. Chapters 4 and 5 examine two recent cases. *ChampionsWorld*, which arose out of the staging of international exhibitions in the United States, posed a challenge to the scope of the United States Soccer Federation's authority over professional soccer and its relationship with Major League Soccer. *Namoff* is an ongoing concussion lawsuit that has the attention of all of American soccer.

Chapters 6 and 7 are based in English football. *R v. Terry* is the well-publicized racial abuse case against former England captain John Terry. *HMRC v. The Football League* deals with the alarming rise in club insolvencies and their significant public cost. Chapter 8 is dedicated to *Bosman*, Europe's most famous sports law case, which ultimately secured players' freedom of movement and completely revolutionized the game. In Chapter 9, UEFA regulations that provide for the punishment of clubs for the conduct of their supporters are challenged before the Court of Arbitration for Sport in Switzerland. Finally, *UEFA and FIFA v. Commission* tested the public's access to the World Cup and European Championship on free television.

My hope is that *On Level Terms* proves to be an enlightening and entertaining read for everyone from industry professionals and attorneys to law students to fans around the world with an interest in the history and inner workings of the game.

Comments? Tweet them to me: @tphilipakos.

Chapter 1

FRASER V. MLS

POETICALLY, IT WAS ON AMERICA'S Independence Day, 4 July 1988, that the United States Soccer Federation, the governing body of soccer in the United States, was awarded the right to host the 1994 FIFA World Cup. In consideration for that award, U.S. Soccer promised to establish a proper first division professional soccer league in the United States as soon as possible. Two years later, Alan Rothenberg, a prominent attorney at Latham & Watkins, was elected as president of U.S. Soccer; he would oversee both the staging of the World Cup and the development of a new league, which would come to be known as Major League Soccer. FIFA, somewhat controversially, had pressed for the election of Rothenberg, who had previously organized the stunningly successful 1984 Olympic soccer tournament. Rothenberg's election would prove to be a pivotal moment in American soccer history.

By the early 1990s, the National Football League (NFL) had already emerged as the country's most popular sports league; Major League Baseball (MLB), despite being bruised by labor battles, was still "America's pastime" and was not far behind; and the National Basketball Association (NBA) and National Hockey League (NHL) were in the midst of major growth periods, fueled by star power and aggressive marketing; while soccer, in any form, barely registered in the American sports consciousness. The country's last notable professional soccer league, the North American Soccer League (NASL), was a fairly distant memory, having folded in the mid-1980s after less than two decades of play that had occasional bright moments but relatively marginal impact. As American soccer historian David Wangerin wrote in *Soccer in a Football World*, most people exhibited "at best indifference and at worst cold-blooded hostility to what they still saw as a foreign game, one they had never seen played to any standard." An American soccer subculture existed, but it was small, fragmented, and struggling for engagement with the game. In the World Cup, many hoped for a tipping point. Rothenberg argued this was America's last chance to become a soccer nation.

While the World Cup was being organized, Rothenberg set to work on planning the new league, along with Sunil Gulati, a Columbia University economics professor, and Mark Abbott, an attorney recruited by Rothenberg from Latham & Watkins.[1] Indeed, the American World Cup would be a rousing success, achieving total and average attendance records that still stand today. But Rothenberg always understood that even if the tournament did generate a burst of momentum for the sport, that momentum, no matter how expertly harnessed, would not sustain a new league and give it a real foothold in the American sports marketplace. The competitive environment was daunting. The specter of the sport's past failure loomed large. Without question, this was a venture teeming with risk. As such, the league's architects took on a conservative approach, seeking, above all else, stability. More specifically, they focused on positioning the new league such that it might enjoy slow, steady growth, while minimizing risk by avoiding the business and legal pitfalls inherent in the traditional model sports league. To achieve this, Rothenberg would decide that it was necessary to abandon the traditional model altogether.

MAJOR LEAGUE SOCCER AND THE SINGLE ENTITY MODEL

Rothenberg envisioned Major League Soccer as a "single entity" league. Whereas the traditional model sports league—e.g., the NFL, MLB, the NBA, and the NHL—is generally an association of separately owned and independently operated member clubs, the single entity model league features common ownership and centralized operation. In an interview for Beau Dure's *Long-Range Goals: The Success Story of Major League Soccer*, Rothenberg stated:

> I had thought of [the single entity model] years before when I was doing a lot of work with the NBA and other leagues and was a sports lawyer and commentator and saw all the day-to-day structural problems resulting from the way other leagues were created and felt that if I ever had the chance to start a league from scratch,

that would be the right structure. . . . Starting with a blank slate, it made the most sense from a business standpoint.

Gulati added:

I think a number of the investors in the league fully believed that we needed something different to get the league off the ground and stabilized, and that was the notion behind the single entity structure. If, in its infancy, you weren't going to have that model, the league didn't make economic sense.

In February 1995, Major League Soccer (MLS) was formed as a limited liability company under Delaware law. MLS would own the league's clubs, maintain league and club intellectual property and broadcast rights, control league and club operations, and directly employ and compensate players, among other uniquely centralized features. MLS investors would manage the league's business affairs through a management committee and would share the league's profits and losses based on their respective ownership interests.

The traditional model breeds certain fundamental business concerns. The individual clubs do not necessarily share perfectly aligned interests prompting consistent action in the best interests of the league as a whole, which is particularly problematic because any individual club's practices may have a significant ripple effect throughout the league. Further, any individual club's economic instability is likely to jeopardize the success of other clubs and the league as a whole. As MLS organizers were well aware, these were among the principal factors in the NASL's demise. The NASL was marked by a lack of control, as expansion, financial and competitive balance, and player spending all went unchecked. The NASL's marquee club was the New York Cosmos, under the ownership of entertainment conglomerate Warner Communications, which spent lavishly to assemble and promote glittering teams—famously including Pelé and Franz Beckenbauer, two iconic players—that attracted spectacular crowds in the late 1970s. As other clubs were spurred to compete, they would spend to unsustainable levels. Meanwhile, interest in the league slowly waned. Overexpansion and financial and competitive disparity certainly damaged the product, though some, including David Wangerin, considered whether the country's early interest was simply a fad that was inevitably destined to fade. Across the league, millions of dollars in losses mounted, year after year. In 1978 and 1979, every NASL club operated at a loss; in 1979, aggregate losses exceeded $20 million, the highest in the league's history. The early 1980s saw a wave of club collapses. In 1980, the league featured 24 clubs; by 1983, only 12 clubs were still standing, and just barely. Even the Cosmos suffered a fall from grace—Pelé retired, attendance dwindled, and Warner faced serious financial troubles in some of its other business lines. In 1984, the league tried to stem the tide by establishing a salary cap and other cost controls, but it was too little, too late. After the 1984 season, the NASL ceased operations.

One NASL figure that had pleaded for collective restraint was Lamar Hunt. The American sports pioneer was a founder of the NASL, the owner of the league's Dallas franchise (the Tornado), and a presence that gave credibility to the league. In 1981, Hunt made several proposals to control costs—specifically, to increase the number of American and Canadian players on the field (thereby weaning clubs off of expensive foreign talent), to establish a $20,000 average salary for North American players, and to limit losses to $400,000 per team. The proposals were not adopted, and Hunt would dissolve the Tornado at the end of the season. Over 15 years in the NASL, Hunt lost approximately $20 million—yet he would become a founding investor in MLS. Hunt drew confidence from MLS's single entity model, telling the *New York Times* that it was "much more viable and intelligent" than the NASL's traditional model.

MLS organizers would use the single entity model to concentrate decision making on the best interests of the league as a whole, with particular emphasis on exercising control over league growth, product development and marketing, competitive balance, and labor costs. Indeed, the model's heaviest impact would be felt in the player market. With common ownership, MLS could readily eliminate competition among its clubs for players, and thereby significantly suppress player compensation. In a statement years later, MLS commissioner Don Garber would confirm, remarkably bluntly, "MLS was founded on the principle that our owners would not be competing against each other for a player's services."

While such an extreme form of player market restraint is uniquely available to a single entity league with common ownership, traditional model leagues have for many years established various restraints on player mobility and player compensation (e.g., free agency restrictions, salary caps, and individual salary restrictions). However, the traditional model leagues—most notably, the NFL, NBA, and NHL—have had to establish such player market restraints, as well as other desired restraints (e.g., club ownership restrictions, including sale and relocation restrictions), with some exposure to attack under antitrust law. As commentators debate the economic value of the traditional model versus the single entity model, it is clear that the traditional model's primary weakness is an inherent antitrust vulnerability. In contrast, the single entity model is at once both a means to facilitate implementation of certain desired practices and a means to shield those practices from antitrust scrutiny.

ANTITRUST LAW AND TRADITIONAL MODEL SPORTS LEAGUES

As described by Tulane University law professor Gabe Feldman, the role of antitrust law (widely referred to as competition law outside of the United States) is "to act as a gatekeeper, ferreting out anticompetitive conduct." More specifically, antitrust law is designed to promote competition and prevent unfair practices that may lead to monopolies or suppression of competition. The principal U.S. antitrust statute is the Sherman Antitrust Act. For professional sports leagues, the Sherman Act provision of greatest concern has been Section 1, which declares to be illegal "[e]very contract, combination . . . or conspiracy, in restraint of trade or commerce,"[2] though courts have settled on prohibiting only "unreasonable" restraints of trade. A restraint (e.g., a professional sports league's free agency restriction) is "unreasonable" if its anticompetitive effects (e.g., reducing players' choice of employers and earning potential) outweigh its procompetitive benefits (e.g., promoting competitive balance, which enhances the league product and maximizes fan interest and league revenues). Section 2 targets any entity that "shall monopolize, or attempt to monopolize, or combine or conspire . . . to monopolize."[3]

Thus, the Sherman Act creates a distinction between concerted action and unilateral action. Section 1 requires a "contract, combination . . . or conspiracy," which requires an agreement between at least two entities, otherwise there can be no violation; Section 2 only requires action by a single entity. This distinction is particularly important because it can be significantly easier to prove a violation of Section 1 than a violation of Section 2.[4] The Sherman Act was designed to respond to concerted action more strictly than unilateral action because, as the U.S. Supreme Court noted in *Copperweld Corp. v. Independence Tube Corp.*, concerted action "inherently is fraught with anticompetitive risk."[5] Therefore, it becomes advantageous for an enterprise to be viewed as a single entity rather than consisting of multiple entities. For this reason, traditional model sports leagues have repeatedly argued that, despite being comprised of separately owned and independently operated member clubs, they are in fact single entities and thus incapable of violating Section 1. This argument, though, has consistently been rejected.

Copperweld has represented the Supreme Court's most definitive treatment of the distinction between concerted action and unilateral action under the Sherman Act. In *Copperweld*, the Court decided that a corporation and its wholly owned subsidiary were a single entity whose coordinated actions were not violative of Section 1. The Court defined concerted action as that which "deprives the marketplace of the independent centers of decisionmaking that competition assumes and demands."[6] The Court reasoned that a parent and its wholly owned subsidiary constitute a single entity insofar as they share a "complete unity of interest,"[7] where "[t]heir objectives are common, not disparate, and their general corporate objectives are guided or determined not by two separate corporate consciousnesses, but one," much like a "team of horses . . . under the control of a single driver."[8] With such unity of interest, parties are more properly "viewed as a single economic unit."[9] The Court did not consider the single entity status of any other corporate relationships. Subsequently, lower courts would use *Copperweld* to extend single entity status beyond a parent and its wholly owned subsidiary, but, without clear guidance, the courts have applied the opinion in differing ways and produced differing single entity tests.

Despite such evolving and expanding application, courts have overwhelmingly refused to grant single entity status to traditional model sports leagues, thereby holding the concerted actions of their member clubs within the scope of Section 1. In so ruling, courts have typically focused on the fact that the member clubs of traditional model sports leagues are independently owned and operated businesses that are actual or potential competitors for players, coaches, management personnel, fan support, and certain revenues. Such a view has been maintained despite acknowledgment of the unique nature of the business of professional sports leagues, which is fundamentally dependent upon some degree of agreement and joint action among member clubs. Moreover, it is recognized that each member club has a stake in the success of the other member clubs and the league as a whole, a semblance of an economic unity of interests. Nonetheless, traditional model sports leagues have failed to qualify for single entity status and exemption from Section 1. Instead, traditional model sports leagues have typically been classified as joint ventures—a business structure in which multiple, distinct, and sometimes competing entities jointly engage in some economic activity—whose intra-venture concerted activity is subject to Section 1 and deemed unlawful when anticompetitive effects are measured to outweigh procompetitive benefits.

Alan Rothenberg, after consulting with antitrust counsel on these issues, ultimately concluded that a league properly structured as a single entity might pass a "unity of interest" test and protect its desired practices from antitrust scrutiny under Section 1.

MLS TAKES SHAPE

MLS organizers presumed that the single entity model, with its theoretical business and legal advantages and its overarching principle of shared risk and reward, would be especially attractive to potential league investors. To some extent, it was. However, a practical problem would come to light. Wealthy entrepreneurs generally found the individual control and public stature that traditionally came with sports property ownership to be highly desirable. As a result, initial investment interest in the league was relatively modest. Alan Rothenberg discussed the issue with Beau Dure:

> The interesting story about trying to sell it—when I first got out trying to raise money, I of course went to [Yankees owner] George Steinbrenner in New York, who looked at this thing and huffed that this is communism. About a year and a half later, somehow our investment book got to him through somebody else, and he called me, and it was in the midst of the baseball strike. Our business plan hadn't changed; it was still single-entity. And he said to me, this is brilliant! I sat there laughing. The same plan was communism one day, and a year and a half later it was brilliant.

But that kind of does tell you the story as far as what the reaction to single-entity was from various business people. It ranged from exactly that—communism to a brilliant concept. The typical sports owner is a great entrepreneur and generally a pretty strong individual. To introduce him to a concept that somehow restrains individualism to a certain extent was in some cases foreign to their way of doing business.

MLS would be forced to compromise.

Eventually, the league would halve its entry fee to $5 million and create a new class of stock for "investor-operators," who would gain significant operational control over the clubs in their respective areas. Under their original operating agreement, investor-operators would hire and pay the salaries of their coaches and management personnel and would pay all of their local office and local promotion costs and one-half of their stadium costs. In addition, they would license local broadcast rights, sell home game tickets, and conduct local marketing on behalf of the league. Although the league would still directly employ players and allocate them to clubs, investor-operators would have some ability to select their own players through the league's amateur draft and through intra-league trades (and player selection would soon expand). In return for their services, the league would pay investor-operators a management fee largely corresponding to their respective club's performance. The management fee would equal

> the sum of one-half of local tickets and concessions; the first $1,125,000 of local broadcast revenues, increasing annually by a percentage rate, plus a 30 percent share (declining to 10 percent by 2006) of any amount above the base amount; all revenues from overseas tours; a share of one-half the net revenues from the MLS Championship Game and a share of revenues from other exhibition games.[10]

Although the league still owned the clubs, investor-operators would be able to transfer their operating rights, with certain limits, and retain much of the value generated through their individual operations and investment in their respective clubs.

Despite carving out this special class of stock, much of the single entity model remained in place. The investor-operators would control the majority of seats on the league's board, which would be responsible for centralized operations such as hiring the commissioner and approving national broadcast contracts and marketing decisions, league rules and policies (including team budgets), and investment interest transfers. Further, the league would be responsible for all expenses not borne by individual investor-operators directly, and the league would distribute to its investors in equal portions all revenues remaining after investor-operator management fees. To be sure, though, MLS no longer had a pure single entity model.

The launch of MLS had to be pushed back from 1995 to 1996, but soon enough ownership capital reached a healthy $75 million, broadcast and sponsorship contracts were finalized, playing facilities were prepared, and coaches and players were recruited. Ultimately, MLS settled on ten original clubs—seven under the control of investor-operators and three to initially be run by the league. Lamar Hunt would operate two clubs, in Kansas City and Columbus. On 6 April 1996, MLS officially kicked off, with the San Jose Clash defeating D.C. United, 1–0, before a national television audience on ESPN and a sellout crowd at San Jose State University's Spartan Stadium. The inaugural season would far exceed expectations, and optimism abounded.

But the best laid plans of professional sports leagues often go awry. One of Alan Rothenberg's primary fears would very soon be realized—an antitrust challenge from the league's players. And the league's tinkering with the single entity model would leave it in a precarious position.

PLAYER DISSATISFACTION

Amid the excitement surrounding MLS's first season, many of the league's players were dissatisfied. MLS had imposed an initial salary cap—more specifically, a limit on total player compensation for each club—of $1.135 million, which made for meager individual salaries. But this was not the main focus of the players' indignation. They were frustrated by a lack of fairness and good faith, accusing the league of taking a very hard line in initial contract negotiations and then backtracking on promises to renegotiate contracts after the first year. They were frustrated by a lack of security, as all contracts were nonguaranteed. Most of all, they were frustrated by the absence of a free player market. Mark Semioli, who was selected by the Los Angeles Galaxy in MLS's first amateur player draft, explained that limited compensation and security "would not be as egregious if you knew if the L.A. Galaxy didn't want you, that you could always talk to the [New York/New Jersey] MetroStars, or you could always talk to the Kansas City Wizards and say, 'Look, they just cut my contract, but can I sign with you?'"

MLS players had two options: to avail themselves of the benefits of either labor law or antitrust law. U.S. labor law—chiefly, the National Labor Relations Act[11]—gives employees the right to form a union to serve as their exclusive bargaining representative. Once a union is recognized, the law requires the employer(s) of unionized employees and the union representing those employees to bargain in "good faith" over wages, hours, and other terms and conditions of employment. In other words, as long as a collective bargaining relationship is in place, employers generally may not unilaterally impose terms and conditions of employment, at least not before good faith negotiations have reached an "impasse." The product of collective bargaining is shielded from attack under antitrust law by a doctrine known as the non-statutory labor exemption, which was designed to "give effect to federal labor laws and policies and allow meaningful collective bargaining to take place," as the Supreme Court stated in *Brown v. Pro Football*.[12] Thus, the traditional model sports leagues have generally established and protected various player mobility and player compensation restrictions through collective bargaining with players. In the alternative, by not forming a union (or dissolving an existing union[13]), employees may wield the antitrust sword as a means to gain leverage and secure desired gains.

The league's players chose not to unionize and moved towards litigation. They did not expect to be able to force meaningful change through collective bargaining with the league. They saw a strike as a nonviable option, because most players in the league had limited employment alternatives and thus limited ability to withstand a significant work stoppage. Garth Lagerwey, selected by D.C. United in the league's inaugural draft,[14] explained:

> If we unionized, the only threat we had was to strike, and that
> wasn't a credible threat . . . So the only mechanism we had to try
> to achieve a labor agreement was the threat of litigation. Any time
> you try to address a problem by suing somebody, it's probably a

bad idea. It's not the best way to mediate a solution, it's not the best way to solve a problem. . . . But having said that, the impression that we had—rightly or wrongly—was that the league was not going to negotiate with us under any circumstances. As a result, we felt that this was the only path that we had. . . . I can tell you unequivocally that was the impression that we had, that we simply had no other choice. Not only was the league not going to negotiate with us, but they were not going to speak to us.

The players would form a nonunion trade association, known as the Major League Soccer Players Association. Curiously, the MLS Players Association would come under the direction of the NFL Players Association (NFLPA).

In February 1997, less than a year after the launch of MLS, eight players sued the league under various antitrust theories. MLS executives were outraged over the suit in general and the NFLPA's role in particular. In a memo obtained by the *Newark Star-Ledger*, Doug Logan, the league's first commissioner, charged that the suit was "provoked, financed, led and encouraged by other actors in the sports labor movement"—namely, the NFLPA. Logan told *Soccer Digest*, "[The NFLPA is] a group that pretends to represent soccer players under contract. We do know that no MLS player under contract is paying for any lawyers or paying any dues." Don Garber, who succeeded Logan, would later tell *Bloomberg News* that the NFLPA was "hellbent to break single entity." After all, the NFL had been on a quest for single entity status and antitrust immunity for decades, so if there was even the slightest chance that an enhanced NFL single entity argument could grow out of any precedent derived from MLS, it would certainly be in the interest of the NFLPA to step in and nip it in the bud.

There were certain players who questioned the suit and the NFLPA's involvement. U.S. national team and D.C. United star Jeff Agoos[15] told Beau Dure:

A lot of people I knew really didn't want to go the lawsuit route. There was no stability in the league, we were all sort of in this together, and we wanted to make sure that the league was viable and that there was a place for players who came after us. The NFLPA really turned the screws . . . I always question why the NFL really were involved in this. . . . It just seemed like the NFL were trying to protect their own interests. I really question why they would want to represent us. I know they weren't doing it out of the goodness of their hearts. I had serious questions as to what they were in it for, and I just didn't agree with the lawsuit.

But the train had left the station.

FRASER V. MLS (DISTRICT COURT)

The players filed their complaint in the United States District Court for the District of Massachusetts and named Major League Soccer, the league's investor-operators, and U.S. Soccer as defendants. The complaint had three main prongs:

- In Count I, the players claimed that MLS and its investor-operators had combined to restrain trade in violation of Section 1 of the Sherman Act by contracting for player services centrally and effectively eliminating competition for players.
- In Count III, the players claimed that MLS monopolized, attempted to monopolize, or combined or conspired with U.S. Soccer to monopolize the market for Division I professional soccer players in the United States in violation of Section 2 of the Sherman Act.
- In Count IV, the players claimed that the actual formation of MLS violated Section 7 of the Clayton Act, which prohibits acquisitions or mergers the effect of which "may be substantially to lessen competition, or to tend to create a monopoly"[16] in any line of commerce.

MLS eventually moved for summary judgment—that is, judgment without a trial—on Counts I and IV. The players filed a cross-motion for summary judgment, seeking to block MLS from asserting a single entity defense on Count I.

U.S. District Judge George O'Toole Jr. ruled on the motions for summary judgment on 19 April 2000.[17] His analysis began with the players' Sherman Act Section 1 claim and the league's single entity defense. With his focus on the league's organizational form as a limited liability company, Judge O'Toole determined that "MLS's operations should . . . be analyzed as the operations of a single corporation would be, with its operator-investors treated essentially as officers and shareholders."[18] Therefore, he concluded that MLS and its investor-operators constituted a single entity, and activity between the league's members could not violate Section 1, unless the league's members act "not in the interest of the entity, but rather in their own self-interest."[19]

The players made several arguments aimed at proving that MLS investor-operators did in fact have divergent self-interest, which would invoke the "independent personal stake" exception to the single entity rule, but Judge O'Toole rejected each argument. The players noted that the investor-operators receive management fees that are calculated in large part according to their local club-generated revenues. Judge O'Toole countered that "[t]he management fee arrangement exists in addition to, not in place of the overall profit and loss sharing,"[20] and "successful local operation of a team benefits the entire league."[21] The players also pointed out that investor-operators have the ability to harvest the value of the clubs they operate by selling their operational rights. Judge O'Toole countered that "management fees and operational rights notwithstanding, every operator-investor has a strong incentive to make the league—and the other operator-investors—as robust as possible,"[22] because his personal stake "is not independent of the success of MLS as a whole enterprise."[23]

Judge O'Toole emphasized that he found MLS's player policies as the most compelling reason not to apply the independent personal stake exception. He stated:

> No operator has an individual player payroll to worry about; the league pays the salaries. Moreover, the MLS investor gets the lower-cost benefit in exchange for having surrendered the degree of autonomy that team owners in "plural entity" leagues typically enjoy. The reason an individual team owner in one of those other leagues is willing to bid up players' salaries to get the particular players it wants is because by paying high salaries to get desirable players, the owner can achieve other substantial benefits, such as increased sales of tickets and promotional goods, media revenues, and the like. The MLS operator-investors have largely yielded that opportunity to the central league office. Plainly, there are trade-offs in the different approaches. The MLS members have calculated that

the surrender of autonomy, together with the attendant benefit of lower and more controlled player payrolls and greater parity in talent among teams, will help MLS to succeed where others, notably NASL, failed. That is a calculation made on behalf of the entity, and it does not serve only the ulterior interests of the individual investors standing on their own.[24]

Although the players had highlighted a degree of investor-operator self-interest, in Judge O'Toole's view it was insufficient to apply the independent personal stake exception, which he maintained other courts in the circuit had applied conservatively.

The players also urged Judge O'Toole to look past MLS's organizational form, which they characterized as "a sham designed to allow what is actually an illegal combination of plural actors to masquerade as the business conduct of a single entity."[25] To make the argument, the players turned to *Copperweld*. As a reminder, *Copperweld* held that although a corporation and its wholly owned subsidiary were two distinct legal entities, the economic reality was that they functioned as a single enterprise, and as a result coordinated action between them was not violative of Section 1. In other words, the Supreme Court had stressed economic reality over organization form in its single entity analysis. Therefore, the players proposed that "the 'economic reality' test should be applied not only to ignore formal legal distinctions between separate corporations as the court did in *Copperweld*, but conversely to *envision* distinctions in what is formally a single legal entity when doing so would accurately describe how the business of the entity actually operates."[26] Judge O'Toole asserted the argument "may have some superficial appeal, but on close examination it appears that it rests on a misconception of the scope of the *Copperweld* principle."[27] Specifically, he found that "*Copperweld* does not support the proposition that a business organized as a single entity should have its form ignored, or its 'veil' pierced,"[28] for the purpose of Section 1 scrutiny, and "[m]erely posing that proposition suggests how troublesome it would be as a practical matter."[29] He added, "[p]ractical objections aside, the theory is also fundamentally incompatible with the axiom the *Copperweld* Court's analysis started with—that coordination of business activities within a single firm is not subject to scrutiny under § 1."[30]

Therefore, Judge O'Toole ruled in favor of the league on the players' Section 1 claim. In summary, he stated:

> MLS is what it is. As a single entity, it cannot conspire or combine with its investors in violation of § 1, and its investors do not combine or conspire with each other in pursuing the economic interests of the entity. MLS's policy of contracting centrally for player services is unilateral activity of a single firm. Since § 1 does not apply to unilateral activity—even unilateral activity that tends to restrain trade—the claim set forth in Count I cannot succeed as a matter of law.[31]

As Alan Rothenberg had envisioned, the single entity structure had successfully shielded MLS from Section 1 liability—at least for the moment.

Judge O'Toole also ruled in favor of the league on the players' Clayton Act Section 7 claim. As stated above, Section 7 of the Clayton Act prohibits acquisitions or mergers that may substantially reduce competition. But Judge O'Toole determined that the relevant test under Section 7 looks to whether competition has been reduced in *existing* markets, and, prior to the formation of MLS, there had been no active market for Division I professional soccer in the United States. Therefore, he concluded, despite the fact that MLS's structure reduced competition for players' services, "[t]here can be no § 7 liability because the formation of MLS did not involve the acquisition or merger of existing business enterprises, but rather the formation of an entirely new entity which itself represented the creation of an entirely new market."[32] He continued:

> Where there is no existing market, there can be no reduction in the level of competition. There are no negative numbers in this math; there is nothing lower than zero. Competition that does not exist cannot be decreased. The creation of MLS did not reduce competition in an existing market because when the company was formed there was no active market for Division I professional soccer in the United States.[33]

MLS had scored twice.

In September 2000, a three-month jury trial commenced on the players' remaining Sherman Act Section 2 claims. As previously stated, Section 2 of the Sherman Act is directed at any entity that "shall monopolize, or attempt to monopolize, or combine or conspire . . . to monopolize." The players made three Section 2 claims, alleging MLS *monopolized* the market for Division I professional soccer players in the United States; *attempted to monopolize* that market; and *combined or conspired with U.S. Soccer to monopolize* that market by preventing any other entity from being sanctioned as a Division I league or otherwise competing against MLS.

U.S. Soccer's sanctioning of MLS as the country's Division I league was, at best, a bit awkward. At the outset, there were three entities bidding for Division I status. In a December 1993 vote, U.S. Soccer selected its own president's bid, Alan Rothenberg's Major League Professional Soccer, Inc. (MLPS), which later became Major League Soccer. One of the competing bids came from the American Professional Soccer League (APSL), a league that was already in existence but was, without question, a minor league. Two years earlier, the APSL had applied for Division I status but was granted Division II status instead. The third bid came from an organization calling itself League One America, which intended to play something that hardly could be called soccer—with a field divided into color-coded zones, players confined to specific zones, a multiple-point scoring system based on the zone from which the shot came, and so on—and for that reason did not warrant serious consideration. In the end, MLPS received 18 votes, the APSL received 5 votes, and League One America received none. Rothenberg maintained that he did not participate substantively in U.S. Soccer's selection of the MLPS bid.

Now, seven years later, MLS players were arguing that MLS and U.S. Soccer, under Rothenberg's direction, had engaged in a conspiracy to suppress competition from the APSL as part of a greater conspiracy to suppress competition for players' services. The players further argued that the APSL was a fully viable league and as such should have been granted Division I status alongside if not instead of MLS. None of these arguments would be convincing. There was no evidence to suggest that Rothenberg had exerted undue influence on the vote, and there was no evidence to suggest that U.S. Soccer had otherwise improperly selected MLS as the country's Division I league. Moreover, it was clearly apparent that the APSL was far from a viable league.

As *Soccer America*'s Ridge Mahoney wrote, "That the APSL, which consisted of seven teams at the time [of the December 1993 sanctioning vote], could have some day attained the status of a full-fledged professional league if not for the U.S. Soccer decree is far-fetched, if not ludicrous." The argument for two Division I leagues was simply not reasonable. "If there were two competing leagues, the quality of play would have been so pathetic, it would have been gone overnight," said Rothenberg in his testimony. "There weren't enough players to go around." This was difficult to refute. The jury's decision, though, would not be based on any of these issues.

A monopolization claim (the players' first Section 2 claim) requires a plaintiff to prove that the defendant (1) possesses monopoly power, which is generally defined as the power to control prices or exclude competition, and (2) has engaged in some wrongful conduct by which the monopoly power in question was acquired, preserved, or abused. An attempt to monopolize claim (the players' second Section 2 claim) requires a plaintiff to prove the defendant (1) has the intent to achieve monopoly power and (2) is engaging in some wrongful conduct with a dangerous probability of achieving monopoly power. In making either claim, to establish the existence or possibility of monopoly power, the plaintiff must define the relevant market. A number of courts have also required proof of a relevant market to sustain a conspiracy to monopolize claim (the players' third Section 2 claim), as Judge O'Toole did here. Every relevant market has a product dimension and a geographic dimension. In *Fraser*, the players alleged the relevant product market was all Division I professional players and the relevant geographic market was the United States. But the jury ultimately rejected the alleged market.

At the close of evidence, Judge O'Toole submitted a 15-question special verdict form to the jury, and on 11 December 2000, the jury returned its verdict after answering only the first two questions, finding the relevant product market to be all professional players, not just Division I professional players, and the relevant geographic market to be worldwide, not just the United States. Judge O'Toole had directed the jury to end its inquiry on all Section 2 claims if it found that the players had failed to prove the existence of their market. Most significant, and contentious, was the relevant geographic market question. MLS had argued that professional players had alternative opportunities for employment in international leagues as well as the A-League, as the APSL had since become known, and indoor leagues in the United States. With respect to international opportunities, while certain leagues might only be available to a limited number of players, due to work permit issues or other factors, MLS offered testimony that its players had, prior to or after joining MLS, played in 67 professional soccer leagues of different divisions from 46 countries. With respect to other domestic opportunities, MLS testified that several players had actually turned down MLS contracts to play in the A-League or an indoor league. Generally, the average player often had a choice between being a role player in MLS or a star player in the A-League or an indoor league. In the eyes of the jury, MLS had successfully demonstrated a broad labor market, one in which MLS did not possess monopoly power. The players' failure to establish their alleged market doomed their Section 2 claims, regardless of any alleged wrongful conduct that might satisfy an element of the cause of action. After the jury answered the relevant market questions, Judge O'Toole dismissed all three Section 2 claims.

The players appealed the summary judgment on the Sherman Act Section 1 and Clayton Act Section 7 claims and the jury verdict on the Sherman Act Section 2 claims.

FRASER V. MLS (COURT OF APPEALS)

Fraser's next venue was the United States Court of Appeals for the First Circuit, which hears appeals from the U.S. District Courts in Maine, Massachusetts, New Hampshire, Puerto Rico, and Rhode Island. On 20 March 2002, more than five years after the players filed their initial complaint, the First Circuit issued its opinion.[34]

Most significant was the Sherman Act Section 1 question. At the outset, the First Circuit noted that circuit precedent rejected single entity status for traditional model sports leagues, citing *Sullivan v. NFL*.[35] Of course, MLS was something different, and the district court had recognized it as a single entity, relying on *Copperweld*. Upon review, however, the First Circuit determined that the case for granting single entity status to MLS had "not been established."[36] In its analysis, it saw two functional differences between this case and *Copperweld* that were significant for antitrust policy. It focused specifically on the investor-operators' diversity of interests and their control over the league.

First, the First Circuit found that MLS clubs had "a diversity of entrepreneurial interests that goes well beyond the ordinary company."[37] The court observed:

> MLS and its operator/investors have separate contractual relationships giving the operator/investors rights that take them part way along the path to ordinary sports team owners: they do some independent hiring and make out-of-pocket investments in their own teams; they retain a large portion of the revenues from the activities of their teams; and each has limited sale rights in its own team that relate to specific assets and not just shares in the common enterprise. One might well ask why the formal difference in corporate structure should warrant treating MLS differently than the National Football League or other traditionally structured sports leagues.[38]

Therefore, MLS clubs did not possess the "unity of interests" required under *Copperweld*, but were in actual or potential competition with each other. MLS had established the investor-operator arrangement in its efforts to attract capital, but the arrangement had produced an antitrust vulnerability.

Second, the First Circuit found that the investor-operators were "not mere servants of MLS,"[39] but "effectively, they control it, having the majority of votes on the managing board,"[40] and "where, as here, the stockholders are themselves potential competitors,"[41] an "especially serious"[42] problem arises. It described MLS has having two roles: "one as an entrepreneur with its own assets and revenues; the other (arguably) as a nominally vertical device for producing horizontal coordination, i.e., limiting competition among operator/investors."[43] The court explained that such agreements, between competing entities that have the ability to make decisions, are a distinct concern of antitrust law. It stated:

> Whatever efficiencies may be thought likely where a single entrepreneur makes decisions for a corporate entity (or set of connected entities), the presumption is relaxed—and may in some contexts be reversed—where separate entrepreneurial interests can collaborate; the fixing of above market prices by sellers is the paradigm.[44]

The court added that "[t]his does not make MLS a mere front for price fix-ing, but it does distinguish *Copperweld* by introducing further danger."[45] The district court's application of single entity status had been firmly rejected.

So, if not a single entity, then what? The answer was, a hybrid. The First Circuit concluded that "MLS and its operator/investors comprise a hybrid arrangement, somewhere between a single company (with or without wholly owned subsidiaries) and a cooperative arrangement between existing com-petitors."[46] Next, the court considered the possible approaches to such an arrangement for the purposes of Section 1 analysis. In so doing, it articulated a practical problem: "Once one goes beyond the classic single enterprise, including *Copperweld* situations, it is difficult to find an easy stopping point or even decide on the proper functional criteria for hybrid cases."[47] Ulti-mately, the court determined that the question did not need to be answered. In its view, regardless of the answer, the jury verdict on the relevant market precluded a victory for the players on the Section 1 claim. It explained:

> In all events, we conclude that the single entity problem need not be answered definitively in this case. The case for expanding *Cop-perweld* is debatable and, more so, the case for applying the single entity label to MLS. But even if we assume that section 1 applies, it is clear to us that the venture cannot be condemned by per se rules and presents at best a debatable case under the rule of rea-son. More significantly, as structured by plaintiffs themselves, this case would have been lost at trial based on the jury's rejection of plaintiffs' own market definition.[48]

The players' case had been tripped up.

The First Circuit's references to "per se rules" and the "rule of reason" concerned two Section 1 standards of review. Per se analysis is applied to certain agreements that are classified as inherently anticompetitive—e.g., price-fixing agreements, which are presumed to be per se illegal regardless of procompetitive effects or motives. Here, the First Circuit found that rejection of the per se rule was "straightforward."[49] Rule of reason analysis is applied to all other agreements—including, in most cases, professional sports leagues' agreements—and is used to determine whether the challenged agreement sup-presses or promotes competition, by weighing anticompetitive effects against procompetitive effects. Under rule of reason analysis, the plaintiff bears the initial burden of showing that the challenged action had an anticompetitive effect in a relevant market. In this case, the relevant market requirement was crucial, since the jury had already rejected the relevant market alleged by the players. "In theory, there may be a broader market which plaintiffs might show (without contradicting the jury findings) in which unrestricted salary competition between the MLS operator/investors might result in somewhat higher player salaries," the First Circuit stated. "In that event, assuming that the single entity defense failed, a basis for liability might exist."[50] However, the court said it had "been given no reason to think that any other market would have been alleged and made the subject of proof if the section 1 claim had gone to trial along with the section 2 claims."[51] Furthermore, even if the players had sought to amend their complaint after summary judgment, the court had "great doubt whether such an amendment would have been permitted,"[52] since adding a new market theory at an advanced stage of the proceedings "would have substantially altered the contours of the case—potentially requiring new discovery and expert analyses based on the new alleged market."[53] The court concluded:

> We thus have every reason to think that if the section 1 claim had not been dismissed on summary judgment it would have been presented at trial with the same market analysis alleged in the complaint. It follows that had the district court allowed the section 1 claim, it too would have been defeated by the jury's finding that the market alleged in the complaint had not been proved. Accordingly, any error in dismissing the claim based on a single entity theory was harmless so long as the jury verdict stands, a matter we address in the next section. The outcome, as the plaintiffs shaped their own case, would have been the same.[54]

Ultimately, MLS saw its single entity status rejected, but it still prevailed on the Section 1 claim.

On all three Sherman Act Section 2 claims, the district court's judgment was affirmed. The players attacked the jury verdict, arguing it had been tainted by any or all of several alleged district court errors. Most notably, the players contended that the district court had wrongly refused to give two requested instructions on market definition—the most significant instruction being that the jury should include in the relevant market only those leagues that are "sufficiently attractive and practically available to a large enough number of MLS players to prevent MLS from having the power to pay wages below competitive market levels"[55]—but the First Circuit determined these instructions had not been properly made. Of the remaining alleged errors, which concerned the inclusion or exclusion of certain testimony and evidence, the First Circuit found nothing significant enough to have had any effect on the jury verdict.

With respect to the conspiracy to monopolize claim, at trial and on appeal, the players argued that proof of a relevant market was not required. The First Circuit acknowledged that "[c]onspiracy to monopolize claims are not often the subject of much attention, since almost any such claim could be proved more easily under section 1's ban on conspiracies in restraint of trade."[56] The court went on to highlight mixed case law on the issue, maintaining that "a black or white rule is not inevitable."[57] However, the court stated, "there may in principle be some cases in which one could argue that a conspiracy claim should be provable without a showing that the alleged market is a real economic market,"[58] but "[t]his case is not among them."[59] The court found the exclusivity agreement by which U.S. Soccer sanctioned MLS as the country's only Division I professional soccer league to be "garden variety"[60] and "not inherently unlawful."[61] It concluded: "The exclusivity agreement sought by MLS might be unlawful if it threatened adverse competitive effects but not otherwise; and this in turn required proof that someone who was the only purchaser of Division I soccer player services in the United States would control prices in an economic market."[62]

The district court's summary judgment on the Clayton Act Section 7 claim was also affirmed. The First Circuit established that "[t]he district court was saying no more than that, after the failure of the NASL and prior to the formation of MLS, there was no enterprise engaged in providing Division I soccer in the United States and thus that a combination that added Division I soccer in this country could hardly reduce competition where none before existed."[63] According to the First Circuit, this was "plainly correct insofar as the creation of MLS added a new entrant without subtracting any existing competitors."[64] The First Circuit went on to consider the question of "whether section 7 can be used to prevent a merger that itself increases competition where it can be confidently predicted that prevention will or probably will increase competition *even more*,"[65] which the district court had rejected. While the First Circuit speculated that "there might be cases where the facts might compel the conclusion that turning down a pro-competitive merger (compared to the status quo) would produce an even more competitive realignment,"[66] it concluded, "[t]hat is not this case."[67] The court reasoned:

> Here, there is no possible way to predict just what would happen if the current version of MLS were precluded. Players assert that, had the operator/investors not formed MLS, they would have entered the market as a traditionally structured league. But as the district court noted, it is "not inevitable that the league would be formed and would operate the same way as previous sports leagues." Fraser, 97 F.Supp.2d at 142. More importantly, it is quite possible these investors would have found the alternative structures unattractive and simply abandoned their effort altogether—hardly a procompetitive outcome.[68]

It continued:

> Even the alternative result suggested by players—that another, more traditionally structured league like the APSL would have received the Division I sanction instead—appears on the surface no more pro-competitive. The evidence indicates that the APSL was not as well financed or well managed as MLS (hence the USSF's decision to certify MLS and not the APSL), thus increasing the risk that the new Division I league would fail in the long run. In addition, elevating the APSL to Division I status would not necessarily increase competition significantly, since the APSL, an existing minor league, may have already been in the relevant market.[69]

The players appealed to the U.S. Supreme Court, but their petition was denied. Their fight had ended.

"Major League Soccer is pleased that these years of litigation are now behind us," commissioner Don Garber said. "We are excited to concentrate on the tasks at hand, the foremost of which is working with our players and focusing on the continued development of professional soccer in the United States." Jeffrey Kessler, an attorney for the players, said, "It's time for the players to move on to the next step: to come together and form a union." He added, "We expect that, eventually, the players will get their fair shake."

THE EVOLUTION OF MLS AND THE SINGLE ENTITY QUESTION

MLS may have prevailed in *Fraser*, but the league does remain vulnerable to another antitrust challenge. The First Circuit's rejection of single entity status was significant and could prove influential in another circuit. Moreover, it must be stressed that MLS clubs' diversity of interests has greatly expanded since *Fraser*. Now more than ever, these clubs are in actual competition, most notably for players, fan support, and corporate partners. From that competition, a group of elite clubs has been emerging, and it is reasonable to believe that their ambition could increasingly come into conflict with the centralized structure in years to come. Thus, it seems the league's evolution threatens to push it further away from the fundamental legal standards of single entity enterprise. As a practical matter, though, MLS players are unlikely to launch an antitrust attack in the foreseeable future. As evidenced by *Fraser*, antitrust litigation is slow, expensive, and unpredictable, and MLS players still would have to find a way to demonstrate that MLS possesses market power. This generally makes litigation a weapon of last resort.

Still, the MLS Players Union could use the threat of an antitrust challenge in an attempt to gain bargaining leverage in labor negotiations. In 2011, the NFL Players Association and the National Basketball Players Association both made this threat and then made good on it, dissolving their respective unions and filing antitrust actions, to varying effect, before labor agreements were ultimately reached. In 2012, the NHL Players Association made the same threat but stopped short of antitrust action. In the 2015 labor negotiation or subsequent labor negotiations, MLS players could conceivably make this threat as well. Of course, for it to have any effect, MLS would need to find the threat to be credible, which it may not.

In the meantime, MLS rests on its victory in *Fraser*.

Chapter 2

THE NASL AND THE NASL PLAYERS ASSOCIATION

THE ONLY WORK STOPPAGE IN American soccer history didn't even last a week, and it actually involved more working than stopping. On 13 April 1979, North American Soccer League (NASL) players announced that they were going on strike. All 24 clubs were scheduled to play the following day, and all 24 clubs announced that they would play as scheduled, with replacement players as needed. But the need for replacement players would not be overwhelming. Despite voting in favor of the strike, most of the league's players crossed the picket line and took the field. The strike was officially called off on 18 April 1979. Only one round of matches was affected, and not significantly.

The 1979 NASL player strike is generally treated as little more than an anecdote in the telling of American soccer history, one that recalls most notably the drama of the threat of deportation for the league's foreign players and the comedy of the makeup of the league's replacement players. But it should be remembered that the strike was just one battle in a very long war, one in which players fought the league for union recognition and collective bargaining over three and a half years, from July 1977 to December 1980. The conflict would heavily involve the National Labor Relations Board and federal courts. In the end, the players prevailed. By that time, though, the end was nigh for the league.

THE FORMATION OF THE NASL PLAYERS ASSOCIATION

In the United States, the National Labor Relations Act[1] gives employees the right to organize and to bargain collectively with their employers through representatives of their own choosing. A labor union is an organization that represents employees in a particular work site, and its primary responsibility is to negotiate and administer a collective bargaining agreement, which is a contract between an employer and a union that sets terms and conditions of employment. Once a union is established, the National Labor Relations Act requires employers to bargain with the union in "good faith" over terms and conditions of employment until an agreement or an "impasse" is reached. In American professional sports, labor organizing took off in the 1950s, when the Major League Baseball Players Association (MLBPA), National Football League Players Association (NFLPA), National Basketball Players Association (NBPA), and National Hockey League Players Association (NHLPA) were formed. Though largely ineffectual in their early years, by the mid-1960s these player unions had matured in solidarity and seriousness and began to transform their respective leagues. But despite such precedent, through the first nine seasons of the NASL's existence, from 1968 through 1976, the league's players had not yet organized.

It was the executive director of the NFL Players Association, Ed Garvey, who would initiate the NASL labor movement. In the summer of 1977, Garvey began meeting with NASL players for the purpose of forming an NASL player union, to be called the NASL Players Association. The NFL Players Association gave Garvey its authorization and even advanced him the funds necessary for the organizing efforts, which Garvey promised would be repaid as soon as the NASL Players Association began generating revenue from dues and licensing arrangements. To support his efforts, Garvey would recruit John Kerr, a Scottish-born Canadian international and NASL veteran, upon Kerr's release from the NASL's Washington Diplomats.

In July 1977, Garvey circulated a memorandum to NASL players asking them to authorize his group to act as their collective bargaining representative. Why had Garvey taken an interest in NASL players? He offered an explanation in the memo:

> Some of you might wonder why we are extending our hand to be of assistance to you. The reason is that we believe all professional

athletes should work together in order to improve wages and working conditions. . . . We believe we can do this collectively, as any one individual union will be too weak operating on its own to achieve major gains.

Whether Garvey was being completely genuine was up for debate. Garvey's memo continued:

One thing should be made clear. The National Football League Players Association would not establish priorities in bargaining. Only the members of the NASL Players Association would have a voice in your bargaining priorities. You would decide what the minimum salary should be, you would decide on impartial arbitration and other issues troubling you.

While there may have been doubts about a man coming from a rival league, NASL players keen to organize couldn't ignore that Garvey brought two things they desperately needed—resources and experience. Garvey's memo didn't shy from the point:

Frankly, because of the relatively low salaries in the NASL it would not be possible for you to collect much money in dues, certainly not enough to open an office, hire a staff, employ attorneys and take all the other necessary steps to engage in collective bargaining with the NASL.

Kyle Rote Jr. of the NASL's Dallas Tornado was one player who admitted talking with Garvey and favored Garvey's involvement in a player union. Rote told the *New York Times*:

I've talked with Ed about a possible link between the two groups. It is of paramount importance that we form a players' association before the end of the season. . . . They would advise us on matters in which they have experience. We've gone through a lot and made a lot of mistakes. Hopefully they will help us avoid making more mistakes.

He would not be alone. That month, approximately 300 NASL players signed authorization cards designating the NASL Players Association (NASLPA) as their collective bargaining representative.

There are two main ways for a union to formally become the bargaining representative of a unit of employees. Most commonly, an election petition is filed with the National Labor Relations Board (NLRB), which is the federal agency established to administer and enforce the National Labor Relations Act. The petition must be supported by a "showing of interest" from at least 30 percent of employees in the unit; the authorization cards referenced above would serve as proof of interest. Upon the filing, a representation hearing is scheduled. If it is determined that the unit is appropriate and a question of representation exists, an election is ordered; otherwise, the petition is dismissed. In an election, a simple majority of the employees in the unit is required for union certification.[2] Alternatively, an employer may voluntarily recognize a union that has majority support, which eliminates the need for an NLRB petition and election. The MLBPA, NFLPA, NBPA, and NHLPA had been underestimated by their respective employers and received voluntary recognition. The NASLPA would not be as fortunate.

Garvey first asked NASL commissioner Phil Woosnam to recognize the NASLPA on 5 August 1977. A week later, Woosnam told Garvey that the owners were not prepared to recognize the union at that point but would consider it at an owners meeting in Portland on 29 August. In the meantime, Garvey, not willing to rest on Woosnam's promise, filed an election petition with the NLRB, and a representation hearing was set for 8 September. When 29 August arrived and the owners assembled in Portland, Garvey sent them a request for recognition via telex. Garvey did not receive a reply. Woosnam claimed that the owners had not received the message. But he did confirm that the owners had decided to withhold recognition until after the upcoming representation hearing. "We're waiting for the hearing in New York," Woosnam said. "Since they filed a petition I have to attend this hearing. There is nothing we can do until after that is over." Garvey was irritated. "That's just nonsense," he said. "If they wanted to recognize us we could work out the arrangements with or without the NLRB. It's simply nonsense." These early exchanges, marked by distrust and animosity, were a sign of things to come.

Not until the following summer, on 30 June 1978, did the NLRB issue a Decision and Direction of Election,[3] which represents its decision to conduct an election. Months of deliberation[4] focused on three main questions. The two most important questions were closely related: first, whether the NASL and its clubs were "joint employers" of the league's players and, second, whether a league-wide bargaining unit of players was appropriate. The NASLPA maintained that the NASL and its clubs were joint employers, and it sought to establish a league-wide bargaining unit (the prevailing arrangement in the other major professional sports leagues). However, the NASL contended that each club was an autonomous entity and a separate, single employer of its own players, meaning the league and its clubs lacked joint employer status, and therefore only single club bargaining units were appropriate. The NASL further argued that since the NASLPA had not requested representation in single club units, the election petition should be dismissed. The third question was whether the bargaining unit should include players employed by the league's Canadian clubs.

On the joint employer question, the NLRB found that the league exercised a significant degree of control over clubs' labor relations in areas including, but not limited to, the terms of individual player contracts, player acquisition and release, player discipline, and dispute resolution. Therefore, it decided that a joint employer relationship existed. Its decision stated:

> Considering all the circumstances herein, we agree with the Petitioner that the League and the individual clubs are joint employers of the players on each team. We have long held that "the critical factor in determining whether a joint employer relationship exists is the control which one party exercises over the labor relations policy of the other." Although . . . the individual clubs operate their respective teams on a daily basis with a considerable degree of autonomy, it is clear from all of the foregoing that the League, through the commissioner, exercises a significant degree of control and influence over the clubs, including the terms and conditions of employment of players. We therefore find that the League and the clubs are in a joint-employer relationship.[5]

With the joint employer relationship having been established, the next question was whether the league-wide unit of players was appropriate. Here, the NLRB's exact responsibility is important—specifically, it need not determine the *only* appropriate unit or the *most* appropriate unit, but only whether the petitioned-for unit is appropriate. Therefore, although the Board recognized that each club had substantial autonomy, and acknowledged that such autonomy "might support a finding that single-club units may be appropriate,"[6] it asserted that "these facts do not establish that such units are alone appropriate or that the petitioned-for overall unit is inappropriate."[7] It found that "the record clearly supports the finding that the league-wide unit is an appropriate unit."[8] In making this decision, the Board incorporated the reasons underlying its finding of a joint employer relationship. It concluded:

> [I]t is clear that the League, through the commissioner, exercises a substantial degree of control over the individual clubs, including the terms and conditions of employment of the players, so much so in fact that it would be difficult to imagine any degree of stability in labor relations if we were to find appropriate single-club units. This is especially true in light of the fact that the clubs have joined together in a single association which controls, in many areas, their operations. Accordingly, we find that the league-wide unit of 17 clubs is appropriate for the purposes of collective bargaining.[9]

These were crucial victories for the players.

As to the third question, the 17 clubs referenced by the Board were the league's American clubs (actually, by the time the decision was issued, the league had added five more American clubs, bringing the total number of American clubs to 22). The Board had chosen not to exercise jurisdiction over the league's two Canadian clubs, the Toronto Metros (renamed the Toronto Blizzard in 1979) and the Vancouver Whitecaps. The Board reasoned:

> [O]ur exercise of jurisdiction is not so broad as to include the two soccer teams located in Canada. These two teams, the Toronto Metros and the Vancouver Whitecaps, are owned and operated by either Canadian citizens or Canadian corporations, all of whose stockholders live in Canada. They pay business license fees and

taxes to Canadian authorities. Players and other employees are subject to both the Canadian personal income tax and Canadian labor laws. All team offices are located in Canada, and the clubs pay one-half of their regular season games in Canada. Additionally, and as noted above, the Metros and the Whitecaps pay all registration and affiliation fees to the Canadian Soccer Association, not to the United States Soccer Federation. In view of these factors, we shall exclude the two Canadian teams from our exercise of jurisdiction herein.

In a separate position, one Board member dissented from the majority's decision to exclude the players of the Canadian clubs.[10]

With these questions answered, an election was scheduled. The election was held between 27 July and 4 August 1978, and the players voted 271 to 94[11] to be represented by the NASLPA. On 1 September 1978, the NLRB certified the NASLPA as the exclusive bargaining representative of NASL players employed by the league's American clubs. In a little more than a year, Ed Garvey had succeeded in formally organizing the players. But his work was not about to get any easier.

THE NASL REFUSES TO BARGAIN

The NASL would continue to refuse to bargain with the NASLPA, despite now having a legal obligation to do so. In part, this had to do with the presence of Ed Garvey. Derek Carroll, chairman of the NASL's labor relations committee and president of the NASL's New England Tea Men, would admit to the *Washington Post*, "We just don't think [Garvey's] track record is favorable and we have refused to meet with him." Two NASL owners, Lamar Hunt and Joe Robbie, were also NFL owners and had firsthand experience with Garvey. Not surprisingly, Hunt and Robbie were among those NASL owners who most strongly opposed bargaining with the NASLPA. Since 1971, when Garvey became the NFLPA's first executive director, his critics had accused him of "zealotry or excessive idealism at best, or serving his own political ambitions at the expense of the players at worst," as Michael Oriard wrote in *Brand NFL*. Whatever his motivations, Garvey had guided the NFL players in highly aggressive action against the NFL in the 1970s. In 1972, NFL players filed two antitrust suits against the league, *Kapp v. NFL*[12] and *Mackey v. NFL*,[13] which together attacked the amateur draft, the standard player contract, and a free agency restriction known as the Rozelle Rule. In 1974, the NFLPA called a strike that lasted five weeks; after the strike failed, the NFLPA filed charges with the NLRB alleging that the league had engaged in unfair labor practices during the strike. Between 1974 and 1976, these three cases produced rulings that the league was in violation of federal antitrust and labor laws. In 1977, the NFL and the NFLPA finally established a new collective bargaining agreement, which provided the players with significant gains in several areas: increased benefits, impartial arbitration in noninjury disputes, a reformed waiver system, and elimination of the Rozelle Rule. As one might expect, the NFL's relationship with Garvey had grown hostile. In fact, so chaotic was this period that even the NFL players' support of Garvey had waned. In light of these events, NASL owners viewed Garvey as a virus poised to infect their league. But John Kerr was absolutely correct when he stated the following: "As far as [the NASL owners] not wanting Garvey, they have no say in the matter. He's a part of the NASLPA. He was elected by the players when the union was formed. That's over."

The NASL's other main point of contention was over league-wide bargaining. The league claimed it would be disastrous and insisted that there should only be bargaining on a club-by-club basis. As one owner explained to the *Washington Post*:

> We're struggling for survival right now. There's no way we can bargain for all 24 clubs as a group. It has to be done on an individual basis. How can the multi-rich Cosmos be compared with the Rochester Lancers, who are being kept alive on a string? We can't put that club out of business. The average salaries on one team can't be matched by other teams.

Another owner remarked:

> The NLRB ruled we should bargain as a group simply because the other major league sports have been doing that. . . . We don't have the big TV money or the gate-sharing receipts that those other sports have. We'd be glad to sit down with Garvey and bargain if

he set it up on an individual basis. We pay the players' salaries, not the league.

There was no doubt that the league and its clubs were struggling. It was mostly their own fault, for expanding too rapidly and failing to implement adequate revenue sharing and cost control mechanisms, among other reasons. But whatever the reasons, the reality of the moment was that they were struggling, and badly. In the 1978 season, every club would operate at a loss. Would league-wide bargaining really push them to the brink? It wasn't exactly clear, but John Kerr was certainly unconvinced:

> Right now they're just using stalling tactics. Everything else in the league is done on a league-wide basis, why not this? We have a league-wide draft, a league-wide waiver system, and a standard league contract. Why shouldn't we have a league-wide union? Their claims are a joke.

What was clear, though, was that the league was not going to bargain with the players until they were forced to do so. To push the league closer to that point, the players filed an unfair labor practice charge with the NLRB, alleging that the league's refusal to bargain constituted a violation of its rights under the National Labor Relations Act (NLRA). Their complaint was filed on 30 October 1978.

THE STRIKE

As the 1979 season was getting set to kick off, the NLRB had yet to issue a decision on the unfair labor practice charge, so the union began discussing a strike—that is, a concerted refusal to perform work—as a means to force recognition and bargaining. The NLRA provides employees with the right to strike and establishes two categories of lawful strikes: (1) "economic strikes," which have the purpose of obtaining some economic concession, such as higher wages, shorter hours, or better working conditions; and (2) "unfair labor practice strikes," which have the purpose of protesting some unfair labor practice, such as a refusal to bargain. The proposed

NASLPA strike would fall into the latter category. At a March 15 press conference, Garvey stated:

> We want soccer fans to understand that if there is a strike, it is over one issue only: recognition of our union. We have not asked for a single dollar. We have not asked for a pension, for insurance or even impartial arbitration. We have only asked that the owners give us the respect of meeting us at the bargaining table as the law requires them to do. . . . We will either strike or wait for the NLRB to take action.

A few days later, the union set a March 30 deadline for recognition, which predictably came and went with no such result. The union started gearing up more seriously for a strike. When it was put to a vote, the players voted to strike, 252 to 113. On April 13, the strike was announced. "All it would take to end the strike is recognition of the union by the owners," Garvey declared. The following day, all 24 clubs were scheduled to be in action. The owners were determined to play through the strike, and their technical staffs immediately began searching for replacement players. In the event of an unfair labor practices strike, employers are permitted to hire replacement employees, but the striking employees can be neither discharged nor permanently replaced. "We deplore the action the union is taking when there are legal issues still pending before the National Labor Relations Board which have yet to be decided," said Derek Carroll. "A strike can only hurt soccer, the players themselves, and the teams." He added, "We believe that many of the players have been misled into believing that they will be deported if they play in the face of a strike called by the union."

The deportation question was critical. Foreign players made up 55 percent of the league's playing force, and nearly 100 percent of the league's star power. A strike could not be sustained if the foreign players did not participate, and their participation was not a given. It was largely the American players who were the union activists—they earned an average of just $12,000 per year, they generally felt themselves to be second-class citizens, and they were determined to improve their status. Bobby Smith, the Cosmos' player representative, an American, would confirm, "There are a lot of angry Americans in the league." In contrast, the foreign players generally had considerably higher salaries and considerably less interest in rocking the boat. Smith would charge that "a majority of the foreigners really don't care about the league or the protection of players." To be sure, many of them had come to the NASL for an easy life. As described by David Wangerin in *Soccer in a Football World*, "Spending a few lazy summers earning a hefty paycheque alongside some of international football's household names, before a largely naïve public, was a lot more comfortable than toiling in the Football League (in England)." But the threat of deportation would certainly be enough to get the foreign players to participate in the strike.

It is difficult to say for certain whether Garvey knowingly misled the foreign players, as was Carroll's accusation, since there seemed to be some legitimate confusion on the issue, even within the federal government. Garvey had interpreted existing immigration regulations to mean that foreign players who worked during a strike could be deported. In late March and early April, he so told the players. When the strike began, it appeared that the Immigration and Naturalization Service (INS), a Department of Justice agency that handled matters of legal and illegal immigration and naturalization,[14] shared Garvey's view. Several INS regional offices reportedly made statements about being prepared to take deportation action. Nevertheless, the owners tried to assure their foreign players that they could play without fear of deportation, and they went before a federal judge in Washington, D.C., to obtain a restraining order against such action. Senior judge George Hart denied the motion based upon the fact that no deportation proceeding had yet been initiated, but he stated that he would be inclined to block deportation if it was in his jurisdiction. "I don't believe it would be constitutional to deport an alien under the circumstances of this case," Hart said.

Amid the confusion, most of the foreign players decided to trust the owners and suit up on April 14. Many Americans did the same. Overall, nearly three-quarters of the players crossed the picket line—this after about 69 percent of players voted in favor of the strike. Besides some of the foreign players' deportation fears being calmed, there were three more key reasons for the turnaround. First, there were players who didn't trust Garvey. "We are not antiunionists.... It's just that the reports we are getting about Garvey are not so good," said one Cosmos foreign player who did not wish to be identified to the *New York Times*. Second, there were players who feared for their jobs. As Garvey would later say:

All athletes fear for their jobs because of supply and demand. The owners can always find another player to replace them. This situation is magnified a hundred times in the soccer league here because the foreign players fear that the owners, who must apply for their certification, will keep them out of the country next year.

Third, there were players who were concerned about damaging the league and the sport. "We agree in principle with the need for a players association," said Tampa Bay Rowdies team representative Farrukh Quraishi, who was born in Iran, was raised in England, and attended college in the United States, "but we cannot support a strike action which could threaten the very existence of the game we are trying to establish in the United States." "American soccer has to be the first priority," said Cosmos winger Dennis Tueart, an Englishman. "This is still a baby sport here and you have to be very careful before you take any step that could knock out the foundation."

About 17 of the 24 clubs would be at or near full strength. Of those 17 clubs, the most significant was the Cosmos, the league's marquee attraction. About a week earlier, Cosmos players had voted 20 to 2 in favor of the strike, the two voting against being Italian star Giorgio Chinaglia and English midfielder Terry Garbett. But their final decision was made the day before their match away to the Atlanta Chiefs. As a heated debate raged outside of Giants Stadium in New Jersey, the players missed their flight to Atlanta. At first, team representative Bobby Smith convinced his teammates to observe the strike. But Steve Ross, chairman of Warner Communications, the owner of the club, and Krikor Yepremian, the general manager, eventually swung the majority of the players the other way, with only Smith and a handful of young American players standing firm. The team boarded a bus for the airport, where a private jet had been arranged to take them to Atlanta. Smith, near tears, berated his teammates as they left. He spoke for the entire union leadership. This was a huge blow to the strike.

The Fort Lauderdale Strikers, Memphis Rogues, and Rochester Lancers were among the heavily strike-depleted teams that day. The Strikers were missing 16 of their 23 players. Their replacement players included their 44-year-old head coach, Ron Newman, who took the field alongside his 21-year-old son, who was one of the team's reserve defenders, and several players picked off the streets. In front of the team's home fans, the Strikers lost 4–0 to the Washington Diplomats. Memphis saw all but one of its players participate in the strike, and its makeshift side would also feature its head coach, 36-year-old Eddie McCreadie, plus a former player turned agent in goal, along with a mix of youth players and miscellaneous amateur players. The Rogues were routed 6–0 by the Detroit Express. The Lancers, without key starters and a bench, flew in eight amateur players from Rochester and several more from in and around New York City to make up the numbers. Head coach Dragan Popovic did not dress, but he did say, "I felt like crying." The Lancers fell 5–2 to the Tulsa Roughnecks. As soccer writer Michael Lewis wrote in a piece on the strike years later, "The strike left the sport with a black eye and some of the most bizarre moments in professional soccer history."

There would be no more such scenes. On April 17, the INS, in a change from its original position, declared that foreign players with proper work visas could not be deported for playing during the strike. This was the result of an advisory opinion issued by Attorney General Griffin B. Bell and the Justice Department's Office of Legal Counsel. The Justice Department had decided that the law was meant to prevent strikebreakers from being brought into the country once a work stoppage began, not to throw out foreign workers who were already certified and living in the country. Garvey realized that the government's ruling had gone against him, and he had little remaining power to sustain the strike. On April 18, the strike was called off and the players were ordered to return to work. "I knew late last night that the strike would be over today," said Gary Etherington, the Cosmos' young English-American player who had participated in the strike. "We had a long meeting with Garvey and players from other teams last night and it was obvious that the strike was not successful." Etherington confirmed that the reversal of the decision concerning the foreign players was "the final blow." He also added, "I agree with the fact that the foreign players were misinformed about their status with the authorities and also about the benefits of a union." If it wasn't already apparent, the strike proved that the number of foreign players in the league presented an unusual and complex labor situation in the NASL.

Although the strike had failed, Garvey said that the union would regroup and continue to pursue collection bargaining through the NLRB and the courts. And it turned out that they had a favorable ruling on the way.

NASL V. NLRB

The unfair labor practice charge that the players had filed several months before the start of the season was ruled upon less than two weeks after the end of the strike. On 30 April 1979, the NLRB ordered the NASL to bargain collectively with the NASLPA.[15] According to the NASLPA's complaint, the NASL "had engaged in and was engaging in unfair labor practices,"[16] as the league "refused, and continues to date to refuse, to bargain collectively with the Union as the exclusive bargaining representative although the Union has requested and is requesting it to do so."[17] In its answer to the complaint, the NASL once more contested the validity of the NASLPA's representative status and certification, on several grounds. But the NLRB found that the issues raised by the league were not "properly litigable in this unfair labor practice proceeding"[18] and that the league had indeed violated the NLRA by refusing to bargain collectively with the union. The NLRB directed the league to "cease and desist therefrom, and, upon request, bargain collectively with the Union."[19] "Much was said during the strike by management about waiting until the NLRB considered new arguments by the NASL," Garvey remarked. "The board has rejected these arguments and has made it clear that the NASL stands in violation of the law."

The NASL, though, was still not ready to concede defeat. The next battleground would be a federal court, as the league petitioned the U.S. Court of Appeals for the Fifth Circuit to review and set aside the NLRB's decision. About a year later, on 21 March 1980, the Fifth Circuit issued its decision in *NASL v. NLRB*,[20] which enforced the NLRB's order. The court reexamined the issues of whether a joint employer relationship existed between the league and its clubs and whether a league-wide bargaining unit of players was appropriate, and concluded:

> Our review of the record reveals sufficient evidence to support the National Labor Relations Board's determination that the League and its member clubs are joint employers, and that a collective bargaining unit comprised of all NASL players on clubs based in the United States is appropriate. Finding petitioners' due process challenge to be without merit, we deny the petition for review and enforce the collective bargaining order on the cross-application of the Board.

In its analysis of the joint employer question, the court confirmed that the league "exercises a significant degree of control over essential aspects of the clubs' labor relations,"[21] such that it "supports the Board's factual finding of a joint employer relationship among the League and its constituent clubs."[22] On the question of whether the league-wide bargaining unit was appropriate, the court reasoned:

> [T]he facts successfully refute any notion that because the teams compete on the field and in hiring, only team units are appropriate for collective bargaining purposes. Once a player is hired, his working conditions are significantly controlled by the League. Collective bargaining at that source of control would be the only way to effectively change by agreement many critical conditions of employment.

Once again, the league's arguments had failed. Garvey called the decision "an important step forward."

It was a step that finally led to actual bargaining. On 12 August 1980, the league and the players held their first bargaining session. Less than a week later, the players' bargaining position was further strengthened.

MORIO V. NASL

The NASLPA had filed a series of unfair labor practice charges in 1979, which were eventually consolidated on 14 February 1980. As previously stated, upon a union's certification, employers have a duty to bargain; therefore, employers generally may not unilaterally impose terms and conditions of employment, at least not before good faith negotiations have reached an impasse. Since the NASLPA's certification on 1 September 1978, the NASLPA charged, the NASL had unilaterally changed terms and conditions of employment by engaging in the following acts and conduct:

1. Requiring players to obtain permission from their respective clubs whenever a particular brand of footwear, other than that selected by each of the clubs, was desired;

2. Establishing a new winter indoor season, which was held for the first time from November 1979 to March 1980;
3. Requiring players to play in the winter indoor season;
4. Expanding the 1980 summer season by two games and two weeks; and
5. Reducing the maximum roster of all clubs during the summer season from 30 to 26 players.

The duty to bargain carries with it the obligation not to undercut the union by entering into individual contracts with employees. The NASLPA also charged that the NASL had unlawfully bypassed the union and dealt directly with employees in the unit by soliciting, negotiating, and entering into individual contracts.

NLRB Regional Director Winifred D. Morio of New York petitioned the U.S. District Court for the Southern District of New York for a temporary injunction pending the final disposition of these unfair labor practice charges in *Morio v. NASL*.[23] Specifically, the NLRB sought to require the NASL to "maintain the present terms and conditions in effect until Respondents negotiate with the Union—except, of course, for the unilateral changes—unless and until an agreement or a good faith impasse is reached."[24] It also sought to require the NASL to "render voidable, at the option of the Union, all individual player contracts, whether entered into before or after the Union's certification on 1 September 1978."[25] As Judge Constance Motley would emphasize, this was "not a request to have all individual contracts declared null and void,"[26] but a request "to render voidable only those unilateral acts taken by the Respondents"[27] (with the exception of the unilateral provision that provided for the season in progress), as it was "consciously limited . . . to prevent any unnecessary disruption of the Respondents' business."[28]

On 18 August 1980, Judge Motley concluded, "there is reasonable cause to believe that Respondents have engaged in unfair labor practices and that Petitioner is entitled to the temporary injunctive relief sought in this action."[29] The NASL had claimed that it had the right to refuse to bargain with the union because it was pursuing an appeal to the NLRB's determination that a league-wide bargaining unit was appropriate, but Judge Motley disagreed, stating:

> Respondents' duty to bargain with the Union arose from the time
> the Union was certified as the exclusive bargaining representative

of the players [on] September 1, 1978. The fact that Respondents were pursuing their right to appeal did not, absent a stay of the Board's order, obviate their duty to bargain with the Union and does not constitute a defense to an application for relief under Section 10(j) of the [National Labor Relations] Act where, as here, Respondents have apparently repeatedly refused to bargain with the Union and have continued to bypass the Union and deal directly with employees.[30]

Thus, Judge Motley reestablished the terms and conditions of employment prior to the unilateral changes. Further, Judge Motley rendered voidable all individual contracts. It was established in court that 96.8 percent of existing individual contracts were signed after the union's certification and the remaining 3.2 percent of existing individual contracts had been signed prior to the union's certification. With respect to those signed after certification, Judge Motley concluded that they were "apparently in violation of the duty of the Respondents to bargain with the exclusive bargaining representative of the players,"[31] since "[t]his duty to bargain carries with it the negative duty not to bargain with individual employees."[32] With respect to those signed prior to certification, Judge Motley concluded they had been used to "forestall collective bargaining,"[33] and "there simply is no incentive for Respondents to bargain with the Union with those contracts in place."[34] In support of his ruling, Judge Motley cited *National Licorice Co. v. NLRB*, in which "the Supreme Court held that the Board has the authority, even in the absence of the employees as parties to the proceeding, to order an employer not to enforce individual contracts with its employees which were found to have been in violation of the NLRA."[35]

The U.S. Court of Appeals for the Second Circuit would affirm Judge Motley's ruling.[36]

THE NASL'S FIRST COLLECTIVE BARGAINING AGREEMENT

Judge Motley's order prohibited the NASL from going ahead with its indoor season until good faith bargaining produced a collective bargaining agreement or an impasse. A month later, the league said an impasse had been reached. The players disagreed, and the NLRB began to investigate. True to form, the league went ahead with its indoor season anyway, with an injunction still in place and the question of bargaining impasse still open.

However, the Department of Labor and the INS would not certify the NASL players or approve visa applications for the Canadian teams to enter the country. "We have informally indicated that if and when the court authorizes the [season] to proceed, we'll certify," said Carl Gerig of the Department of Labor to the *Washington Post*. "That hasn't happened." Mike Heilman of the INS explained, "To us, the injunction clearly banned the playing of the winter season. If there is no winter season, there is no job. Our position, then, is we will not approve petitions related to the winter season." To avoid this roadblock, the indoor season carried on with U.S. teams not playing in Canada and Canadian teams not playing in the United States. Nevertheless, Garvey sensed the end was near. "It's unprecedented—for three years they've refused to bargain with us," Garvey said, "and now it's finally caught up with them."

In late November, the NLRB went back to the U.S. District Court for the Southern District of New York, filing a petition for an order adjudging the NASL in civil contempt for failing to comply with the injunction. In the words of NLRB deputy assistant general counsel Joseph P. Norelli, this "would put the whole kibosh on the indoor season." NASL attorney Robert Rolnick maintained that the league "had conducted extensive bargaining" and was in "total compliance" with the law. But the league had finally run out of ways to escape the union.

Over the next two weeks, the league and the union engaged in marathon bargaining sessions, and on 5 December 1980, they signed the NASL's first collective bargaining agreement. The agreement included a minimum salary, guaranteed contracts, and impartial arbitration of disputes. "We're very pleased with the contract. . . . It has been a long, tough war for three years and now we want to help the NASL succeed," said Garvey. Unfortunately, the NASL would not survive much longer. The main reasons were described in Chapter 1, but the inability of the league and the union to cooperate, as described in this chapter, played a role as well. When the league's first collective bargaining agreement expired in November 1983, only nine struggling clubs remained. A second collective bargaining agreement was signed in April 1984, but that season would be the league's last.

Chapter 3

NASL V. NFL

THE NFL'S CROSS-OWNERSHIP BAN

Beginning in the 1950s, the National Football League (NFL) commissioners maintained a "cross-ownership" policy against its owners taking interests in other sports businesses. The underlying rationale was that the NFL was in competition with all other sports businesses, and the policy was necessary to prevent any dilution of the resources, energies, and loyalties of its club owners.

In 1966, the cross-ownership policy was, as described by author David Harris in *The League*, "little more than a loosely enforced, informal, and largely unarticulated understanding rather than a constitutional requirement." In 1966, the NFL and the upstart American Football League (AFL) agreed to a merger, and NFL commissioner Pete Rozelle sought to establish a formal cross-ownership policy (and other ownership policies) as part of the final agreement. The result was that the NFL's Supplementary Merger Agreement bound "all present franchises of the NFL and AFL" to "present NFL [ownership] policies," but only "with respect to changes of club ownership after February 1967." Rozelle had originally hoped for a constitutional amendment but was ultimately forced to settle for the continuance of an informal cross-ownership policy that included exemptions for existing owners, since several of them—including Lamar Hunt, who owned the NFL's Kansas City Chiefs and the NASL's Dallas Tornado—stood in violation. Nevertheless, Rozelle had gained some momentum on the issue, and he would continue to push for a formal and comprehensive policy. In 1972, Rozelle made further progress when the owners passed a resolution stating that "no person owning a majority interest in or in direct or indirect operational control of a member club may acquire any interest in another major team sport." In addition, the owners agreed to make a "best effort" to dispose of interests in competing sports. The resolution was effective through the following year's spring meeting.

When the 1972 resolution came up for renewal, the NFL owner who over the next several years would be the loudest critic of cross-ownership, and of Lamar Hunt's NASL ownership in particular, stepped to the fore: Philadelphia Eagles owner Leonard Tose. Earlier that year, Hunt had held a press conference in Philadelphia announcing the arrival of a new NASL franchise, the Philadelphia Atoms, to be led by local contractor Thomas McCloskey, who had been lured into the investment by Hunt at the Super Bowl. (The story goes, McCloskey was in Los Angeles for the Super Bowl with eight friends and no tickets; Hunt learned of McCloskey's situation, arrived on the scene with nine tickets, fanned himself with them, and asked McCloskey, "How would you like to have a soccer franchise in Philadelphia?") Hunt's press conference was captured on the front of *The Philadelphia Inquirer*'s sports page. Tose took exception:

> I was indignant. I confronted [Hunt] personally and tried to stand up close to him so he would get my message. . . . [W]hat he has done is taken the prestige of the NFL and turned it in to bring a team into Philadelphia to compete . . . rather than coming to Philadelphia to help me. . . . The mere fact that [Hunt] sits in our meetings and [then reports] whatever we do to the [NASL] to me is reprehensible. . . . It turns my stomach. It is against everything I have been taught. It is un-American.

Tose demanded a report from Hunt on his "best efforts" to divest himself. Hunt—self-composed and nonconfrontational by nature, Tose's complete opposite—was unshaken by the attack and simply replied that he was working on it.

In actuality, Hunt's devotion to the NASL did not seem to be wavering at all, even in the face of millions of dollars in losses. In an interview with David Harris, Hunt would explain, "I felt I made a commitment, which I had made publicly—to attempt to build and help develop a team in Dallas. . . . I guess I am a little hardheaded from that standpoint and I don't want to be known as a quitter." Hunt would continue to serve as the NASL's most prominent advocate, working tirelessly to promote and raise capital for the league. From 1972 to 1978, Hunt and Rozelle would trade letters on the subject of Hunt's cross-ownership. In 1974, Rozelle received a letter from Hunt in which Hunt reported that his soccer interest was difficult to sell because there were no buyers for existing teams, but he offered the following reassurance: "I . . . think I see the light at the end of the tunnel and have some ideas that could conceivably accomplish it at the right time." When reminded of the letter several years later, Rozelle quipped, "That was a long tunnel."

Meanwhile, another NFL owner had joined Hunt as an NASL owner, though somewhat indirectly. In 1972, shortly after the NFL's cross-ownership resolution was passed, Miami Dolphins owner Joe Robbie and his wife, Elizabeth, attended a gathering at Miami's Jockey Club hosted by Dolphins limited partner Harper Sibley that was organized to raise capital for the city's struggling NASL franchise, the Miami Gatos. That night, the franchise was rescued, and Harper Sibley coaxed Elizabeth Robbie into becoming a limited partner. The following year, Elizabeth raised the stakes, becoming a general partner in the franchise, which was renamed the Miami Toros (later the Fort Lauderdale Strikers). Joe Robbie, though, was not entirely disconnected from the investment. Joe and Elizabeth had shared rather than separate wealth, and the financing of the Toros largely originated from the profits made from the Dolphins. The financial liability was not insignificant. In the first three years of the Robbie family's involvement, the Toros lost some $900,000. In subsequent years, Joe became more directly involved with the NASL. Along with Hunt, Robbie served as a member of the NASL's planning committee, weighing in on issues such as expansion and prospective owner vetting. Robbie also contributed to efforts to improve NASL operations by sharing studies and specifics of NFL operations, including certain information that other NFL owners considered to be confidential. Rozelle would grow increasingly irritated:

> [Joe Robbie] said . . . in League meetings that his wife had an interest in [the soccer club] and that she was the one involved . . . from what we've heard of the Robbie situation, it would appear that it is Mr. Robbie who is on the soccer committees, not Mrs. Robbie, and it is

> Mr. Robbie attending meetings, not Mrs. Robbie. I would say that . . .
> there is a conflict . . . with the spirit and intent of ownership policy.

Indeed, there was a conflict with the spirit and intent of the policy, but not the letter of the policy.

In 1973, the cross-ownership resolution was extended until 1975. In 1976, the resolution was extended in perpetuity. But little changed. Its opponents had been willing to continue passing the resolution realizing that it didn't have teeth. It would not force Hunt into any immediate and undesirable sale. It did not even address the Robbie situation. By 1978, Rozelle's patience on the issue had run out. He was ready to step up his battle to effectively eliminate cross-ownership. This time, though, he would have more substantial backing from his owners. At the NFL's 1978 annual meeting, Leonard Tose kicked off discussion of the cross-ownership issue with another attack on Lamar Hunt, which had become a tradition of such meetings. Tose's latest inspiration was an article that appeared in *American Way*, the in-flight publication of American Airlines. With magazine in hand, Tose told the room, "I was flying someplace and I picked up this magazine. . . . What particularly disturbed me . . . was the fact that Mr. Hunt was quoted as saying soccer is going to replace football." Tose waved the magazine in the air and exclaimed, "[T]his is the type of thing Lamar is doing." Minnesota Vikings owner Max Winter was equally disturbed by NASL competition. Winter argued that the NASL's Minnesota Kicks "are hurting the Vikings, our sports dollar . . . they are drawing and we are losing ground as far as media exposure and fan participation."

If the NFL ever perceived the NASL as a potentially significant threat to its business, it would have been precisely at this point in time. In 1977, the Cosmos drew 77,691 and 73,669 and the Seattle Sounders drew 42,091 and 56,256 en route to their meeting in the Soccer Bowl, the league's championship game, which the Cosmos won, 2–1. (The Soccer Bowl did not boast a gaudy attendance number, but only because it was played at Portland's Civic Stadium, which had a modest capacity that could not serve overwhelming demand.) In the winter of 1977–78, the NASL audaciously expanded from 18 to 24 clubs. In 1978, the Cosmos won their second consecutive championship in front of 74,901 (played, this time, at Giants Stadium in New Jersey). In that season, NASL aggregate attendance reached 5.3 million, a league record, while the Cosmos' average attendance reached nearly 43,000, second best in the world, behind England's Manchester United. After the season, the NASL earned a three-year broadcast contract with ABC. In *Soccer in a Football World*, David Wangerin described the moment:

> Soccer had never been so popular. While the joy of playing it had been obvious for some time, Pelé had heightened interest in watching it and reading about it. Newspapers across the country now carried NASL results and wrote features on college and high school teams. . . . Magazines with titles such as *Soccer Corner* and *Soccer Express*—and, for a time, even a weekly soccer tabloid— appeared on newsstands. Bookstores made space for *All About Soccer, Inside Soccer*, and *The International Book of Soccer*. . . . The unfailing barometer of television advertising now featured soc- cer players muddying their clothes or working up a thirst for the benefit of commerce.

Wangerin further noted, "the handsome mansion the NASL had built for itself still lacked a sturdy foundation," as "[n]obody had made any money yet, least of all the Cosmos," and "most of the league's membership remained anonymous outside a tiny circle of obsessive fans," but to many it did appear on the surface as though "soccer's time had finally come."

In this environment, the frustrations and fears of Tose and Winter could perhaps be understood. And at the 1978 annual meeting, criticism of Hunt and cross-ownership did not end with them. New England Patriots owner Billy Sullivan was close to Hunt, but one of his sons, Chuck, felt compelled to speak up on the issue. Chuck Sullivan stated that his family had turned down various opportunities to purchase MLB's Boston Red Sox, the NBA's Boston Celtics, the NHL's Boston Bruins, and the NASL's Boston Tea Men, saying, "it was our feeling that our family had become identified with the NFL and identification with . . . other enterprises would take away from our primary objective of promoting the NFL." Sullivan continued, "If Lamar Hunt were to devote more time to the promotion of the Kansas City Chiefs and less time to the promotion of other sports interests, I think the NFL would signifi- cantly benefit." Tampa Bay Buccaneers owner Hugh Culverhouse shared the Sullivans' point of view, and said that he had turned down the opportunity to purchase the NASL's Tampa Bay Rowdies for similar reasons. New York

Giants owners Wellington Mara suggested that Hunt should sell either his football or his soccer interests, and do it soon. Hunt maintained that he had been making a good faith effort at divestiture, but to many owners his words rang hollow. "Every year Lamar would just sit and take the criticism," recalled Steve Rosenbloom, son of Los Angeles Rams owner Carroll Rosenbloom. "Every year he'd say, 'I'm working on it,' and then do nothing." The Robbie situation was also addressed, and most agreed that it should be prohibited. Robbie was not present at the meeting to defend his position.

There was now a groundswell of support for meaningful action on cross-ownership. Specifically, the majority of owners wanted comprehensive prohibition, including family interests, with a hard deadline for divestiture and significant penalties for noncompliance. And they wanted this written into the league's constitution. Three months later, at the league's June executive session, the owners held a series of votes on the issue. By those votes, the owners directed the league office to draft a constitutional amendment. Hunt was frustrated, though characteristically reserved. Robbie was furious, and he made that clear. But they were in a distinct minority.

By late June, Rozelle proposed to amend Article IX of the NFL Constitution and Bylaws by adding a new Section 9.4 as follows:

A. No person (1) owning a majority interest in a member club, or (2) directly or indirectly having substantial operating control, or substantial influence over the operations, of a member club, or (3) serving as an officer or director of a member club, nor (4) any spouse or minor child of any such person, may directly or indirectly acquire, retain, or possess any interest in another major team sport (including major league baseball, basketball, hockey and soccer).

B. The prohibition set forth in subsection (A) hereof shall also apply to relatives of such persons (including siblings, parents, adult children, adult and minor grand children, nephews and nieces, and relatives by marriage) (1) if such person directly or indirectly provided or contributed all or any part of the funds used to purchase or operate the other sports league entity, or (2) if there exists between such person and any such relative a significant community of interest in the successful operation of the other sports league entity.

C. The Commissioner shall investigate, to the extent he deems necessary or appropriate, any reported or apparent violation of this Section and shall report his findings to the Executive Committee prior to imposition of disciplinary action by the Committee.

D. Beginning on February 1, 1980, any person who, after notice and hearing by the Executive Committee, is found to have violated subsection (A) or (B) above will be subject to fines of up to $25,000 per month for each of the first three months of violations; up to $50,000 per month for each of the next three months; and up to $75,000 per month thereafter. In addition, violations of more than six months' duration may be dealt with by the Executive Committee pursuant to Article VIII, Section 8.13(B).

E. If such person does not pay such fine to the League Treasurer within 20 days of its assessment, the unpaid amount thereof may be withheld, in whole or in part, by the Commissioner from available funds in possession of the League Office belonging to the member club with which the person in violation is affiliated.

It was an especially aggressive move. It was not "necessary or reasonable," according to Hunt. "The whole tenor of the proposal is considerably different [from previous policy]," he said. "It asks for forced divestiture with a time limit that would to say the least, be punitive. . . . It would make it very, very difficult to sell [my other interests] at a fair price." Robbie responded, "I am flatly, unalterably opposed to it. That wipes my family out in every direction."

Washington Redskins partner Edward Bennett Williams, a legendary trial attorney, had long been firmly opposed to cross-ownership prohibition,[1] even more vocally than Hunt and Robbie, and he had asked the league to obtain an opinion as to its legality two years earlier. At the June executive session, when the owners voted to draft an amendment, Robbie, a prominent attorney himself, asked what had become of Williams' request. In July, after the amendment had been drafted, Robbie received a letter from Covington & Burling, the league's outside counsel, which stated that cross-ownership prohibition would be legal. Both Robbie and Williams disagreed. Robbie said, "I think it's illegal. I think it's contrary to public policy, especially as it related to family . . . I don't see any reason why a person can't have an investment in more than one major league team sport." Williams issued a warning to the league: "I told them they would have certain litigation if they enacted this."

It did not take long for Williams to be proven right. The NFL set a special meeting for October to discuss and vote on the draft amendment. But the NASL was ready to step in.

NASL V. NFL (DISTRICT COURT)

By August 1978, the NASL had voted to retain counsel and take action. Joe and Elizabeth Robbie's son, Mike, voted in favor. Lamar Hunt abstained. In September, the NASL's attorneys paid a visit to the NFL's headquarters. Pete Rozelle, speaking to David Harris, recalled:

> The draft amendment had got into their hands, and they came marching over here to our office. They sat us down for several hours and told us that they were going to sue us unless we voluntarily retracted the amendment. They weren't just going to sue if we passed it; they were going to sue if we put it on the agenda. They, in effect, said, if you don't stop it right now, we will sue. We told them we weren't going to stop.

The NASL made good on its threat.

On 28 September 1978, the NASL filed a complaint in the U.S. District Court for the Southern District of New York. The NASL sought an injunction that would prohibit the NFL from enacting the proposed cross-ownership ban, a declaratory judgment that the proposed cross-ownership ban violated antitrust law, and treble damages. The complaint named 21 of the NASL's 24 franchises as plaintiffs and 25 of the NFL's 28 franchises as defendants. The unnamed parties were Hunt's Kansas City Chiefs and Dallas Tornado, the Robbies' Miami Dolphins and Ft. Lauderdale Strikers, plus the NFL's Seattle Seahawks and the NASL's Seattle Sounders—the Nordstrom family was the majority owner of the Seahawks and a minority owner of the Sounders. Not surprisingly, Leonard Tose pointed a finger squarely at Hunt: "Hell, I don't know if [Hunt] is a plaintiff on the record, but he is the guy who originated it. . . . I don't think any of this would have happened if Mr. Hunt hadn't started this." Hunt expressed that the suit placed him in "an awkward position" in which he was "divorced from himself either way."

On 21 February 1979, New York Southern District Judge Charles S. Haight Jr. issued a preliminary injunction against the implementation of the cross-ownership ban.[2] A preliminary injunction is a court order that restrains a party from a disputed action until its lawfulness can be determined in a full trial. Traditionally, courts examine the following four factors in determining whether to grant a preliminary injunction:

1. whether the moving party is likely to suffer "irreparable harm" in the absence of an injunction;
2. whether the moving party is likely to prevail at trial, referred to as the "likelihood of success on the merits";
3. the balance between the harm to the moving party if an injunction is denied and the harm to the nonmoving party if an injunction is granted, often referred to as the "balance of hardships"; and
4. the public interest.

For decades, though, circuit courts have applied these four factors in differing ways. The majority of circuits have used some variation of the traditional four-part standard, with some circuits weighing all the factors and others treating one or two of the factors as threshold issues and weighing the other factors.[3] The Second Circuit, which covers New York, Connecticut, and Vermont, has long maintained a less stringent three-part test, requiring the moving party to show:

1. irreparable harm;
2. either a likelihood of success on the merits or sufficiently "serious questions" going to the merits to make them a fair ground for litigation; and
3. a balance of hardships tipping decidedly in its favor.[4]

This standard permits a district court the flexibility to grant a preliminary injunction when the moving party's probability of success is unclear or less than likely.

At the time of the NASL's motion, while there was some confusion within the Second Circuit concerning the preliminary injunction standard, the essence of the three-part test described here was in place, and its leniency on the "likelihood of success" prong would provide the NASL a relatively easy road to relief. Judge Haight did not go as far as to make a specific finding on the NASL's likelihood of success, but held that the presence of "merits issues of sufficient doubt"[5] sufficed for the purposes of the test. Judge Haight also concluded that the NASL made the requisite showing of a threat of irreparable harm and that the balance of the hardships tipped in its favor. Therefore, the preliminary injunction was granted. In an early win for the NASL, the status quo would be preserved until a full trial on the merits.

At trial, the NASL's challenge of the NFL's cross-ownership ban came under Section 1 of the Sherman Act. Section 1 declares to be illegal "[e]very contract, combination . . . or conspiracy, in restraint of trade or commerce."[6] Despite its sweeping language, courts have held that Section 1 only prohibits agreements that "unreasonably" restrain trade. A restraint is "unreasonable" if its anticompetitive effects outweigh its procompetitive benefits. The NASL perceived two principal anticompetitive effects of the cross-ownership ban. First, the NASL claimed that the cross-ownership ban would obstruct its ability to compete with the NFL and other sports in the limited market for "sports ownership capital and skill," a submarket of the broad market for capital. According to the NASL, NFL owners "comprise a significant (and highly desirable) part of [the] market for sports ownership capital and skill,"[7] and "[g]roup restrictions on the investment decisions of such owners, therefore, necessarily constitute an unreasonable restraint of trade."[8] Second, the NASL argued that this anticompetitive effect leads directly to another, since the coercions and restraints placed upon present and potential owners served to undermine the NASL's ability to compete with the NFL and other sports in the market for major professional sports, a submarket of the broad market for entertainment. In support of this second argument, the NASL highlighted a statement made by Rozelle in a memo that accompanied the draft amendment when it was dispatched to NFL owners:

> The NFL's success depends on fan interest and loyalty. The League competes with other major team sports for that interest and loyalty, as well as for gate receipts, television revenues, advertising dollars, and media coverage. Connections with NFL personnel may well enhance those competing team sports, both in fact and in the public's perception, at the expense of the NFL.[9]

The NASL characterized this statement as a "smoking pistol."[10]

The NFL submitted that in such competition between and among leagues, it acted as a single economic entity; therefore, Section 1 did not apply to its conduct because Section 1 explicitly requires an agreement (a "contract, combination . . . or conspiracy"), and an agreement requires more than one entity. The league was attempting to sustain this argument despite being comprised of member clubs that were separate legal entities. The NASL contended that the NFL's single entity defense "disregards more than twenty years of decisions . . . which consistently have applied Section 1 of the Sherman Act to the NFL defendants,"[11] and "Section 1 has also been consistently applied to other professional team [sports]."[12] But Judge Haight was not willing to immediately dismiss the NFL's single entity argument. He observed:

> [T]he courts do not reject the concept [of the NFL as a single economic entity] out of hand. On the contrary, Judge Grim's characterization [in *United States v. National Football League*] of a professional sports league as "truly a unique business enterprise" is echoed in later cases, most recently by Judge Pregerson's observation in [*Los Angeles Memorial Coliseum v. NFL*] that "[t] he relationship between the teams does not fit the traditional competitive mold."[13]

Judge Haight recognized that, in contrast with other industries, some cooperation was essential in the professional sports business:

> Single companies can, and do, make bearings and mufflers. No interdependence or joint action is necessary to make a bearing or a muffler. . . . The professional sports league is entirely different. The individual teams cannot, and do not, make the league product. Interdependence and concerted activity are essential to the existence of that product.[14]

As a result:

> A tension unmistakably arises between the concept of a league, whose members must combine and cooperate if the league is to

function at all, and the Sherman Act § 1's prohibition of combinations in restraint of trade.[15]

In his analysis of professional sports league antitrust cases, Judge Haight derived a resolution of this tension.

On the one hand, Judge Haight proposed that Section 1 properly applies where a league's member clubs individually compete against each other in an identifiable market—for instance, in cases concerning the player market, which previously resulted in consistent rejection of the single entity argument. On the other hand, he proposed:

> [If] joint league conduct neither implicates nor impinges upon competition between the member clubs, then the professional sports league, that unique business enterprise not fitting the usual competitive mold, may properly be regarded as a single economic entity; and in those circumstances, § 1 of the Sherman Act has no office to perform. That is so, even if the joint league conduct disadvantages another competitor in the entertainment industry.[16]

With respect to the present case, Judge Haight determined that "[c]ompetition between the NASL and NFL in the entertainment industry is one on one: league against league."[17] He explained:

> Judge Curtis was quite right in *San Francisco Seals* [*v. National Hockey League*], when he said that the "main purpose" of a professional sports league is "producing sporting events of uniformly high quality," the member teams "acting together as one single business enterprise, competing against other similarly organized professional leagues." It is the league product—its sporting events—which competes against the comparable product of competing leagues.[18]

Judge Haight described the competition between leagues as "the primary economic competition in professional sports,"[19] and he found the competition to be between "single economic entities"[20] and "uncomplicated by any relevant competition between the member clubs of a league"[21] such that "no antitrust implications arise."[22] Thus, Judge Haight concluded that Section 1 of the Sherman Act did not apply to the NFL's cross-ownership ban, despite the ban's anticompetitive nature. In summary, he stated:

> The anticompetitive intent of the cross-ownership ban is not an illegal intent, because the NFL, which competes against other professional sports leagues as a simple economic entity, seeks to promulgate the ban in furtherance of that entity's marketplace efficiency. The ban is an exercise in entity housekeeping; and as a matter of economic reality, it is a one family, fully detached house. I need not further mix the metaphors. I have found that the cross-ownership ban has a conceded anticompetitive intent, and, in its impact on the NASL, will probably have an anticompetitive effect. I conclude that, in the circumstances of the case, neither intent nor effect falls within the Sherman Act.[23]

The NFL's single entity defense had succeeded.

Judge Haight further concluded that although a market for sports ownership capital and skill may exist, as a submarket of the broad market for capital, the NASL had failed to prove its claim that the market was limited to individuals in control of member clubs of major professional sports leagues. He rejected the NASL's perception of the market, saying it was too narrow, because it disregarded potential individual or corporate investors. Judge Haight chose not to define the scope of the market. Instead, he chose to rest his decision on the single entity theory. He stated: "Having concluded that the NASL's suggested 'sports ownership capital and skill' submarket does not exist, I need not decide whether the NASL and NFL are in actual competition with each other in the suggested area. But if competition does exist in such a submarket, it is, again, competition between two single economic entities."[24]

The decision was issued on 17 November 1980. Judge Haight entered a judgment dissolving the preliminary injunction and dismissing the complaint. However, in consideration of "the importance of the legal issues raised, and the adverse effect upon the [the NASL] if [the NFL] were now to promulgate a cross-ownership ban,"[25] the judgment dissolving the injunction was stayed (suspended), and the injunction was continued, pending appeal.

NASL V. NFL (COURT OF APPEALS)

The NASL did launch an appeal, and the NFL's cross-ownership ban would not survive it. The U.S. Court of Appeals for the Second Circuit issued its decision on 27 January 1982.[26] First, the Second Circuit considered whether Section 1 of the Sherman Act should apply to the NFL's cross-ownership ban. Although the district court had held that the NFL and its member clubs acted as a single economic entity and therefore Section 1 did not apply, the Second Circuit disagreed. In its analysis, the Second Circuit found that NFL clubs are "separate economic entities engaged in a joint venture"[27] and observed that "[t]he theory that a combination of actors can gain exemption from § 1 of the Sherman Act by acting as a 'joint venture' has repeatedly been rejected by the Supreme Court and the Sherman Act has been held applicable to professional sports teams by numerous lesser federal courts."[28] While the district court had attempted to distinguish those previous cases from the present one, the Second Circuit was "unpersuaded."[29] Among those previous cases, the Second Circuit highlighted one in particular that raised issues between leagues—*Radovich v. NFL*,[30] which concerned an NFL boycott of a player who had previously played in a rival league. In *Radovich*, the Supreme Court held that the boycott violated Section 1 even though it might not implicate or impinge upon competition between member clubs. Thus, the Second Circuit determined:

> The characterization of [the] NFL as a single economic entity does not exempt from the Sherman Act an agreement between its members to restrain competition. To tolerate such a loophole would permit league members to escape antitrust responsibility for any restraint entered into by them that would benefit their league or enhance their ability to compete even though the benefit would be outweighed by its anticompetitive effects.[31]

Moreover, the Second Circuit pointed out that the cross-ownership ban was designed not only to protect the NFL as a league or single economic entity from competition from the NASL, but also to protect individual NFL clubs as separate economic entities from competition from individual NASL clubs, and cited Leonard Tose's Philadelphia Eagles and Max Winter's Minnesota Vikings and their respective competition with local NASL clubs as examples. The Second Circuit concluded:

The sound and more just procedure is to judge the legality of such restraints according to well-recognized standards of our antitrust laws rather than permit their exemption on the ground that since they in some measure strengthen the league competitively as a "single economic entity," the combination's anticompetitive effects must be disregarded.[32]

The single entity theory had been rejected.

Having established that Section 1 was applicable to the cross-ownership ban, the Second Circuit considered two standards of Section 1 review—specifically, whether the cross-ownership ban should be (1) condemned as per se unlawful or (2) subjected to rule of reason analysis. As noted by the Second Circuit, combinations or agreements are per se violations of Section 1 only if they are "so 'plainly anticompetitive'"[33] and "so lacking in any 'redeeming virtue'"[34] that they are "presumed illegal without further examination."[35] In the Second Circuit's view, the cross-ownership ban did not meet these conditions. Instead, the court deemed it appropriate to apply rule of reason analysis—generally the favored standard of review for agreements between members of joint ventures, including professional sports leagues. In rule of reason analysis, the relevant inquiry is "whether the challenged agreement is one that promotes competition or one that suppresses competition,"[36] which is determined by weighing the anticompetitive effects against the procompetitive effects.

The Second Circuit clearly recognized the cross-ownership ban's anticompetitive intent and effect:

> The voluminous trial record discloses that the NFL's cross-ownership ban would foreclose NASL's teams from continued enjoyment of and access to a significant segment of the market supply of sports capital and skill, thereby restraining at least some NASL teams from competing effectively against NFL teams for fan support and TV revenues. Any resulting restraint would benefit not merely the NFL as a league but those NFL teams that would be otherwise weakened individually and disproportionally (as compared with other NFL teams) by competing NASL teams.[37]

The NFL had argued that there was no such thing as a limited market or submarket for sports capital and skill—there was only a general market, where capital was "fungible," or interchangeable, and where the cross-ownership ban's effect would be negligible. The NFL further argued that in this general market, any difficulty that the NASL experienced in attracting capital should be attributed to its poor financial state, not to the cross-ownership ban. The NASL had argued that a separate market for sports capital and skill existed and was limited to existing owners in major professional sports leagues. Whereas the district court had rejected "the extremes of both the [NASL] and [NFL] perceptions"[38] and declined to make more specific findings, the Second Circuit leaned toward the NASL's position. It stated: "Since we have rejected the 'single economic theory' in the context of this case, it is necessary to determine whether the record discloses a separate market for sports capital and skill. We are satisfied that it does."[39]

The Second Circuit found a sports capital and skill market existed that, "while not limited to existing or potential major sports team owners, is relatively limited in scope and is only a small fraction of the total capital funds market."[40] The court reasoned:

> Because of the economic interdependence of major league team owners and the requirement that any sale be approved by a majority of the league members, an owner may in practice sell his franchise only to a relatively narrow group of eligible purchasers, not to any financier. The potential investor must measure up to a profile having certain characteristics. Moreover, on the supply side of the sports capital market the number of investors willing to purchase an interest in a franchise is sharply limited by the high risk, the need for active involvement in management, the significant exposure to publicity that may turn out to be negative, and the dependence on the drawing power and financial success of the other members of the league.[41]

The Second Circuit also found that existing owners in major professional sports leagues constituted a "significant portion"[42] of the sports capital and skill market. The court stated the NFL's intent to prohibit cross-ownership supported these findings:

Indeed the existence of such a submarket and the importance of the function of existing team owners as sources of capital in that market are implicitly recognized by the defendants' proven intent in adopting the cross-ownership ban. If they believed, as NFL now argues, that all sources of capital were fungible substitutes for investment in NASL sports teams and that the ban would not significantly foreclose the supply of sports capital, they would hardly have gone to the trouble of adopting it.[43]

Finally, the court confirmed that it was not required to prove the precise boundaries of the sports capital market or the exact percentage foreclosed, but that it was sufficient to "establish . . . the general outlines of a separate submarket of the capital market and that the foreclosed portion of it was likely to be significant."[44]

With the foregoing established, unless the cross-ownership's ban had procompetitive effects that outweighed its anticompetitive effects, it would be prohibited by Section 1 of the Sherman Act. The NFL's alleged procompetitive effects—most notably, the assurance of NFL owners' undivided loyalty in competing against the NASL in the sale of tickets and broadcast rights and the assurance that NFL owners would not disclose confidential information to the NASL—were rejected. Therefore, the Second Circuit concluded:

Although there may be some merit in NFL's contentions that the ban would prevent dilution of the good will it has developed, that it would avoid any disruption of NFL operations because of disputes between its owners or cross-owners, or that it would prevent possible inter-league collusion in violation of the antitrust laws, these procompetitive effects are not substantial and are clearly outweighed by its anticompetitive purpose and effect. Its net effect is substantially to restrain competition, not merely competitors. It therefore violates the rule of reason.[45]

The Second Circuit reversed the district court's order granting judgment for the NFL and remanded the case to the district court with directions to enter a permanent injunction against the cross-ownership ban and to consider damages.

Nearly a year later, on 6 December 1982, the U.S. Supreme Court denied the NFL's petition for certiorari (a petition for review). Interestingly, though, Supreme Court Justice William H. Rehnquist, in a rare written dissent from a denial of certiorari, argued that the NFL had acted as a single economic entity. He wrote:

> The NFL owners are joint ventures who produce a product, professional football, which competes with other sports and other forms of entertainment in the entertainment market. Although individual NFL teams compete with one another on the playing field, they rarely compete in the market place. The NFL negotiates its television contracts, for example, in a single block. The revenues from broadcast rights are pooled. Indeed, the only inter-team competition occurs when two teams are located in one major city, such as New York or Los Angeles. These teams compete with one another for home game attendance and local broadcast revenues. In all other respects, the league competes as a unit against other forms of entertainment.[46]

Justice Rehnquist's dissent would provide some hope for the single entity argument in professional sports in the future.

Nevertheless, the NASL had prevailed. The league was able to keep Hunt and Robbie in its ranks, and it was also free to recruit as many NFL owners as were willing to listen. It was also hoping to obtain a significant award of monetary damages. Since 1980, the league had been drowning, and it was desperate for something that would help keep its head above water. But the NASL would have to wait two years for a jury verdict on the damages question, and when it came, in the summer of 1984, the NASL was awarded a nominal amount: $1. At the end of the year, the NASL ceased operations.

MODERN CROSS-OWNERSHIP

Ultimately, the main beneficiary of *NASL v. NFL* would be Major League Soccer (MLS). In 1995, Lamar Hunt, still owner of the Kansas City Chiefs, and Robert Kraft, the owner of the NFL's New England Patriots, had a clear path to become key founding investors in MLS. In 1997, NFL owners passed a resolution (by a 24–5 vote, with the Detroit Lions, Cincinnati Bengals, Chicago Bears, Washington Redskins, and Buffalo Bills voting against and the Oakland Raiders abstaining) reaffirming their previous cross-ownership ban, but it would not apply to MLS. It read, in part:

> Be it *Resolved*, as follows:
>
> That the controlling owner of an NFL club may acquire an interest in a major league baseball, basketball or hockey ("other major sports league") franchise (subject to prior notice to the Commissioner and to such covenants and safeguards as the Commissioner and Finance Committee may determine are appropriate to address actual or perceived conflicts of interest that may arise in the particular situation), but only if such other franchise is located (1) within the home territory of the owner's NFL club, or (2) within a neutral area, i.e., any area that is not within the home territory of any NFL club . . . [47]

Since then, three more NFL owners have joined MLS. In 2004, St. Louis Rams owner Stan Kroenke bought the operating rights for the Colorado Rapids from Anschutz Entertainment Group; in 2007, Seattle Seahawks owner Paul Allen bought a 25 percent stake in the expansion Seattle Sounders; and in 2014, Atlanta Falcons owner Arthur Blank was awarded to right to launch an expansion franchise in Atlanta.

Chapter 4

CHAMPIONSWORLD V. UNITED STATES SOCCER FEDERATION

OVER THE PAST TEN YEARS, as Europe's biggest clubs have sought to build their brands and expand their global footprints, they have increasingly turned to the United States as a key market, recognizing the country's ever-growing interest in the sport. Among other activities, these clubs have made the United States a regular summer destination, taking part in various preseason exhibition matches and tournaments, generally with great fanfare. Such visits provide opportunities to capture the hearts and minds of thousands of American fans. They also provide significant appearance fees, which can reach as high as $2 million to $2.5 million per match. "And please don't forget," Real Madrid manager Carlo Ancelotti once told the *New York Times*, "that the players love coming to the U.S.A."

The International Champions Cup is the latest major annual summer exhibition event involving international clubs being staged in the United States. In summer 2013, the inaugural edition of the tournament was played in Indianapolis, Los Angeles, Miami, New York, Phoenix, and San Francisco.[1] Its participants were England's Chelsea and Everton; Italy's AC Milan, Inter Milan, and Juventus; Spain's Real Madrid and Valencia; and Major League Soccer's Los Angeles Galaxy. In the final, Real Madrid defeated Chelsea before a crowd of more than 67,000 in Miami. The preceding matches drew an average attendance of more than 37,000.[2] All matches were televised live and posted relatively solid ratings. The tournament was created by Relevant

Sports, the soccer division of RSE Ventures, a sports, entertainment, and technology business owned by Stephen Ross, whose main sports property is the NFL's Miami Dolphins. The International Champions Cup's predecessor was the World Football Challenge, which was launched by CAA Sports, a division of Creative Arts Agency, in 2009, and was produced in partnership with Soccer United Marketing (SUM), the marketing arm of Major League Soccer (MLS), in 2011 and 2012.[3] The World Football Challenge featured a mix of elite European clubs plus MLS and Liga MX (Mexican top division) clubs. In 2012, RSE Ventures acquired the rights to the World Football Challenge and rebranded and restructured the event.

Before RSE, CAA, or SUM entered the space, a New Jersey–based promoter named ChampionsWorld made the first effort to bring top European clubs to the United States on a regular basis. ChampionsWorld was founded in 2001. Among other activities, it organized the ChampionsWorld Series—a summer series of exhibition matches, with participants including AC Milan, Barcelona, Bayern Munich, Chelsea, Juventus, Liverpool, Manchester United, Roma, and others—in 2003 and 2004. Prior to ChampionsWorld, MLS had promoted more than 40 international exhibitions between 1996 and 2002, but they were not part of a regular event, and they generally did not involve clubs of quite the same caliber. When SUM was founded in 2002, it expressed an interest in acquiring all or part of ChampionsWorld, but SUM's talks with ChampionsWorld failed. In response, SUM created SUM International to promote high-caliber international matches. An SUM memorandum stated that "leaving the field open to ChampionsWorld and other promoters will prove extremely damaging to SUM and MLS."[4]

When the ChampionsWorld Series kicked off, it was successful in attracting large crowds. In 2003, average attendance was 45,427 per match. In 2004, average attendance was 39,811 per match. But ChampionsWorld suffered substantial losses in both years. It was drowning under the costs of staging the event. In January 2005, ChampionsWorld filed a voluntary petition for reorganization under Chapter 11 of the Federal Bankruptcy Code in the U.S. Bankruptcy Court for the District of New Jersey, listing assets of less than $89,000 and liabilities of more than $3.5 million.[5] In May 2005, ChampionsWorld ceased operations. Its founder and CEO was Charlie Stillitano, who had previously managed the 1994 World Cup matches at Giants Stadium in New Jersey and served as the first general manager of MLS's New York/New Jersey MetroStars (now New York Red Bulls). On the company's failure, Stillitano explained to the *New York Times*, "We expanded too quickly, and promoting a top-quality event was very costly, with expenses unique to the soccer world."

Among the "expenses unique to the soccer world," most notable were the fees paid to the United States Soccer Federation (USSF), the governing body of soccer in the United States. U.S. Soccer required the promoters of matches involving foreign national teams or foreign clubs to pay a percentage of their match revenues in sanctioning fees and required the posting of a performance bond to secure the fees. For all or nearly all of ChampionsWorld's matches, U.S. Soccer and ChampionsWorld entered into contracts, or "match agreements," which set forth ChampionsWorld's agreement to pay a fee and put up a bond in exchange for U.S. Soccer's agreement to sanction the matches in question. Believing that these fees contributed substantially to its failure, ChampionsWorld sued U.S. Soccer and MLS. In 2001, the Los Angeles Memorial Coliseum Commission had sued U.S. Soccer and MLS on a similar basis, but the case was eventually settled for an undisclosed amount. ChampionsWorld's bankruptcy reorganization plan provided for the commencement and prosecution of the lawsuit as the company's only remaining material asset, to be liquidated and distributed among its creditors.

A highly complex case would unfold over the next six years.

CHAMPIONSWORLD V. UNITED STATES SOCCER FEDERATION: BACKGROUND

On 2 May 2006, ChampionsWorld filed a complaint in the U.S. District Court for the Southern District of New York, which later transferred the case to the U.S. District Court for the Northern District of Illinois. The complaint included antitrust claims (Counts 1 through 3), Racketeering Influenced and Corrupt Organizations (RICO) Act claims (Counts 4 and 5), and contract claims (Counts 6 through 10). In the words of Judge Harry D. Leinenweber of the Northern District of Illinois:

> At the heart of the controversy is the question of whether the USSF has the authority to oversee professional, as well as amateur, soccer in the United States. The USSF claims that it has this power. ChampionsWorld argues that USSF improperly arrogated this

power to itself and used it to unreasonably restrain trade and to extract over $3 million in arbitrary and "backbreaking" fees from ChampionsWorld and to cause it many millions more in damages, substantially contributing to ChampionsWorld's demise.[6]

ChampionsWorld pointed to a historically cozy relationship between U.S. Soccer and MLS, and alleged that U.S. Soccer and MLS were engaged in a scheme primarily designed to restrain the competitive threat to MLS posed by ChampionsWorld, whose matches had triple the attendance of MLS matches between 2003 and 2004. U.S. Soccer and MLS denied any wrongdoing.

U.S. Soccer maintained that it had required the promoters of international matches to pay sanctioning fees and put up performance bonds since the early 20th century. ChampionsWorld disputed this, arguing that U.S. Soccer bylaws did not require fees and bonds from nonmembers[7] until 1999. U.S. Soccer's sanctioning fees are generally calculated as follows:

- 5.25 percent of the gross gate receipts of matches involving one foreign club;
- 9 percent of the gross gate receipts of matches involving two foreign clubs;
- 11.25 percent of the first $200,000 and 15 percent of the balance of gross gate receipts of matches involving a foreign national team.

With respect to performance bonds, U.S. Soccer generally requires the greater of the following:

- $3,750 per foreign club per game;
- $25,000 for any match involving a foreign national team; or
- an estimate of anticipated percentage payments that will be due to U.S. Soccer, CONCACAF, and FIFA after the match,[8] such estimate to be at the sole discretion of U.S. Soccer.[9]

ChampionsWorld disputed that all promoters had to put up performance bonds, and claimed that MLS clubs benefited from using a collective "blanket bond" of $50,000. In 2001 and 2002, U.S. Soccer set performance bonds for

ChampionsWorld matches at the base amount. In 2003, U.S. Soccer set performance bonds for all but one ChampionsWorld match higher than the base amount—most often, $100,000—though, at ChampionsWorld's request, U.S. Soccer significantly reduced the bond amounts for some of those matches. In 2004, U.S. Soccer set performance bonds for all ChampionsWorld match above the base amount—generally, $75,000—and did not agree to reduce the amounts for any matches.

U.S. Soccer insisted that it made decisions regarding fee amounts and bond amounts independent of anyone at MLS. In making the claim that U.S. Soccer and MLS worked together to run it out of business, ChampionsWorld relied on

> a series of e-mails and communications, mostly between, among others, [Sunil] Gulati, [Don] Garber, [Mark] Abbott, and Kraft Soccer's Brian O'Donovan, to demonstrate that, e.g., MLS and/or SUM improperly sought special breaks on sanctioning fees; MLS and/or SUM could use USSF's structure, contacts, and/or members to their benefit; MLS and/or SUM affiliates were improperly consulted regarding [ChampionsWorld's] sanctioning fee and bond amounts; or that they were gleefully plotting [Champions-World's] demise.[10]

U.S. Soccer and MLS would contest the admissibility of many of these documents and the conclusions that ChampionsWorld drew from them.

ARBITRATION PROCEEDINGS

On 4 May 2007,[11] Judge Leinenweber granted motions by U.S. Soccer and MLS to stay (suspend) the claims against them pending arbitration before the FIFA Players' Status Committee, one of FIFA's dispute resolution bodies.[12] ChampionsWorld's claims were potentially subject to two different dispute resolution agreements. The first arose from FIFA regulations agreed to by Charlie Stillitano, summarized as follows by Judge Leinenweber:

> In brief, FIFA requires any person arranging international professional men's soccer matches to be a licensed "match agent." Pursuant to this directive, in 2004, Stillitano submitted to FIFA a

written "match agent license application." As part of the application, Stillitano declared that he was familiar with, and unconditionally accepted, FIFA's "Match Agent Regulations" ("MARs"). Article 22 of the MARs addresses dispute resolution, providing: "[i]n the event of a dispute between a match agent and a national association, . . . the complaint shall be submitted to the FIFA Players' Status Committee for consideration and resolution." The MARs also provide for appeal of FIFA's arbitration decisions to the independent Court of Arbitration for Sport (the "CAS").[13]

The second dispute resolution agreement appeared in the match agreements between U.S. Soccer and ChampionsWorld, which included the following forum selection clause:

> The parties hereby consent to the exclusive jurisdiction of the courts of the State of Illinois in connection with any action or proceeding arising out of or relating to the Agreement. In addition, it is expressly agreed that any judicial action or proceeding relating to this Agreement shall be brought in the Federal or State courts which cover Chicago, Illinois.[14]

ChampionsWorld made three arguments that it had not agreed to arbitrate its dispute with U.S. Soccer:

> First, ChampionsWorld argues that Stillitano's license application did not bind it. Second, ChampionsWorld argues that, USSF, as a nonsignatory to the license agreement, cannot enforce that agreement's arbitration provision. And third, ChampionsWorld contends that the forum selection clause in the ChampionsWorld-USSF sanctioning agreements trumps any rights the license application might give USSF.[15]

Judge Leinenweber rejected all three arguments and determined that the dispute was arbitrable. He relied in part on the Federal Arbitration Act, which, he noted, "embodies a strong federal policy in favor of arbitration."[16]

In November 2007, ChampionsWorld filed a claim for arbitration before FIFA. The following month, FIFA's Director of the Legal Division and its Deputy Head of Players' Status issued a letter stating that FIFA was not in a position to intervene in the matter, in part because its regulations provided that only individuals (not corporations) may be parties to its dispute resolution process. ChampionsWorld continued to make requests for a formal decision. In August 2008, FIFA issued another letter in which it reiterated its original position and for the first time stated that ChampionsWorld's antitrust and RICO claims were not within the categories of disputes that FIFA's dispute resolution bodies were allowed to hear. This prompted ChampionsWorld to file a motion for Judge Leinenweber to lift the stay. U.S. Soccer objected on the ground that it had not been informed of ChampionsWorld's efforts before FIFA and wanted the opportunity to present its own case for arbitration. Judge Leinenweber decided to grant U.S. Soccer a period of 60 days to see if it could persuade FIFA to change its position.

On 4 September 2008, U.S. Soccer filed a claim for arbitration before FIFA and named Stillitano, rather than ChampionsWorld, as the respondent. U.S. Soccer did not raise claims that implicated the antitrust laws or RICO. Specifically, U.S. Soccer asked FIFA to decide whether its rules authorized U.S. Soccer to (1) sanction matches such as ChampionsWorld's, (2) impose sanctioning fees and require the posting of performance bonds to secure those fees, and (3) notify FIFA if a match agent refused to pay a sanctioning fee or post a performance bond. The original petition also asked (4) whether U.S. Soccer, FIFA, and/or CONCACAF had to return any of the sanctioning fees to Stillitano. First, there was a question of jurisdiction. On 2 December 2008, the Players' Status Committee determined that it had jurisdiction over U.S. Soccer's petition. ChampionsWorld appealed to the Court of Arbitration for Sport. On 15 July 2009, the Court of Arbitration for Sport affirmed that the Players' Status Committee was competent to answer the first three questions, but not the fourth, noting that the Players' Status Committee's had jurisdiction over disputes "only to the extent that they implicate FIFA's statutes and regulations."[17] With this decided, the case moved back to the Players' Status Committee, which, on 10 February 2010, found that under FIFA's statues and regulations:

1. U.S. Soccer had the authority to require matches between foreign national teams or clubs in the United States to be sanctioned by it;

2. U.S. Soccer had the right to charge sanctioning fees for such matches and require the posting of performance bonds to secure those fees; and

3. U.S. Soccer had the right to notify FIFA in the event that a FIFA-licensed match agent refused to pay a sanctioning fee or post a performance bond in connection with such games.

Further, the Players' Status Committee concluded that those principles had applied since at least 2001, when Stillitano and ChampionsWorld began promoting international matches, even though FIFA's statutes had only explicitly recognized members' sanctioning authority over club games played on their territory since 2004.

CHAMPIONSWORLD V. UNITED STATES SOCCER FEDERATION: MOTIONS FOR JUDGMENT ON THE PLEADINGS

Once the Players' Status Committee had issued its decision, U.S. Soccer and MLS returned to the Northern District of Illinois to file motions for judgment on the pleadings—that is, judgment based on the complaint and answer alone, without a trial—which challenged the legal sufficiency of ChampionsWorld's claims. On 21 July 2010, Judge Leinenweber upheld nine of ChampionsWorld's ten claims.[18] In that ruling, Judge Leinenweber found as a matter of law that U.S. Soccer did not have the authority to govern professional soccer in the United States.

U.S. Soccer's Authority to Govern Professional Soccer

Before dealing with the motions for judgment on the pleadings, Judge Leinenweber addressed the issue of U.S. Soccer's authority, since it was "central to most of the claims and defenses."[19] He began by stating, "It is undisputed that USSF has the authority to govern *amateur*, though not necessarily professional, soccer in the United States."[20] This authority over amateur sports was derived from federal legislation. In 1978, the Amateur Sports Act established a vertical structure for the management of certain amateur sports in the United States. At its head is the United States Olympic Committee; immediately below are national governing bodies for each Olympic sport, including the United States Soccer Federation for soccer. In 1998, the Amateur Sports Act was amended and renamed the Ted Stevens Olympic and Amateur Sports Act,[21] to reflect changes in the conduct of Olympic events. Among its most notable revisions, the statute prohibited national governing bodies from having "eligibility criteria related to amateur status or to participation in the Olympic Games, the Paralympic Games, or the Pan-American Games that are more restrictive than those of the appropriate international sports federation," because amateurism was no longer a requirement for participation in most sports. Alaska Senator Ted Stevens, for whom the act was named, said, "The addition of the word 'Olympic' to the popularly used title 'Amateur Sports Act' is meant to take into account the participation of professional and quasi-amateur athletes in some of the sports of the Olympic Games and Pan-American Games, but at the same time continue to reflect the unique role the USOC and national governing bodies have in the national framework of truly amateur sports activities."[22] The Amateur Sports Act gave national governing bodies (NGBs) "monolithic control" over the amateur sports they govern.[23] Judge Leinenweber observed that while "[t]his type of control would normally violate the antitrust laws,"[24] and "[t]he ASA does not expressly state that NGBs have . . . an [antitrust] exemption in the governing of amateur sports,"[25] the courts have "consistently found that Congress implicitly exempted NGBs, in the oversight of *amateur* sports, from the antitrust laws,"[26] citing *Behagen v. Amateur Basketball Association,*[27] *Eleven Line v. North Texas Soccer Association,*[28] and *JES Properties, Inc. v. USA Equestrian, Inc.*[29]

But U.S. Soccer claimed that the Amateur Sports Act gave it monolithic control over *professional* soccer as well. "At first glance," Judge Leinenweber wrote, "this argument seems counterintuitive."[30] He pointed out, "the ASA (known as the 'Olympic and Amateur Sports Act') repeatedly uses the word 'amateur' to qualify such terms as 'athlete,' 'competition,' and 'sports organization,'"[31] and "[t]he entire statute is, in fact, peppered with the word 'amateur,' while the word 'professional' hardly, if ever, appears."[32] U.S. Soccer argued that "amateur" was "a term of art and must not be read in its ordinary sense."[33] It reached the conclusion that it had authority over professional soccer through the following line of reasoning:

1. The International Olympic Committee rules provide that the international federation for each sport has the responsibility for determining eligibility requirements for its sport in the Olympic games.
2. FIFA, the international federation for soccer, has allowed professionals to participate in Olympic soccer teams since 1984.

3. Under the Amateur Sports Act, an "amateur athlete" is one who meets the eligibility standards of his or her sport's national governing body.
4. As the national governing body for soccer, U.S. Soccer must establish the eligibility criteria for amateur athletes.
5. But U.S. Soccer may not maintain eligibility standards more restrictive than FIFA's.
6. Since FIFA permits paid professional players to participate in the Olympics and related competitions, U.S. Soccer must do the same.
7. Since professional soccer players are eligible to participate in the Olympics, professional soccer players are amateur athletes under the Amateur Sports Act.

Judge Leinenweber stated that he "cannot accept USSF's reasoning in the last step."[34] He contended, "Just because FIFA allows professionals to play in the Olympics, it does not necessarily follow that all professional soccer players are now 'amateur' players *for all purposes*; nor that USSF has authority over all professional soccer players and, by extension, all professional soccer matches because they are now 'amateur' events."[35] In his view, the legislative intent of the Amateur Sports Act amendment upon which U.S. Soccer's argument relied was only to create a "limited exception"[36] for the participation of professionals in the Olympics and related competitions without seeing the U.S. Olympic Committee and the national governing bodies lose control over these competitions.

Nevertheless, U.S. Soccer further argued that FIFA required it to approve all matches between foreign national teams or clubs in the United States, and therefore it was legally obligated to exercise authority over professional soccer matches or it could be subjected to disciplinary measures. For this reason, U.S. Soccer claimed that it had "implied immunity"[37] from antitrust laws with respect to its oversight of professional soccer. In support of its position, U.S. Soccer cited the FIFA Players' Status Committee decision that found it had the authority to sanction matches between foreign national teams or clubs in the United States, the right to charge sanctioning fees and require the posting of performance bonds, and the right to notify FIFA if a match agent refused to pay a fee or post a bond. But Judge Leinenweber found that the exercise of those rights "would arguably constitute unreasonable restraints of trade under the Sherman Act."[38] He also noted that the Court of Arbitration for Sport had determined that the jurisdiction of the Players' Status Committee was limited to interpreting FIFA's statues and regulations. "Indeed," Judge Leinenweber wrote, "it is clear that FIFA has no power to grant USSF an exemption, either express or implied, from the antitrust laws."[39] He added, "Furthermore, it seems far-fetched to believe that FIFA would discipline USSF for obeying the antitrust laws of the United States."[40]

U.S. Soccer had one remaining argument. It contended that "Congress was not only aware, but expected that the NGBs appointed under the [Amateur Sports] Act would be subject to the rules and regulations of their respective [international federations], and yet Congress chose not to limit or interfere with those obligations."[41] Therefore, it reasoned, "Congress can be assumed to have approved USSF's authority over professional soccer, absent an express statement to the contrary."[42] But according to Judge Leinenweber, this was "turning the presumption upside down."[43] He wrote, "Surely, Congress expected NGBs generally to follow the rules of their international federations [IFs]. But that does not mean that Congress intended for IFs to be able to unilaterally authorize their NGBs to violate the antitrust laws of the United States without Congressional approval of any kind."[44] He continued, "Furthermore, USSF offers no reason why Congress would have known of (and therefore tacitly approved) USSF's practice of sanctioning professional soccer matches at the time it passed or amended the ASA. It seems unlikely that this practice could have been apparent to Congress when it is only this year, after a lengthy arbitration process, that FIFA has clarified that it condones such a practice."[45] Judge Leinenweber concluded:

> [A]s a matter of law, the ASA does not give USSF authority to govern professional soccer in the United States, except to the extent necessary for USSF to govern the participation of professional players in the Olympics and related events. USSF is not entitled to an exemption from the antitrust laws regarding professional soccer, except to the extent necessary for USSF to oversee Olympic and related events. USSF has no clear mandate from Congress to govern the whole of professional soccer in the U.S.[46]

With this established, Judge Leinenweber went on to find that Counts 1 through 9 of ChampionsWorld's complaint were sufficiently pled to survive the U.S. Soccer and MLS motions for judgment on the pleadings. The ruling's potential broader consequences, beyond the motions for judgment on the pleadings, were not immediately clear, but it seemed U.S. Soccer's standing with FIFA and the practice of foreign national teams and clubs playing in the United States could be in jeopardy.

ChampionsWorld's Antitrust Claims (Counts 1 Through 3)

In Counts 1 through 3 of its complaint, ChampionsWorld made claims against U.S. Soccer and MLS for (1) conspiracy to restrain competition under Section 1 of the Sherman Act, (2) conspiracy to monopolize under Section 2 of the Sherman Act, and (3) attempt to monopolize under Section 2 of the Sherman Act. As discussed in previous chapters of this book, Section 1 declares to be illegal "[e]very contract, combination . . . or conspiracy, in restraint of trade or commerce,"[47] while Section 2 is directed at any entity that "shall monopolize, or attempt to monopolize, or combine or conspire . . . to monopolize."[48] The law allows successful plaintiffs to recover treble damages (triple the amount of monetary damages). ChampionsWorld alleged that U.S. Soccer and MLS conspired to "damage ChampionsWorld's ability to compete by charging excessive sanctioning fees and requiring unreasonable performance bonds, all under the color of an authority to govern professional soccer that USSF did not possess,"[49] in order to "enhance MLS's position as the premier professional soccer league in the United States."[50] Judge Leinenweber found the allegations sufficiently pled, and denied the motions for judgment on the pleadings regarding Counts 1 through 3. A year later, on 14 September 2011, ChampionsWorld would voluntarily dismiss Counts 2 and 3, leaving Count 1, the Section 1 claim, as its only antitrust claim.

ChampionsWorld's RICO Claims (Counts 4 and 5)

When the RICO Act[51] was passed in 1970, its primary target was the Mafia, which had grown in power and infiltrated legitimate business since the Prohibition era. But even at the time of RICO's passage, its scope extended beyond organized crime to "white-collar" crime, and in the years since the law's passage, its scope has significantly expanded to reach a broad range of activities. RICO may be pursued criminally or civilly by the U.S. Department of Justice or civilly by private individuals or entities that have suffered damage to their business or property. So, while RICO may still be commonly associated with the mob, the same statute used by the federal government to prosecute New York's "five families" was used by ChampionsWorld to challenge U.S. Soccer and MLS. In the present case, the statute's application was significant considering its serious consequences—specifically, its provision for treble damages, just as under the antitrust laws.

Of the two RICO claims in its complaint, ChampionsWorld would voluntarily dismiss Count 4 on 14 September 2011, leaving only Count 5. In Count 5, ChampionsWorld alleged RICO violations under Section 1962(c), which declares:

> It shall be unlawful for any person employed by or associated with any *enterprise* engaged in, or the activities of which affect, interstate or foreign commerce, to conduct or participate, directly or indirectly, in the conduct of such enterprise's affairs through a *pattern* of *racketeering activity* or collection of unlawful debt [emphasis added].[52]

RICO provides a long list of "predicate acts" prohibited by federal and state law—including murder, gambling, robbery, bribery, extortion, fraud, and many others—that can be used to show "racketeering activity."[53] RICO defines "pattern of racketeering activity" as at least two acts of racketeering activity within 10 years, and the Supreme Court has held that the acts in question must be related and demonstrate continuity in order to constitute a pattern. ChampionsWorld alleged that U.S. Soccer and MLS "formed an association-in-fact enterprise, operating together 'to carry out the extortionate fraudulent scheme' of obtaining sanctioning fees and performance bonds, in unreasonable and discriminatory amounts, without any actual authority to do so."[54] Specifically, ChampionsWorld alleged that U.S. Soccer and MLS committed extortion by "obtain[ing] property from [ChampionsWorld] on at least two dozen occasions . . . with consent from [ChampionsWorld] that was induced by the wrongful use of fear through economic threats and by the color of official right."[55] ChampionsWorld also alleged that U.S. Soccer and MLS committed mail and wire fraud in that they "orchestrated a scheme to defraud [ChampionsWorld] of money through the employment of the material misrepresentation that USSF had the exclusive legal authority to sanction all professional soccer matches in the United States."[56] ChampionsWorld counted 24 predicate acts over five years, with each act simultaneously alleged as extortion and mail and/or wire fraud. Judge Leinenweber found that ChampionsWorld had sufficiently pled a pattern of racketeering activity.

According to ChampionsWorld, U.S. Soccer and MLS had legitimate purposes of promoting soccer in the United States, "but that the two had an additional, nefarious purpose to monopolize all professional U.S. soccer matches."[57] According to ChampionsWorld, U.S. Soccer and MLS had "a common purpose, with overlapping officers and an organization structure that provided for continuity with differentiated roles between the two entities."[58] ChampionsWorld charged that certain individuals had dictated U.S. Soccer's sanctioning fees with the purpose of harming MLS's competitors. Champions-World also highlighted U.S. Soccer's support in MLS's development, noting, among other things, that U.S. Soccer provided MLS with $5 million in seed money and eventually forgave the loan in exchange for certain marketing benefits, and also separately helped fund Project 40, an MLS player development program, and stadium development for certain MLS clubs. Judge Leinenweber found that these allegations sufficiently pled an "association-in-fact." The motion for judgment on the pleadings regarding Count 5 was denied. (The motion for judgment on the pleadings regarding Count 4, which was later voluntarily dismissed, was also denied.)

ChampionsWorld's Contract Claims (Counts 6 Through 10)

In Count 6, ChampionsWorld made a "fraudulent inducement" charge against U.S. Soccer. It alleged that U.S. Soccer knew it did not have the authority to govern professional soccer and intended for ChampionsWorld to rely on the false claim, that ChampionsWorld reasonably relied on the false claim, and that this reliance proximately caused monetary loss to ChampionsWorld. Judge Leinenweber upheld the claim.

In Count 7, ChampionsWorld made an "unjust enrichment" charge against U.S. Soccer and MLS, which requires a plaintiff to allege "that the defendant retained a benefit to the plaintiff's detriment, and that the retention of that benefit violates fundamental principles of justice, equity, and good conscience."[59] MLS argued that there could be no claim of unjust enrichment against it because only U.S. Soccer had received the sanctioning fees. But ChampionsWorld responded that U.S. Soccer's sanctioning fee policy also allowed MLS to demand fees from ChampionsWorld when the two organizations staged doubleheader matches. For example, in July 2003, U.S. Soccer gave ChampionsWorld a discount for sponsoring a doubleheader match with MLS, and ChampionsWorld was then compelled to pay a $50,000 fee to MLS, on the basis that, as Judge Leinenweber described it, "MLS had conferred a benefit on ChampionsWorld by deigning to be a cosponsor."[60] Judge Leinenweber upheld the claim.

In Count 8, ChampionsWorld alleged that its contracts with U.S. Soccer were invalid due to a lack of consideration. Specifically, ChampionsWorld argued that, in exchange for the sanctioning fees it paid to U.S. Soccer, it received no goods or services of any kind besides U.S. Soccer's promise to sanction its events, and since U.S. Soccer had no authority to sanction the events, U.S. Soccer's promise was illusory and actually not a promise to do anything. Judge Leinenweber stated, "An illusory promise is not sufficient consideration to support a contract."[61] Therefore, he found the claim sufficiently pled.

In Count 9, ChampionsWorld alleged that its contracts with U.S. Soccer were invalid due to "unconscionability"—meaning, generally, that they were unjust or extremely one-sided and contrary to good conscience. Judge Leinenweber found the claim sufficiently pled.

Finally, in Count 10, ChampionsWorld pled "economic duress" as a basis for restitution. Judge Leinenweber found the allegations insufficient to support an economic duress claim.

CHAMPIONSWORLD V. UNITED STATES SOCCER FEDERATION: MOTIONS FOR SUMMARY JUDGMENT

Clearly, there was a tension between FIFA's view and Judge Leinenweber's view on the scope of U.S. Soccer's authority. That tension was resolved by the Court of Arbitration for Sport.

Prior to Judge Leinenweber's July 2010 ruling, ChampionsWorld had appealed the FIFA Players' Status Committee's February 2010 ruling to the Court of Arbitration for Sport. ChampionsWorld named FIFA as a respondent, and FIFA submitted briefs and arguments to the panel. On 12 July 2011, the Court of Arbitration for Sport affirmed the FIFA Players' Status Committee's ruling as a reasonable interpretation of FIFA's statutes and regulations, holding that U.S. Soccer had the authority to sanction and charge sanctioning fees for matches between foreign national teams and clubs in the

United States and to notify FIFA regarding delinquent match agents.[62] U.S. Soccer had the favorable ruling it needed.

Moving back to the Northern District of Illinois, U.S. Soccer filed a petition to confirm the Court of Arbitration for Sport's decision, and U.S. Soccer and MLS filed motions for summary judgment on ChampionsWorld's antitrust, RICO, and contract claims.

U.S. Soccer's Petition to Confirm the Arbitral Award

On 17 August 2012, Judge Leinenweber confirmed the Court of Arbitration for Sport's arbitral award, thereby confirming U.S. Soccer's sanctioning authority.[63] "Frankly speaking," he wrote, "this is a close case."[64]

U.S. Soccer had petitioned for recognition and enforcement of the arbitral award under the 1958 United Nations Convention on the Recognition and Enforcement of Foreign Arbitral Awards, also known as the New York Convention, to which the United States acceded in 1970 and which is enacted in U.S. law as Chapter 2 of the Federal Arbitration Act.[65] The New York Convention provides the foundation for U.S. courts' pro-enforcement policy for arbitral awards arising from relationships with an international dimension. In the words of the U.S. Supreme Court:

> The goal of the Convention, and the principal purpose underlying American adoption and implementation of it, was to encourage the recognition and enforcement of commercial arbitration agreements in international contracts and to unify the standards by which agreements to arbitrate are observed and arbitral awards are enforced in the signatory countries.[66]

Article 1(1) defines the Convention's scope:

> This Convention shall apply to the recognition and enforcement of arbitral awards made in the territory of a State other than the State where the recognition and enforcement of such awards are sought . . . [and to] arbitral awards not considered as domestic awards in the State where their recognition and enforcement are sought.

Section 202 defines a Convention award as:

> An . . . arbitral award arising out of a legal relationship, whether contractual or not, which is considered as commercial. . . . An . . . award arising out of such a relationship which is entirely between citizens of the United States shall be deemed not to fall under the Convention unless that relationship involves property located abroad, envisages performance or enforcement abroad, or has some other reasonable relation with one or more foreign states.[67]

Judge Leinenweber found that U.S. Soccer and ChampionsWorld had construed Section 202 differently, and upon review of previous cases, he determined that the Convention properly applied "if (a) a non-U.S. citizen is a party to the commercial relationship, or (b) the relationship involves property, performance, or enforcement abroad or 'some other reasonable relation with one or more foreign states.'"[68] Thus, Judge Leinenweber turned his attention to the arguments as to whether the commercial relationship between U.S. Soccer and ChampionsWorld involved a foreign party.

U.S. Soccer argued that FIFA was "'integral' to the 'relationship giving rise to the arbitration,' in that it issued Stillitano a match agent license and thus was party to the arbitration agreement."[69] As described by Judge Leinenweber, ChampionsWorld contended, in essence, that its relationship with U.S. Soccer was "between domestic entities and related to soccer matches played in the United States"[70] and was "too domestic to fall within the Convention"[71] because its foreign elements were "too incidental."[72] ChampionsWorld pointed to the fact that FIFA never signed the contracts between U.S. Soccer and ChampionsWorld and claimed that FIFA was "largely inactive"[73] in the parties' relationship. However, Judge Leinenweber noted that the contracts between U.S. Soccer and ChampionsWorld did refer to FIFA—for example, they stated that U.S. Soccer would be responsible for fees owed to FIFA, and they required ChampionsWorld to ensure that its matches were played in accordance with FIFA rules. Furthermore, ChampionsWorld found it necessary to have Stillitano obtain a match agent license from FIFA. Therefore, Judge Leinenweber determined that ChampionsWorld's reliance on the contracts between U.S. Soccer and ChampionsWorld to prove FIFA's irrelevance was "misplaced"[74] and that the relevant relationship "was not, in fact, 'entirely between citizens of the United States.'"[75] Judge Leinenweber stated that his conclusion was "buttressed by the fact that the parties' relationship also bore a reasonable relation to foreign states through FIFA, its members, and their affiliated teams."[76] He summarized:

> FIFA was an interested party throughout—as reflected by the parties' contracts and Stillitano's match agent status. The very nature of [ChampionsWorld's] business was bringing foreign, FIFA-affiliated soccer teams to play matches in the U.S. This is not a case where, as [ChampionsWorld] argues, the relationship is insufficiently "foreign" to warrant enforcement under the Convention.[77]

The Convention recognizes a limited number of defenses to enforcement of an arbitral award, and U.S. courts interpret those defenses narrowly. ChampionsWorld submitted three of these defenses, all of which Judge Leinenweber rejected.

U.S. Soccer and MLS Motions for Summary Judgment: RICO and Contract Claims

Having enforced the arbitral award, Judge Leinenweber then relied upon it to grant summary judgment in favor of U.S. Soccer and MLS on the RICO and contract claims against them.

In Count 5 of its complaint, ChampionsWorld alleged that U.S. Soccer and MLS had formed an association-in-fact enterprise and operated together in committing acts of extortion and mail and wire fraud. Under federal law, mail and wire fraud involve a party's participation in a scheme to defraud.[78] In ChampionsWorld's mail and wire fraud claims, the relevant alleged misrepresentation was that U.S. Soccer "had the exclusive legal authority to sanction all professional soccer matches in the United States."[79] Judge Leinenweber determined that ChampionsWorld had standing to challenge U.S. Soccer's conduct as applied to the types of matches that ChampionsWorld promoted—those involving foreign clubs, affiliated with FIFA—and the Court of Arbitration for Sport ruling established that U.S. Soccer had sanctioning authority over such matches. "Therefore," he concluded, "USSF's statement was not false, and [ChampionsWorld's] mail and wire fraud claims fail."[80] As to the extortion claim, the Hobbs Act prohibits affecting commerce by extortion, with extortion defined as obtaining "property from another, with his consent, induced by wrongful use of actual or threatened force, violence, or fear, or under color of official right."[81] U.S. Soccer argued that because it had a lawful and contractual right to sanctioning fees, as well as a right to notify FIFA about delinquent promoters, there could be no Hobbs Act violation. Judge Leinenweber accepted U.S. Soccer's claim of right and found that ChampionsWorld's argument "ultimately boils down to one of economic duress,"[82] which the Seventh Circuit had "deemed insufficient"[83] to overcome a claim of right and sustain a Hobbs Act claim. Therefore, he concluded that U.S. Soccer's conduct "did not rise to the level of extortion."[84]

Count 6 was ChampionsWorld's "fraudulent inducement" claim. Judge Leinenweber wrote, "[ChampionsWorld] has essentially conceded that its only argument for fraud is that USSF lacked the authority to sanction its game,"[85] and "[b]ecause the CAS Ruling precludes such a finding, USSF is entitled to summary judgment."[86] Count 7 was ChampionsWorld's "unjust enrichment" claim. Judge Leinenweber noted that "when a relationship is contractual, one may plead unjust enrichment only if the contract is invalid or fails to cover the claim."[87] ChampionsWorld argued that the contracts were invalid due to a lack of consideration. But Judge Leinenweber found that U.S. Soccer sanction was adequate consideration. He stated, "there seems to be no dispute that the relevant teams would not have participated in unsanctioned games,"[88] thus "ChampionsWorld . . . received something of value under the contract"[89] and "the contracts do not fail."[90] Count 8 was ChampionsWorld's claim for restitution predicated on the alleged lack of consideration in the contracts, which had already been rejected.

Count 9 was ChampionsWorld's "unconscionability" claim. Here, ChampionsWorld contended that even if U.S. Soccer had sanctioning authority, the match agreements were nonetheless unconscionable, and therefore unenforceable. Specifically, it alleged that "(a) it lacked bargaining power against USSF; (b) no party in bona fide negotiations would require the 'exorbitant fees' and performance bonds that USSF did; and (c) that USSF's fee and bond terms were 'shocking and grossly unreasonable, thereby making USSF's contracts with plaintiff improvident, oppressive and totally one-sided.'"[91] ChampionsWorld claimed it had no alternative to U.S. Soccer's unreasonable terms. In Illinois, an unconscionability finding "may be based on either procedural or substantive unconscionability, or a combination of both."[92] Procedural unconscionability consists of some impropriety during the formation of the contract that deprives a party of meaningful choice; substantive unconscionability concerns whether the contract terms themselves are reasonable. U.S. Soccer argued that ChampionsWorld could prove neither procedural nor substantive unconscionability.

In considering procedural unconscionability, Judge Leinenweber observed, "there can be little dispute that there was a disparity in bargaining power here—if ChampionsWorld wanted to promote matches with FIFA-affiliated teams in the United States, USSF was the only game in town."[93] However, he noted that Illinois courts were "reluctant to hold that inequality in bargaining power alone suffices to invalidate an otherwise enforceable agreement."[94] Furthermore, he found that both parties were "sophisticated actors,"[95] and that ChampionsWorld had been represented by counsel in agreeing to a substantial number of the contracts in question. He concluded that the contracts had "an element of procedural unconscionability, but not so much that they must be invalidated on that basis."[96]

In considering substantive unconscionability, Judge Leinenweber was compelled by U.S. Soccer's argument that ChampionsWorld was a sophisticated actor that had accepted the same terms repeatedly over several years. He added, "Although there is arguably some evidence that, for example, a significant cost-price disparity exists, [ChampionsWorld] has generally either not cited to it, cited to it only be incorporating, *e.g.*, an entire brief, or not provided the Court with a copy of the cited evidence."[97] Therefore, summary judgment was granted in favor of U.S. Soccer.

U.S. Soccer and MLS Motions for Summary Judgment: Antitrust Claim

To succeed in its Sherman Act Section 1 claim, ChampionsWorld had the burden of showing that the challenged action had an anticompetitive effect in a relevant market. Every relevant market has a product dimension and a geographic dimension. ChampionsWorld relied on University of Michigan professor Rodney Fort to provide the market definition. But Judge Leinenweber found Fort's opinion "unreliable and unhelpful on both [product and geographic] dimensions,"[98] and therefore granted a motion to exclude his testimony. Having rejected Fort's testimony, Judge Leinenweber concluded that ChampionsWorld could not "carry its burden on the threshold requirement of demonstrating a cognizable market and concomitant market power in [U.S. Soccer and MLS]." He added, "The Court notes that it is not holding that [ChampionsWorld] could not have established a relevant market, merely that it did not." Therefore, he granted summary judgment in favor of U.S. Soccer and MLS.

After six years, they had prevailed over ChampionsWorld's claims.

PRESENT DAY

U.S. Soccer's sanctioning authority was confirmed, and an important revenue stream was preserved. For the fiscal year ended 31 March 2013, U.S. Soccer reported international match revenues of $4.4 million, up from $2.6 million the previous year.[99] This was U.S. Soccer's fourth largest revenue stream, behind sponsorship, television, licensing, and royalties ($23.4 million), national teams' match revenues ($22.2 million), and registration and affiliation fees ($8.7 million). U.S. Soccer showed a net operating profit of $4.5 million.

Those revenues should see continued growth for at least the short term, as the organization of major events involving foreign teams seems to have matured, and there are no signs that interest in the events will cool off. In summer 2014, the International Champions Cup featured another star-studded cast: England's Liverpool, Manchester City, and Manchester United; Greece's Olympiacos; Italy's AC Milan, Inter Milan, and Roma; and Spain's Real Madrid. On 2 August 2014, the group phase match between Manchester United and Real Madrid at Michigan Stadium drew 109,318 fans—setting a record as the largest crowd ever to see a soccer game in the United States. (The record previously belonged to the 1984 Olympic gold medal final between Brazil and France at the Rose Bowl in Pasadena, California, which drew 101,799.)

As previously mentioned, the International Champions Cup is organized by Relevant Sports. Relevant Sports' CEO is none other than Charlie Stillitano. After emerging from the ChampionsWorld wreckage, he moved to CAA Sports, where he organized the World Football Challenge, before arriving at Relevant Sports. His original vision has essentially been realized. And, a decade on from ChampionsWorld, there is once again a question as to MLS's place in the picture. While the first edition of the International Champions Cup had one MLS participant, the LA Galaxy, the second edition of the tournament had none. In an interview with FOX Soccer's Kyle

McCarthy, Stillitano blamed "logistics," explaining that the ICC's schedule conflicted with MLS's schedule. "We expect this to be an annual event," he went on to say. "Certainly, MLS will be a part of it in the future."

Chapter 5
NAMOFF v. D.C. UNITED

UNTIL FAIRLY RECENTLY, THE MEDICAL community lacked a real understanding of the prevalence and seriousness of brain trauma sustained in sports. Today, although it is difficult to measure accurately, it is generally estimated that there may be more than a million and perhaps as many as a few million cases of mild traumatic brain injury—commonly referred to as concussion, the most common type of traumatic brain injury—among sports participants each year. While doctors and researchers are still learning about brain trauma from concussions and subconcussive hits to the head, there is no longer any doubt about its seriousness.

In the late 1980s and early 1990s, the field of sports neuropsychology—the study of the brain under the influence of sports—was born out of research focused on, not surprisingly, American football, an inherently violent game in which blows to the head are unavoidable. "Throughout most of the Super Bowl era, football was understood to be an orthopedic, an arthroscopic, and, eventually, an arthritic risk," wrote Ben McGrath in the *New Yorker*. "What was missing from this picture was the effect of all that impact on the brain." In the words of Mark Fainaru-Wada and Steve Fainaru in *League of Denial*, their book on brain trauma in the National Football League (NFL), a concussion was long regarded as "the neurological equivalent of a stubbed toe." With little research devoted to concussion, there was confusion among doctors about the injury, yet there seemed to be a consensus that it wasn't serious. "In the late seventies and early eighties, nobody thought mild head injury was a problem," said Dr. Jeffrey Barth, a University of Virginia neuropsychologist who performed pioneering research on sports-related concussions, to the *League of Denial* authors. "When you'd go to the doctor or the

ER with a mild head injury, they'd say, 'Just take a couple days off, take some aspirin, and you'll be okay by Monday.'"

It was, after all, an invisible injury. A concussion often cannot be detected by CTs, MRIs, or other brain imaging techniques. The symptoms may be subtle and may not appear immediately. Nevertheless, Jeff Barth's early research indicated that a concussion was not a minor injury. He found that in some cases, individuals experienced intense symptoms for extended periods. Barth eventually ran a study involving college football players in which he administered a set of neuropsychological tests to gather baseline data and then repeated the tests after a player had sustained a concussion in order to assess any changes in brain function. In this way, he was able to highlight a variety of negative changes in brain function following a concussion. Identifying such changes enabled one to better determine when the injury had healed—that is, when normal brain function had returned—and the player in question should return to play. Barth published his findings in 1989, writing, "Through further data review and analysis, it is our hope that we can provide the football community, and sports medicine psychologists in particular, with a brief and easily administered set of neuropsychological assessment tools that will aid team physicians."

Barth's experiment soon inspired Pittsburgh-based neurospsychologist Mark Lovell and neurosurgeon Joe Maroon to develop their own neurological test for assessment of the NFL's Pittsburgh Steelers. Their original pen-and-pencil test ultimately evolved into a computerized test that was branded as the ImPACT test (Immediate Post-Concussion Assessment and Cognitive Testing). The ImPACT test is now the most widely used test in concussion evaluation and management in high school, college, and professional sports.

After the early work of Barth, Lovell, and Maroon, concussions took off as a research subject, with ever-increasing study into diagnosis, management, long-term effects, and other areas. Today, sports-related concussions are a prominent public health issue. Much of the credit for the public's increased awareness of the issue goes to the *New York Times* and its reporter Alan Schwartz, who has written more than 100 articles that have exposed the dangers of concussions in sports, earning him a Pulitzer Prize nomination in 2011.

A concussion is generally defined as an injury to the brain that results in temporary loss of normal brain function. A blow to the head or even a rapid deceleration may cause the injury. The brain, which consists of a gelatin-like substance, normally floats inside the skull, cushioned by cere-brospinal fluid. The skull and cerebrospinal fluid provide protection for the brain by absorbing impact, but this protection is not perfect; a violent force may cause the brain to crash against the rough inner wall of the skull, which can cause bruising and tearing of brain tissue and blood vessels. While such damage is difficult to see in brain scans, all concussions set off symptoms. In his book *Concussions and Our Kids*, Dr. Robert Cantu, a neurosurgeon at Boston University and a leading expert in sports-related brain trauma, places concussion symptoms into four major categories:

- *Somatic:* headaches, nausea, vomiting, balance and/or visual problems, dizzy spells, and issues such as sensitivity to light and noise
- *Emotional:* sadness to the point of depression (even suicide), nervous-ness, and irritability
- *Sleep disturbance:* sleeping more or less than usual and trouble falling asleep
- *Cognitive:* difficulty concentrating, troubles with memory, feeling men-tally slow or as if in a fog that will not lift

"Symptoms are clues," says Cantu. "They reveal many things—the sever-ity of the injury and the pace of recovery, for example. The number and combination also can pinpoint areas of the brain affected by a concussion."

Most patients recover within seven to ten days, but approximately 20 per-cent of patients experience post-concussion syndrome, in which symptoms persist for a month or longer—in some cases, several months or even years. According to Cantu, those suffering from post-concussion syndrome often have had concussions that were not managed properly. The standard treatment for any concussion is rest. "It's essential that these athletes not be allowed to physically and cognitively exert while they're still symptomatic and recover-ing from a concussion," Cantu explained to *Sports Illustrated*'s Grant Wahl. "They can't safely work out or play, and if they try to do that they'll aggravate their condition almost certainly, and that could decide whether they ever come back in the future." With proper care, even post-concussion syndrome patients eventually recover. But once a player has sustained a concussion, that player is more vulnerable to another concussion. And it is believed that future concus-sions carry a higher risk of complications.

MLS CONCUSSION HISTORY

While sports-related brain trauma is most commonly associated with American football and hockey, the danger extends to several other sports, and especially to soccer. The combination of speed and aggression with which the game is played often produces player-to-player and player-to-ground impacts that may jolt the brain. A recent study published in the *American Journal of Sports Medicine* found that girls' soccer and boys' soccer accumulated the second highest and fifth highest number of concussions, respectively, among 20 high school sports that were monitored over a period of two years. Dr. Cantu told Grant Wahl that soccer provided the third highest number of his patients among professional athletes, behind only American football and hockey.

In the past ten years, several Major League Soccer (MLS) players have seen the effects of concussions and post-concussion syndrome terminate their careers, and, to varying degrees, complicate their post-career lives. Ross Paule was the first and perhaps the worst such case. Paule arrived on the MLS scene in 1997, the league's second year. His first concussion was sustained in 1998, while playing for the Colorado Rapids. Paule recovered and played the next four seasons without incident. Then disaster struck. Paule suffered three concussions in a six-week span in 2003, while playing for the Columbus Crew—first bumping heads with a teammate, next being struck by a deflected shot, and finally getting hit in the back of the head while going up for a header. He sat out just two weeks between the second and third concussions, and then just two more weeks after the third concussion, before returning to play. Looking back, the failure to keep him off the field is stunning. "I'd always been taught that if you're only a little bit injured you can play," said Paule to *ESPN*'s Leander Schaerlaeckens. His reasoning highlights why the decision on return to play should never be in the player's hands. In 2004, Paule again suffered multiple concussions, now from increasingly weaker blows to the head. By 2005, he had little to no tolerance for contact to the head. Early that year, one soft shove rendered him unconscious. Soon after, Paule retired, at age 28.

The league's awakening on concussion evaluation and management was still a few years away—not soon enough for Paule. "I do feel like if I was given better advice to sit out and really let my brain heal before I stepped back out there, it would've made a big difference," he said last year in an interview for the official website of the Colorado Rapids, with whom he had become an MLS All-Star in 1998 and 1999. Now almost a decade since his retirement, Paule still suffers from terrible symptoms, including headaches, visual and balance problems, dizziness, difficulty concentrating, and memory loss. Schaerlaeckens reported that he gets migraines daily. If he turns his head too fast, he may lose his balance. He can watch a movie and then watch it a month later without recalling having ever seen it. "I've just gotten used to it," Paule said. "Which is sad."

Josh Gros estimates that he averaged a concussion a year from the tenth grade of high school through his four years at Rutgers University and into his first three years with D.C. United. In his fourth year with D.C. United, he sustained seven concussions. "It seemed like the longer I went, the easier it was for me to get a concussion," said Gros to Leander Schaerlaeckens. The alarming series of concussions in 2007 produced symptoms that were more pronounced than in the past, including nausea, sensitivity to light, sleep disturbance, and memory troubles. Dr. Cantu told Gros that he was causing long-term brain damage by continuing to play. Gros heeded the warning and retired at the end of the year, at age 25. After his retirement, Gros joined the Philadelphia Union's front office. "I miss [playing] quite a bit," he confessed in an interview for D.C. United's official website. "It was one of the things I cherished most. Obviously, things didn't work out the way I would like, but I am grateful for the four years I got to play and put on that uniform." An industrious midfielder, Gros had been an integral part of the D.C. United team that won the MLS Cup in 2004, and he was selected as an MLS All-Star in 2006. More importantly, and very fortunately, he is now practically free of symptoms.

Alecko Eskandarian, Gros's teammate at D.C. United, would not be as fortunate. Eskandarian, a stocky forward with a rough and tumble style who was the MVP of the 2004 MLS Cup and an MLS All-Star in 2004 and 2006, was forced to retire in 2010 after failing to recover from his fourth career concussion. He has been affected by lingering symptoms ever since. He sustained three concussions in his first three years in the league. Both the first and the second caused him to lose consciousness, and on both occasions he stayed in the game. The third, resulting from a violent collision with New England goalkeeper Matt Reis, forced him to step away from the game for ten months, during which time he struggled with headaches, nausea, and depression. Eventually, Eskandarian returned and enjoyed three years without symptoms. Then, in a 2009 exhibition match between the Los Angeles Galaxy, for whom he was then playing, and A.C. Milan, a clearance smacked him in the face from close range. It broke his nose, gave him whiplash, and knocked him unconscious. Eskandarian played three more games the following month, which would be the last of his career. The concussion symptoms that had faded were back, and this time he couldn't completely shake them. "I'm a soccer player through and through. If I could play, I would. Being an athlete my whole life, shutting it down is the worst type of torture," said Eskandarian to Stefan Bondy for *The Record*. "At the same time, this is my brain. It's not a hamstring or an ankle. I don't care how tough you are. This about living a good life after soccer. . . . I've learned to take nothing for granted." Now an assistant coach for the new NASL's New York Cosmos, Eskandarian still deals with headaches, nausea, and dizziness. "It's daily," he revealed to Leander Schaerlaeckens. "I can't tell you how much life has changed. I was a pretty social guy but intense laughter can trigger vertigo (a form of dizziness). You have no choice but to change your personality and lifestyle to avoid it. It's taken a lot out of me and made me a different person."

And then there is Taylor Twellman. Of the MLS careers cut short by concussions, Twellman's was the most decorated. A former league MVP and five-time All-Star, he stands as one of the most prolific goal scorers in league history, having banged in 101 goals in his eight years with the New England Revolution. Twellman's first three concussions were sustained outside of MLS—the first at the University of Maryland, the second during his stint with German club 1860 Munich, and the third in a U.S. national team training session. After the fourth—this one in an MLS match in 2003, where he took a kick to the face from the LA Galaxy's Danny Califf that left him with a broken orbital bone, nose, and jaw, in addition to the concussion—Twellman for the first time experienced post-concussion symptoms, which kept him out for a month. He suffered a fifth concussion in 2005. But the sixth, in 2008, was the critical blow. Twellman leaped to meet a cross and headed home his 96th career regular season goal; at the same time, Steve Cronin, the LA Galaxy's keeper, leaped to cut out the cross and accidentally punched Twellman in the face. "It was almost like running as fast as you can into a wall," he said to Scott Helman of the *Boston Globe*. Twellman, concussed and bleeding, picked himself up and celebrated with his teammates, until he realized that something was wrong. He turned to his teammate Sharlie Joseph, pointed to his head, and said, "I got a concussion." Then he fell back to the ground. "It's so hard to look back on it," said Jay Heaps, then Twellman's teammate and now head coach of the Revolution. "Here we were celebrating the greatest moment. But it was the moment his career would start to slowly unwind." Twellman stayed in the game and went on to play the final eight games of the season. But he wasn't right. When that finally became clear, the decision was made to sit out the 2008 playoffs.

Twellman's symptoms ran the gamut—migraines, nausea, visual problems, vertigo, sensitivity to light, insomnia, memory loss, and depression. After an agonizing fall and winter, he attempted to come back in the spring. Twellman made his first appearance in seven months in May 2009, but the following week he scored a goal with his head that made his head feel "like a sponge." It would be his last game. Twellman worked with Dr. Cantu in 2009 and 2010, hoping that he might be able to recover and return, but Cantu ultimately told him that he had to hang up his cleats if he wanted a chance for a healthy life. In November 2010, Twellman, then 30 years old, announced his retirement.

Today, he is still ever-present on the American soccer scene, most notably in his role as an ESPN analyst, and his condition has significantly improved, but he has not fully recovered. He still deals with headaches and nausea, and he has to avoid strenuous exercise because it triggers his symptoms. His response has been to turn his personal battle into a public service. Leander Schaerlaeckens referred to Twellman, appropriately, as the "unofficial spokesman for concussion victims in soccer." Twellman speaks on concussions at every opportunity, and he has launched a foundation, ThinkTaylor, with a mission to advance concussion awareness, recognition, and education. "I don't want anyone to be me," he explained to Kevin Baxter of the *Los Angeles Times*. "If I knew what I know now in 2008, I might still be playing."

MLS CONCUSSION PROTOCOL

MLS established league-wide ImPACT testing in 2007. Every player was required to undergo baseline testing before every season, and clubs were encouraged to consult those data when a player sustained a head injury. But the ImPACT test is just one tool in overall concussion evaluation and management. Essentially, clubs were still left to evaluate and manage concussions in their own way, and as long as this was the case, the standard of care across the league could vary. There was room for the league to be more proactive. The loss of Taylor Twellman served as a wake-up call.

In response, MLS formed a Concussion Protocol Committee in 2010, with Ruben Echemendia, a neuropsychologist who directs the National Hockey League's concussion program, as its chair and Twellman as one of its members. The committee took steps to improve concussion education among trainers, coaches, and players, and it developed a set of concussion evaluation and management guidelines that went into effect in 2011. "We recognized that we needed to do more," said Nelson Rodriguez, then MLS executive vice president of competition and game operations.

The stated objective of MLS's Concussion Evaluation and Management Protocol, sometimes referred to as the Return To Play (RTP) Protocol, is to "[p]rovide state of the art professional care and treatment for MLS players" and "[r]educe time lost due to injury." First, it acknowledges the following:

> The Return To Play (RTP) decision-making process is complex and dynamic. Although there has been a virtual explosion of research into the diagnosis and management of sport-related traumatic brain injury in the past 10 years, the RTP decision remains largely a clinical endeavor without firm empirically derived guidelines. The weight of clinical and empirical evidence suggests that the RTP decision-making process should be individualized rather than relying on generic RTP guidelines. Of significance is our current understanding from the research literature that the signs and symptoms of concussion are dynamic and evolve over time. Consequently, symptoms may not be present until hours or days following the initial blow(s).

This is a reasonable qualification. As much as MLS or any other league would like to exercise complete control over concussions, that's not possible. What MLS can do is make every effort to stay in tune with the latest developments in concussion research and apply them as well as possible to each player's care.

Under the guidelines, protection begins with quickly identifying the possibility of a concussion and getting players off the field. "Players who are suspected of having sustained a concussion shall be removed from play immediately and evaluated by team medical staff," the guidelines state. "If after initial evaluation the player is diagnosed with a concussion he shall not be returned to play on the same day." The first step in management is "physical and cognitive rest." The return to play process will not commence until the player is "asymptomatic at rest for at least 24–48 hours," with the specific length of time varying "depending on the nature of the injury, the player's concussion history and psychological status." Once symptom free, the player is referred to the team neuropsychologist for a standardized neuropsychological evaluation. When the player is deemed to be "neurocognitively at or above baseline," he may begin a "gradual process of light aerobic workout, followed by more intense aerobic workouts, strength training, non-contact sport-specific drills, contact sport-specific drills, heading training and finally, full RTP." On a daily basis, recovering players are monitored for a reemergence of symptoms using the Post Concussion Symptom Checklist. The team physician is ultimately responsible for making the return to play decision.

This was a sea change for MLS. "Back in the day, it was, 'Hey, if you can see straight and you know what day it is, then get back out on the field,'" recalled Paul Bravo, Colorado Rapids vice president of soccer operations and technical director, who played in the league from its inaugural season through 2001. "Today there's no way. There's a protocol that we must follow in order to get a player back on the field, and if there's any signs of a concussion, we shut them down. And that's the way it should be." The new protocol put MLS on a par with other American sports leagues, and well ahead of any other soccer league in the world. Yet the following year, a concussion lawsuit arrived at its door.

NAMOFF V. D.C. UNITED

In July 2010, two months before the MLS Concussion Protocol Committee met for the first time, yet another D.C. United player retired as a result of post-concussion syndrome—Bryan Namoff. A ten-year D.C. United veteran who helped the club to the MLS Cup in 2004, the MLS Supporters' Shield in 2006 and 2007, and the U.S. Open Cup in 2008, and ranks third on the club's all-time appearance list with 195 games played, Namoff was 31 years old when he retired. Upon his retirement, Namoff was brought into D.C. United's front office, but his symptoms eventually forced him to leave that position. His next step was an unprecedented one. On 29 August 2012, Namoff and his wife, Nadine, sued D.C. United and its former coach, Tom Soehn, in D.C. Superior Court for their handling of his head injury, seeking $12 million in damages. Namoff later added D.C. United athletic trainer Brian Goodstein, D.C. United former team physician Dr. Christopher Annunziata, and Annunziata's practice, Commonwealth Orthopaedics, to the lawsuit.

Namoff's original injury occurred in a game against the Kansas City Wizards (now Sporting Kansas City) at RFK Stadium in Washington, D.C., on 9 September 2009. In a collision with an opponent, Namoff sustained a blow to the head just behind his right temple. The complaint described "visible snapping of his neck violently back to the left."[1] No member of D.C. United's staff entered the field to examine him. Namoff was able to get up on his own, and despite feeling "lost and out of it,"[2] he finished the game. After the game, Namoff told Goodstein that he "did not feel right, that the lights were hazy, and that he had no peripheral vision."[3] Goodstein retrieved Annunziata and an optometrist. But the complaint alleged that neither Annunziata nor Goodstein evaluated Namoff after the game. Goodstein told Nadine Namoff that Bryan had sustained a concussion.

The following day, 10 September, Namoff participated in pool exercises, but he did not respond well and stopped after approximately 25 minutes. According to the complaint, Namoff "had the physical symptoms of a concussion, including headache, fatigue, and not feeling right,"[4] and he "continuously advised Goodstein of his headaches."[5] On 11 September, Namoff participated in a film session but did not participate in physical activities, as he was still exhibiting concussion symptoms. Nevertheless, the decision was made for Namoff to play in a game against the Seattle Sounders at RFK Stadium on 12 September. The complaint alleged, "From September 9, 2009 up to and including September 12, 2009, [Namoff] was not assessed, evaluated, and/or examined by Dr. Annunizata and Goodstein, or any other agent, servant and/or employee of Commonwealth Orthopaedics and Defendant D.C. United prior to being allowed to return to play."[6] Although the club had administered preseason baseline ImPACT testing, neither Annunziata nor Goodstein repeated the testing for comparative purposes. Tom Soehn had been advised of Namoff's status and symptoms and was involved in the return to play decision. Namoff went on to play the entire game against the Sounders. The complaint stated, "Throughout the game, [Namoff] experienced and exhibited post-concussive symptoms, which were significantly exacerbated by the end of the game."[7] After the game, Namoff reported to Goodstein and Annunziata that he was "having difficulty focusing, that he was dizzy, that the lights were hazy, and that he did not feel right."[8] Annunziata and Goodstein "merely stated that they would monitor him," the complaint said.[9]

Namoff would never play again. Over the next several months, he saw numerous specialists, including Dr. Cantu, and he eventually participated in limited training with the team, but his symptoms did not fade away, leading to his decision to retire in July 2010. By August 2012, when the complaint was filed, Namoff was still dealing with the effects. According to the complaint, as a result of the defendants' negligence:

> he suffered serious and disabling damage to his body, including but not limited to permanent traumatic brain injury; permanent cognitive deficits and memory problems; permanent fatigue; permanent headaches; permanent vestibular problems; permanent visual motion hypersensitivity; and sleep problems; he has incurred, and will continue to incur, medical, hospital, rehabilitative, and pharmaceutical expenses in an effort to care for his injuries; he has suffered, and will in the future suffer a loss of earnings and earnings capacity; he has endured and will continue to endure pain and suffering, disability, mental impairment, emotional distress, metal anguish, humiliation, embarrassment and impairment of the enjoyment and quality of a full and complete life.[10]

Namoff had sustained one concussion in high school and one in college, but none in MLS before the 2009 incident.

Negligence can be defined as the failure to use ordinary care, as would be expected of a prudent person under the same circumstances, for the protection of others against unreasonably great risk of harm. Generally, to sustain a negligence claim, the plaintiff must prove: (1) the defendant owed the plaintiff a duty of care; (2) the defendant breached that duty; (3) the breach was the proximate cause of the plaintiff's injury; and (4) the plaintiff was actually injured. A legally recognized duty is the threshold element. While every person owes to others a general duty of care, certain relationships between parties—e.g., employer-employee, doctor-patient, coach-athlete—establish a special duty of care. The Namoffs' complaint included three counts of negligence and one count of loss of consortium.

- Count I stated that Dr. Annunziata and Goodstein "owed a continuing duty to [Namoff] of exercising that degree of skill, care, caution, diligence, and foresight exercised by others similarly situated in the field providing healthcare services to athletes."[11] It further stated that D.C. United, "acting by and through its agents, servants and/or employees, Dr. Annunziata and Goodstein, breached the duties of care owed to [Namoff],"[12] as it was "negligent in its management, care and treatment of [Namoff]."[13] D.C. United's alleged negligence was cited as the "direct and proximate cause"[14] of the injuries previously listed.
- Count II stated that Tom Soehn also owed a duty of care to the members of his team, including to "ensure the health and safety of a player, such as [Namoff], in returning to play soccer after an injury,"[15] and that Soehn, individually, and D.C. United, acting through its employee Soehn, breached duties of care owed to Namoff, which caused his injuries.
- Count III stated that D.C. United had a duty to "implement and/or enforce ... policies and procedures regarding returning a player to practice or play after sustaining a concussion, and train its employees, agents and servants on the dangers of premature post-concussive practice or play,"[16] which the club failed to carry out, thereby causing Namoff's injuries.
- Count IV stated that, as a result of the defendants' alleged negligence, Bryan and Nadine Namoff suffered "the loss of society, companionship, and consortium of each other, to their great and substantial damage."[17]

In May 2013, the Namoffs filed an amended complaint, alleging that D.C. United, Goodstein, and Soehn were (1) negligent in failing to properly assess Namoff's head injury during the game against the Wizards and (2) negligent in making return to play decisions, and alleging that Annunziata was negligent in treating Namoff's head injury. The Namoffs were seeking damages of $10 million for negligence and $2 million for the impact on his marriage.

NAMOFF V. D.C. UNITED: MOTION TO DISMISS

On 6 June 2013, D.C. Superior Court Judge Natalia M. Combs Greene denied a motion to dismiss the amended complaint. D.C. United, Goodstein, and

Soehn argued that the Namoffs' claims against them were covered by workers' compensation insurance, and under the D.C. Workers' Compensation Act (WCA) the claims must be heard in the D.C. Office of Workers' Compensation. However, Judge Combs Greene established that the D.C. Superior Court retains jurisdiction over workplace injury claims where the defendant is (1) not an employer or co-employee of the plaintiff or (2) an employer that has failed to provide the requisite insurance coverage. Therefore, Judge Combs Greene considered in this case (1) whether D.C. United was Namoff's employer and (2) whether D.C. United provided insurance coverage.

On the employment relationship question, although there was no dispute that Namoff was an employee of MLS, he may have concurrently been a "special employee" of D.C. United. Judge Combs Greene observed that the D.C. Court of Appeals has recognized the following three elements of a special employment relationship: (1) the employee has made a contract for hire, express or implied, with the special employer; (2) the work being done is essentially that of the special employer; and (3) the special employer has the right to control the details of the work. The first element is considered the most important. For an implied special employment relationship to exist, the employee must have given deliberate and informed consent to the new relationship. Another element of an implied special relationship is an expectation of payment. Upon review, Judge Combs Greene decided that the record was insufficient for the court to find the existence of a special employment relationship.

Nevertheless, Judge Combs Greene found that even if D.C. United was a special employer, the court still had jurisdiction to hear Namoff's claims against D.C. United, Goodstein, and Soehn, because D.C. United had not provided workers' compensation insurance for Namoff, and an employer's failure to provide insurance coverage allows an employee to bring a lawsuit against the employer. Judge Combs Greene noted a prior D.C. Court of Appeals explanation that workers' compensation is a quid pro quo arrangement whereby "in return for the purchase of insurance against job-related injuries, the employer receives tort immunity; in return for giving up the right to sue the employer, the employee receives swift and sure benefits."[18] And, importantly, she held that although MLS had provided insurance coverage for Namoff, D.C. United still had a requirement to do the same. Judge Combs Greene cited the D.C. Court of Appeals decision in *USA Waste of Maryland, Inc. v. Love*, in which the court determined that when an employee has two employers for the purposes of the Workers' Compensation Act, "both employers are obligated to provide the employee with workers' compensation coverage."[19] She further held that "an employer obligated to provide coverage may not provide coverage by assigning the responsibility to another employer."[20] She stated, "The basic purpose of the WCA is undermined if an employer does not purchase insurance coverage."[21] In summary, she wrote, "Other jurisdictions deal with the issue of joint and several liability for special and general employers differently, however pursuant to District of Columbia law, the special employer has the same workers' compensation obligations as a general employer."[22] Judge Combs Green also held that the court had jurisdiction to hear Namoff's claims against Dr. Annunziata, who had joined the motion to dismiss, arguing that he was a co-employee of Namoff, which would preclude D.C. Superior Court jurisdiction. Judge Combs Green reasoned that if D.C. United was a special employer, then Annunziata was an independent contractor, not a co-employee, and if D.C. United was not a special employer, then Annunziata could not be a co-employee.

Namoff had met his burden of demonstrating that the court had jurisdiction over the claims against D.C. United, Goodstein, Soehn, and Annunziata; therefore, the motion to dismiss was denied.

MOVING FORWARD

Namoff is now in the discovery phase, in which the parties will gather information in preparation for trial. The parties may also consider the possibility of a settlement. A status hearing has been scheduled for 8 November 2014.

Meanwhile, a similar case is now taking shape. On 5 February 2014, former Portland Timbers forward Eddie Johnson filed a complaint in Oregon state court alleging that the Timbers and its team physicians, athletic trainer, and neuropsychologist were negligent in their care of his head injuries in 2011 and 2012, by failing to properly follow MLS's Return to Play Protocol, among other conduct, which resulted in serious and permanent brain injuries. Johnson is seeking $10 million in damages.

As noted by Kevin O'Riordan of *Business of Soccer*, the combined results of the Namoff and Johnson suits "may eventually impact the RTP Protocol and other players' willingness to seek legal redress for career-ending injuries associated with concussions."

Chapter 6

R V. TERRY

ON 23 OCTOBER 2011, Chelsea visited Queens Park Rangers at Loftus Road. Near the end of the match, with Chelsea trailing 1–0 and down to nine men, there was a dispute between Chelsea's John Terry and QPR's Anton Ferdinand inside QPR's box over a penalty claim from Terry. Shortly after the dispute, Terry returned to Chelsea's half of the pitch and turned to face the opposition. At that point, Ferdinand had some unclear words for Terry and made a fist-pumping gesture towards Terry. Terry's response included the words "fucking black cunt".

It happened in a matter of seconds, in front of a typically noisy crowd, in the final minutes of an intense match. Possibly due to one or a combination of these factors, Ferdinand would claim that he did not hear what Terry said to him on the pitch. But the match was being televised live and was seen by more than 2 million viewers. The incident was almost immediately uploaded to YouTube. On screen, while some of Terry's words were difficult or impossible to discern—in part because the view of Terry's lips was momentarily obstructed, by teammate John Obi Mikel from one angle and by teammate Ashley Cole from another angle—the words "fucking black cunt" seemed quite clear.[1] Ultimately, there would be no dispute that Terry said precisely these words. Rather, the dispute that followed would concern the context and intent of their use. Terry would maintain that in saying those words to Ferdinand, he was repeating an accusation of racial abuse that he perceived Ferdinand had made to him and was dismissing the accusation.

Shortly after the match ended, Terry summoned Ferdinand to Chelsea's changing room, and there was a conversation between them that also involved

Ashley Cole. Terry's motive in summoning Ferdinand would be unclear. It was possible that, contrary to Terry's claim, the utterance at issue was intended as racial abuse, that he had already seen or heard about footage of the incident or otherwise realized that the incident could cause him trouble, and he was seeking out Ferdinand in order to manage the situation. It was also possible that, just as Terry claimed, the utterance at issue was actually repetition of racial abuse of which he perceived he was accused, and he was seeking out Ferdinand in order to confront the accusation as soon as practicable. In their conversation, Ferdinand denied that he heard any racial abuse or that he made any accusation of racial abuse. Terry and Ferdinand agreed that it was just "handbags," or typical verbal sparring between players, and they shook hands.

By the time he emerged from the changing room, Terry was indeed aware that he had been captured apparently racially abusing Ferdinand. Terry was advised to wait until all footage was available before making any comment, but he immediately issued the following statement:

> I've seen that there's a lot of comments on the internet with regards to some video footage of me in today's game. I'm disappointed that people have leapt to the wrong conclusions about the context of what I was seen to be saying to Anton Ferdinand. I thought Anton was accusing me of using a racist slur against him. I responded aggressively, saying that I never used that term. I would never say such a thing and I'm saddened that people would think so. I have known Anton for a long time and spoke to him about it after the game and there was no problem between us. I congratulated him on their win. He has not accused me of any wrongful remark. It was clear it was all a misunderstanding at the time. After the result today I am saddened to be dealing with these wrongful allegations. I am the proud captain of one of the most internationally diverse teams in the Premier League and I absolutely believe that there is no place for racism in sport and indeed in any walk of life.

The incident immediately made headlines, and a national debate would ensue over whether the England captain had committed an act of racial abuse, and, if he had, what the consequences should be.

It was not until about an hour after the match that Ferdinand became aware of the incident, when his girlfriend showed him a YouTube video from her phone in the QPR players' lounge. Ferdinand did not take any immediate action. But the next day, 24 October, London's Metropolitan Police Service (MPS) received a complaint from an off-duty police officer who had watched the match on television, and the Football Association (FA) received a complaint from QPR. Both the MPS and the FA immediately began investigating the incident. On 27 October, Hugh Robertson, Minister for Sport and Tourism, urged the FA to take "strong action" if racial abuse could be proved. On 28 October, the FA interviewed Ferdinand for two hours, during which time Ferdinand confirmed that he wanted a comprehensive investigation. On 31 October, Ferdinand issued the following statement on QPR's official website:

> Today I finalised my statement with the Football Association with regards to the incident that occurred last Sunday at Loftus Road in our Barclays Premier League fixture against Chelsea. I have very strong feelings on the matter, but in the interests of fairness and not wishing to prejudice what I am sure will be a very thorough inquiry by the FA, this will be my last comment on the subject until the inquiry is concluded.

While the dual investigations proceeded, Terry continued playing, not only for Chelsea but for England as well. "I think he is innocent until proved guilty," said then England manager Fabio Capello. "For this reason I selected him." André Villas-Boas, Chelsea manager at the time, had earlier called the situation "a big misunderstanding."

TERRY CHARGED AND STRIPPED OF ENGLAND CAPTAINCY

On 1 December, Scotland Yard, MPS headquarters, passed the findings of the five-week police investigation over to the Crown Prosecution Service (CPS), the government department responsible for prosecuting criminal cases. On 21 December, the CPS announced that Terry would face prosecution under the Crime and Disorder Act 1998. Alison Saunders, Chief Crown Prosecutor for London, stated:

I have today advised the Metropolitan Police Service that John Terry should be prosecuted for a racially aggravated public order offence following comments allegedly made during a Premier League football match between Queens Park Rangers and Chelsea on 23 October 2011. The decision was taken in accordance with the Code for Crown Prosecutors and after careful consideration of all the evidence, I am satisfied there is sufficient evidence for a realistic prospect of conviction and it is in the public interest to prosecute this case. . . . He is now summonsed with a criminal offence and has the right to a fair trial. It is extremely important that nothing should be reported which could prejudice his trial.

The details of the charge were as follows:

On 23rd October 2011 at Loftus Road Stadium, London W12 you used threatening, abusive or insulting words or behaviour, or disorderly behaviour within the hearing or sight of a person likely to be caused harassment, alarm or distress which was racially aggravated in accordance with section 28 of the Crime and Disorder Act 1998. Contrary to section 31 (1) (c) of the Crime and Disorder Act 1998.

Under the Crime and Disorder Act, an offence is racially or religiously aggravated if:

a. at the time of committing the offence, or immediately before or after doing so, the offender demonstrates towards the victim of the offence hostility based on the victim's membership (or presumed membership) of a racial or religious group; or
b. the offence is motivated (wholly or partly) by hostility towards members of a racial or religious group based on their membership of that group.

Terry faced a maximum punishment of a fine of £2,500. Of course, far more significant was the cost to his reputation.

Terry would reiterate that he was innocent. "I am disappointed with the decision to charge me and hope to be given the chance to clear my name as quickly as possible," he told the media. "I have never aimed a racist remark at anyone. I count people from all races and creeds among my closest friends." He continued, "I will fight tooth and nail to prove my innocence. I have campaigned against racism and believe there is no place for it in society."

Chelsea backed its captain. "I will be fully supportive of John Terry," said André Villas-Boas. "John represents this club to a maximum level, and we are very glad to have a player of his quality in our team. We know exactly his human values and personality. They are never in any doubt." A club statement added: "Chelsea FC has always been fully supportive of John in this matter and will continue to be so. The club finds all forms of discrimination abhorrent and we are proud of the work we undertake campaigning on this important issue."

Terry was to appear before West London Magistrates' Court[2] on 1 February 2012. On that day, Terry's lawyers entered a not guilty plea on his behalf. A trial date was set for 9 July, which would leave Terry free to captain England at the European Championship. But on 3 February, the FA stripped Terry of the England captaincy. The FA issued a statement that read in part:

> Following the decision to adjourn the court case against John Terry to July, The Football Association confirm he will not captain the England team until the allegations against him are resolved.
>
> The FA Board expected the trial to be concluded prior to the European Championship. Further to Wednesday's confirmation that the trial will not take place until after the tournament, the Board has discussed the matter in detail and has collectively decided it is in the interests of all parties that John has the responsibilities of captaincy removed at this time.
>
> This decision has been taken due to the higher profile nature of the England captaincy, on and off the pitch, and the additional demands and requirements expected of the captain leading into and during a tournament.

The statement confirmed that Terry had not been excluded from the squad, and that Fabio Capello was free to select him for matches leading up to and during the European Championship. Even so, Capello resigned in protest.

On 1 May, the FA appointed Roy Hodgson as England manager. On 16 May, Hodgson named his 23-man squad for EURO 2012. Liverpool's Steven Gerrard was captain. John Terry was in. And Manchester United's Rio Ferdinand, Anton's older brother, was out. Ferdinand, 33, had been managing a back issue in recent seasons and had not played for England in 11 months, but he was still reliable and respected, and his omission sparked some controversy. For more than five years, Terry and Ferdinand had formed the bedrock of England's defense. Earlier in the month, *The Guardian* had reported that Ferdinand was prepared to play alongside Terry once again, and put aside Terry's incident with his brother in the process. But that wasn't going to happen. Hodgson insisted that he made a football decision. "I selected John Terry for footballing reasons and I left out Rio Ferdinand for footballing reasons," he said. "I realised that when I selected [Terry] there would be people who would raise eyebrows but that's the decision that I've made, that's the decision I shall live with."

At EURO 2012, England, with Terry in the starting 11 for each match, emerged from a group with France, Sweden, and cohost Ukraine and advanced to the quarterfinals, where they were defeated by Italy. Two weeks later, Terry's defensive duties moved to the courtroom.

R V. TERRY

After a four-day trial, chief magistrate Howard Riddle handed down his judgment in *R v. Terry* on 13 July 2012.[3] "[Terry's] case is that his words were not uttered by way of abuse or insult nor were they intended to be abusive or insulting," said Mr. Riddle.[4] "He says they were used after a perceived false accusation made by Mr. Ferdinand, the accusation being to the effect that the defendant had used the term 'black cunt' during their exchanges with each other."[5] "Alternatively," Mr. Riddle said, "the case advanced on the defendant's behalf is that although Mr. Terry genuinely believes that Mr. Ferdinand made a false allegation against him, nevertheless this could be a misunderstanding."[6] Mr. Riddle made clear that the question of whether or not Terry is a racist was irrelevant to the trial:

> It may be worth mentioning here that the issue for this court to decide is not whether Mr. Terry is a racist, in the broadest sense of the word. I have received a substantial volume of unchallenged

evidence from witnesses, both in person and in writing, to confirm that he is not. I understand why Mr. Terry wants to make this point. His reputation is at stake. Although I am grateful to all those witnesses who have taken the trouble to provide information on this point, it does not help me in reaching a verdict. It is not relevant to the issue I must decide.[7]

What was relevant was the following:

The issue between the defendant and the Crown is whether Mr. Terry uttered the words "fucking black cunt" by way of insult. If he did then the offence is made out, regardless of what may have motivated him. . . . The question for me is whether I am sure that the words were used as an insult, or whether it is possible, as the defence assert, that he was, or believed he was, merely repeating an allegation made to him, and dismissing it.[8]

Therefore, context was key.

The Crown accused Terry of directing the words "fuck off, fuck off, yeah, yeah, and you fucking black cunt, fucking knobhead," and possibly one or more other words, at Ferdinand. Terry did not deny that he used the words "fuck off, fuck off," "fucking black cunt," or "fucking knobhead." It was clear that Terry said something after "fuck off, fuck off" and before "fucking black cunt, fucking knobhead," but it was not clear what the missing words were. In order to determine those precise words, both parties agreed that expert lip-readers were required. Both the lip-reader for the prosecution and the lip-reader for the defense were of the opinion that Terry's words were: "Yeah and I [obstruction] you/ya fucking black cunt (pause) fucking knobhead." However, both experts agreed that it was possible that they were mistaken and in particular that "you/ya" may have been "a" or a number of other similar sounds. Furthermore, both experts could not comment on tone of voice and could not say whether the observed words were in the form of a question. In cross-examination, Terry accepted that he appeared to use the word "and." As a result, Mr. Riddle noted, "the only difference between the prosecution and the defence is that the Crown alleged he says 'you/ya fucking black cunt' whereas the defence case is that he said 'a fucking black cunt?'"[9] Mr. Riddle concluded, "There are missing words, and I have not been prepared to speculate as to what they may be."[10]

As to that to which Terry had responded, the accusation that Terry claimed to have perceived was one that Ferdinand denied making. Ferdinand gave the following account of the initial exchanges: "He called me a cunt, and I called him a cunt back. And he gave me a gesture as if to say my breath smelled. I said to him: 'How can you call me a cunt? You shagged your team-mate's missus, you're a cunt.'" Ferdinand's reference was to an alleged affair between Terry and the ex-girlfriend of Terry's former England and Chelsea teammate Wayne Bridge (which resulted in Terry's being removed as England captain and replaced by Rio Ferdinand, from February 2010 to March 2011). Ferdinand claimed that he continued on about the affair, and then made the fist-pumping gesture, which was meant to suggest sex. Although there were a number of discrepancies between Ferdinand's evidence and other evidence, Mr. Riddle found that those discrepancies "do not undermine the central evidence of this witness that on the pitch he did not accuse the defendant of racially abusing him."[11] He further stated: "I am satisfied that there was little or no good reason for him to lie about the central issue in this case. . . . While there are indeed discrepancies in his evidence I think it is unlikely that on the central point he is lying. I have no significant doubts about his integrity."[12]

"So the question for me now," Mr. Riddle stated, "is whether there is a doubt that the offence is made out."[13] He explained, "In all criminal courts in this country a defendant is found guilty only if the court, be it a jury, magistrate, or a judge, is sure of guilt. If there is a reasonable doubt then the defendant is entitled to be acquitted."[14] In this case, Mr. Riddle maintained, "Certainly there is doubt about some of the individual facts."[15] He went on to address each area of doubt.

First, there was the evidence of the lip-readers.

> As far as the precise words that were spoken is concerned, the experts agree that there is a doubt about the word "you." Similarly they both make it clear that lip-reading is unable to identify whether the statement was made as a question or in what tone of voice it was said.[16]

Mr. Riddle accepted the notion—submitted by the lip-reader for Terry and agreed to by the lip-reader for the Crown—that there was "fundamental unreliability"[17] in lipreading.

Second, nobody had given evidence about hearing what Terry said to Ferdinand.

> Either nobody heard it, or nobody was prepared to come to court and tell me what they heard. Anton Ferdinand says he did not hear it. . . . There are a number of possible explanations for this. The first is that with the ball once again coming into play, Anton Ferdinand concentrated on the game rather than on the exchange. So he missed the words. Another possibility, and this is a possibility suggested to me by the defence, is that he did indeed accuse John Terry of calling him a black cunt, knows perfectly well that the words observed on the TV footage were in response to that comment, and is lying about it. I think that is unlikely. Another explanation, not one advanced by either party but which certainly crossed my mind, is that Anton Ferdinand did hear the words, did not want to take it any further, agreed in the changing room that he had heard nothing and stuck by that account. In short he may initially have wanted simply to move on, and as things snowballed found it expedient to stick with that position.[18]

This, combined with the evidence of the lip-readers, was problematic for the prosecution.

Third, there was doubt about what Ferdinand had said to Terry just before Terry responded with the words at issue.

> [Ferdinand's] initial account does not refer to any words being spoken at that stage. This is even though, as was put to him in cross-examination and he appeared to accept, he knew by the time that he made his statement that John Terry was saying that his words were in response to something said by Anton Ferdinand. In fact the camera shots show reasonably clearly that he was saying something. In evidence he said that he was continuing his

taunts about John Terry's affair with a team-mate's wife. I accept the defence argument that it is surprising that this was not made explicit in his initial statement. An initial statement, made shortly after events, is usually a witness's best recollection.[19]

Here Mr. Riddle drew an important conclusion from the video evidence and Terry's testimony:

A related point is the way Mr. Terry's facial expression changed at the moment he uttered the words "black cunt." He tells me, and I accept, that he has received countless taunts, from players and spectators, about an alleged relationship with a team-mates's wife. By the time of this match the taunts had occurred over an 18 month period. He had learned to live with them. They did not anger him. Later I heard evidence from Mr. Buck and Mr. Wilkins about his unusual qualities of self-control and leadership. I also heard about his disciplinary record. He has been sent off four times in 600 matches, and never for abuse. There can be little doubt from this, and from other evidence that I need not repeat here, that Mr. Terry has, over the years, been subjected to the most unpleasant personal abuse and has had to learn to keep calm and continue to play football. On the account given by Anton Ferdinand, there is no obvious reason why John Terry should suddenly become annoyed by the repetition of this taunt. He had heard it before many times. He did not react angrily when the obscene gesture was made. Despite his general self-discipline, it could have been a sudden loss of control. Mr. Penny demonstrated to me from the television clips that the defendant did indeed react to later incidents involving other players, notably the QPR goal keeper. On the other hand the footage of Mr. Terry as he says "black cunt" adds credence to the defence account that something of a different order had just been said to him, something altogether more insulting. Most of us will agree that being accused of racism and making racist comments is shocking and offensive. Society does not tolerate racist comments, nor do England football players, nor does the law. Any ordinary person wrongly accused of making a racist comment would be shocked and angered.[20]

Mr. Riddle had already stated that Terry's account was, "under the cold light of forensic examination, unlikely."[21] But with the above comments, Mr. Riddle was suggesting that Terry's account was not entirely implausible.

Mr. Riddle then turned to Terry's reliability and consistency. In Mr. Riddle's view, Terry's press statement following the match was significant.

> There is then the fact that on the evening of the match, 23rd October 2011, Mr. Terry made a press statement. . . . I do think this is an important point. Mr. Terry tells me that he was advised to wait until all the television footage was available before making a statement. I am satisfied he is likely to have received that advice. A cautious adviser would not have wanted a client to be tied to an account that could later be controverted by other evidence. Mr. Penny is right to put the question that it is important in a PR world to meet a high profile allegation with an immediate response. However it is a high risk strategy if there is a possibility that contradictory evidence will later appear. We know, as Mr. Terry will have known, that there would be a number of recordings of the match from different angles. Overall, the fact that he made an immediate statement, and has maintained that account in detail and co-operatively throughout this process, without significant contradiction to his evidence, is undoubtedly a factor in favour of the defence.[22]

Mr. Riddle also noted that Terry had maintained his account through the MPS and the FA enquiries and through expert and forceful cross-examination. "Nobody has been able to show that he is lying,"[23] Mr. Riddle said. "I have assessed John Terry as a credible witness."[24]

Ultimately, Mr. Riddle determined, given the evidence, that it was "impossible to be sure exactly what were the words spoken by Mr. Terry at the relevant time,"[25] and it was also "impossible to be sure exactly what was said to him at the relevant time by Mr. Ferdinand."[26] Mr. Riddle concluded:

Weighing all the evidence together, I think it is highly unlikely that Mr. Ferdinand accused Mr. Terry on the pitch of calling him a black cunt. However I accept that it is possible that Mr. Terry believed at the time, and believes now, that such an accusation was made. The prosecution evidence as to what was said by Mr. Ferdinand at this point is not strong. Mr. Cole gives corroborating (although far from compelling corroborating) evidence on this point. It is therefore possible that what he said was not intended as an insult, but rather as a challenge to what he believed had been said to him.

In those circumstances, there being a doubt the only verdict the court can record is one of not guilty.[27]

And with that, Terry was acquitted of the racial abuse charges against him.

Many observers criticized the failure to punish Terry. Other observers criticized the decision to bring the case to court in the first place. "It was our view that this was not 'banter' on the football pitch and that the allegation should be judged by a court. The chief magistrate agreed that Mr. Terry had a case to answer, but having heard all of the evidence he acquitted Mr. Terry of a racially aggravated offence," responded Alison Saunders. "That is justice being done and we respect the chief magistrate's decision."

But the chief magistrate's decision did not put Terry in the clear. The FA would now resume its own investigation into the case.

THE FA PROCEEDINGS

On 27 July 2012, the FA charged Terry. The FA's press release stated:

It is alleged that Terry used abusive and/or insulting words and/or behaviour towards Queens Park Rangers' Anton Ferdinand, contrary to FA rules. It is further alleged that this included a reference to the ethnic origin and/or colour and/or race of Anton Ferdinand. This charge is the result of The FA's long-standing enquiries into this matter, which were placed on hold pending the outcome of the criminal trial, and relates to rules governing football only. During this period John Terry remains available to play for England. Terry has until 3 August 2012 to respond.

Specifically, Terry was charged with misconduct pursuant to Rules E.3(1) and E.3(2) of the FA's Rules and Regulations.[28] Rule E.3(1) stated:

> A Participant shall at all times act in the best interests of the game and shall not act in any manner which is improper or brings the game into disrepute or use any one, or a combination of, violent conduct, serious foul play, threatening, abusive, indecent or insulting words or behaviour.

And Rule E.3(2) stated:

> In the event of any breach of Rule E 3(1) including a reference to any one or more of a person's ethnic origin, colour, race, nationality, faith, gender, sexual orientation or disability (an "aggravating factor"), a Regulatory Commission shall consider the imposition of an increased sanction.

In his answer, Terry of course denied the charge. Just before the start of the hearing, Terry announced his retirement from England duty. He said the FA's decision to pursue charges against him meant his position with England had become "untenable."

After a four-day hearing, the FA Regulatory Commission issued its ruling on 27 September 2012.[29] The fundamental difference between the criminal proceedings and the FA disciplinary proceedings was the standard of proof, which was higher in the former than the latter. In the criminal proceedings, the Crown was required to prove Terry's guilt "beyond reasonable doubt." In the FA disciplinary proceedings, the FA was required to prove Terry's guilt on the "balance of probabilities"—in other words, that he "more likely than not" breached the relevant FA rules. Specifically, the 2011/12 FA Handbook, Regulation 7.3, provided that: "The applicable standard of proof shall be the flexible civil standard of the balance of probability. The more serious the allegation, taking into account the nature of the Misconduct alleged and the context of the case, the greater the burden of evidence required to prove the matter."[30]

First, Terry submitted that Regulation 6.8 of the FA's Disciplinary Regulations represented a procedural bar to the FA proceedings. Regulation 6.8 provided that:

> In any proceedings before a Regulatory Commission, the Regulatory Commission shall not be obliged to follow the strict rules of evidence, may admit such evidence as it thinks fit and accord such evidence such weight as it thinks appropriate in all the circumstances. Where the subject matter of a complaint or matter before the Regulatory Commission has been the subject of previous civil or criminal proceedings, the result of such proceedings and the facts and matters upon which such result is based shall be presumed to be correct and the facts presumed to be true unless it is shown, by clear and convincing evidence, that this is not the case.[31]

The Regulatory Commission dismissed the argument, holding that:

> [T]he mere fact that a respondent has been acquitted of a criminal charge whose subject-matter is identical, is not capable of acting as a procedural bar preventing the FA from bringing disciplinary proceedings. This is because of the differing standards of proof. In other words, Regulation 6.8 does not entitle a respondent in Mr. Terry's position to say "I was acquitted, therefore Regulation 6.8 prevents any disciplinary proceedings being brought against me."[32]

Plainly, Mr. Riddle's findings were not binding on the Regulatory Commission. Thus, the FA's case was presented to the Regulatory Commission as follows:

> [I]f the Commission were to find, on the balance of probabilities, that Mr. Terry only used the words "fucking black cunt" by way of forceful rejection/inquiry, the FA would not invite the Commission to find that he should be found guilty of Misconduct, or that any sanction should be imposed. Accordingly, and contrary to media comment, although Mr. Terry himself admits that he directed the words "fucking black cunt" at Mr. Ferdinand, that fact alone is not enough for him to be found guilty of Misconduct in this particular case. The FA accepted that it had to satisfy the Commission that the words were spoken by Mr. Terry by way of an insult to Mr. Ferdinand.[33]

Upon review of the evidence, the Regulatory Commission made the following key findings, on the balance of probabilities:

i. That Mr. Ferdinand did not accuse Mr. Terry of racially abusing him and did not use the word "black" or any words that could have been heard, understood, or misunderstood by anyone to have any kind of reference to, or context with, skin colour, race or ethnicity. We are driven to conclude not just that it is "highly unlikely" (referencing Mr. Riddle's judgment) that Mr. Ferdinand accused Mr. Terry on the pitch of calling him a "black cunt," but that he did not.[34]

ii. That Mr. Terry did not hear, and could not have believed, understood or misunderstood Mr. Ferdinand to have used the word "black," or any word(s) that might have suggested that he was accusing Mr. Terry of racially abusing him.[35]

The Regulatory Commission then listed further aspects of Terry's account that it found "improbable, implausible and contrived."[36] First, the Commission stated that it was "inherently unlikely that if he had been accused by Mr. Ferdinand of calling him something that ended with the words 'black cunt,' that Mr. Terry would have added the world 'fucking' when he threw the words back, if he was genuinely doing so by way of forceful denial."[37] Second, it stated, "His repetition of words that Mr. Terry claims were said to him first by Mr. Ferdinand is implausible if they were really intended to be a denial."[38] Third, it stated, "At no point is his demeanour and facial expression that of someone who is imploring, injured, or even quizzical in the face of an unfounded allegation by Mr. Ferdinand that he (Mr. Terry) had just been racially abusive towards him (Mr. Ferdinand)."[39] The Commission also noted that, following the dispute at issue, Terry was involved in another dispute before the match's end, this one with QPR's goalkeeper, Paddy Kenney, during which Terry said: "You fucking cunt, you fucking cheeky cunt."[40] Finally, and perhaps most compellingly, the Commission pointed to Terry's conduct immediately following the match's end.

> Mr. Terry made no attempt to confront Mr. Ferdinand when the game ended. Instead, he went to acknowledge the support of the

Chelsea fans. If he genuinely believed that he had been the victim of an unjustified accusation of the serious type alleged, it is very surprising that Mr. Terry left it for approximately one hour after the match before he requested a meeting with Mr. Ferdinand. The Commission cannot speculate as to what may have transpired during that hour or so, apart from the likely realization on Mr. Terry's part that what he said may well have been caught on camera and be a source of trouble for him. When they did speak after the game, Mr. Ferdinand's unchallenged evidence is that the first thing Mr. Terry said to him was "What happened?" This is telling. Without first speaking to Mr. Ferdinand, and asking that question, Mr. Terry could not have known what Mr. Ferdinand heard or knew, and whether he intended to pursue matters further.[41]

In light of these findings, the Commission in its ruling stated:

[T]he Commission is quite satisfied, on the balance of probabilities, that there is no credible basis for Mr. Terry's defence that his use of the words "fucking black cunt" were directed at Ferdinand by way of forceful rejection and/or inquiry. Instead, we are quite satisfied, and find on the balance of probabilities, that the offending words were said by way of insult.[42]

The Commission decided that a four-match ban and a £220,000 fine were appropriate sanctions.

After the ruling was made, Terry decided not to appeal and issued an apology in the following statement:

After careful consideration, I have decided not to appeal against the FA judgment.

I want to take this opportunity to apologise to everyone for the language I used in the game against Queens Park Rangers last October.

Although I'm disappointed with the FA judgment, I accept that the language I used, regardless of the context, is not acceptable on the football field or indeed in any walk of life.

As I stated in the criminal case, with the benefit of hindsight my language was clearly not an appropriate reaction to the situation for someone in my position.

My response was below the level expected by Chelsea Football Club, and by me, and it will not happen again.

Looking forward, I will continue to do my part in assisting the club to remove all types of discriminatory behaviour from football.

I am extremely grateful for the consistent support of Chelsea FC, the fans and my family.

Once Terry decided not to appeal, his four-match ban went into effect.

The four-match ban would be widely criticized as too lenient, and it prompted a public protest from several black players. In October 2012, when Kick It Out, the antiracism campaign funded by English football's governing bodies, organized for Premier League players to wear shirts bearing the organization's logo before their matches, Rio and Anton Ferdinand were among about three dozen players who refused to wear the shirts. Afterwards, former West Brom and Coventry player Cyrille Regis, whose nephew, Reading's Jason Roberts, was one of the protesting players, confirmed that the boycott had was at least partly prompted by Terry's ban.

In May 2013, the FA responded by introducing a minimum five-match ban for racial abuse. Not surprisingly, that response would receive further criticism.

Chapter 7

HER MAJESTY'S REVENUE AND CUSTOMS V. THE FOOTBALL LEAGUE

OVER THE PAST TWO DECADES, English football has seen a wave of clubs crash into insolvency—that is, a state of inability to pay debts. Since 1992, when England's top clubs formed the Premier League in a break from the Football League,[1] only one Premier League club has formally entered insolvency proceedings—Portsmouth, in 2010 and 2012—but more than half of the 72 clubs in the Football League have done so, and many of them more than once.[2] Among the more high-profile Football League insolvency cases have been Wimbledon (now Milton Keynes Dons) in 2003 and Leeds United in 2007.

These insolvencies are commonly attributed to a lack of discipline and rationality in player spending as clubs attempt to advance their league position. However, University of Michigan professor and *Soccernomics* coauthor Dr. Stefan Szymanski suggests in a working paper[3] that insolvencies are more significantly influenced by "negative shocks," or consistent underperformance relative to expectations, finding that insolvent clubs generally "have been declining, in the sense of achieving lower league positions and being relegated to lower divisions, for several years before becoming insolvent." Therefore, Szymanski concludes, "it is not clear that discipline and rationality will avoid further insolvency events in the future." In recent years, the Premier League and the Football League have introduced and expanded "parachute payments" to clubs that have been relegated to lower leagues as a means to ease their financial transition, and the appropriateness of the system continues to be examined. Still, the conversation among the game's stakeholders on the issue of financial sustainability remains focused on spending more than anything else, which is perhaps not surprising considering that the arms race is so visible and the numbers are so startling.

Since its formation, the Premier League's revenues (£2.36 billion in 2011–12) have surged, most notably from lucrative broadcast deals, while the Championship's revenues (£476 million in 2011–12) have seen less spectacular but nonetheless substantial growth. In both leagues, though, clubs have spent a significant and increasing percentage of their revenues on player wages, and most have struggled to generate profits. Former Tottenham chairman Alan Sugar famously described the phenomenon of money coming in and going out straight away as the "prune juice effect." From 1992 to 2010, Premier League and Championship player wages increased by 1508 percent and 518 percent, respectively, according to a 2012 High Pay Centre study. The 2012 and 2013 editions of Deloitte's annual football finance survey showed that Premier League clubs' average wages-to-revenue ratio has risen to 70 percent, while Championship clubs' average wages-to-revenue ratio has been between 87 percent and 90 percent. In 2011–12, only half of Premier League clubs and three Championship clubs made an operating profit. The Championship's 24 clubs had an average operating loss of £6.125 million. On the Championship's financial situation, the 2013 Deloitte report noted:

> For many years the division has struggled financially—the combination of clubs adjusting to the impact of relegation from the Premier League and others aspiring to achieve promotion, has now delivered almost a decade of ever increasing operating losses. Championship clubs continue to spend 30% more than they generate—a clearly unsustainable position without owner benefaction, a source of funds upon which the Football League is trying to reduce its member clubs' dependence.

In League One, average revenue was £5 million, the average wages-to-revenue ratio was 93 percent, and the average net loss was £2.4 million. In League Two, average revenue was £3.3 million, the average wages-to-revenue ratio was 70 percent, and the average net loss was £0.3 million. As football clubs maintain such precarious financial positions, insolvencies would seem inevitable.

In a February 2010 piece on football club insolvencies, *The Guardian's* David Conn wrote, "In England, the trails of creditors left unpaid, including a mountain of public money, represent the flipside of football's financial feast, since the Premier League club broke away, for the money, in 1992." In the cases where football clubs have formally entered insolvency proceedings, Britain's tax authority, Her Majesty's Revenue and Customs (HMRC), has generally been owed more money than any other party. And due to a change in insolvency law and a controversial football insolvency policy, HMRC has generally received a very small percentage of what it is owed. In effect, this represents a public loss. Eventually, the taxman decided to fight back through the courts.

INSOLVENCY LAW AND FOOTBALL POLICY

In England, the law provides for three main insolvency procedures: liquidation, administration, and company voluntary arrangements.[4] The liquidation or "winding up" of a company may be voluntary or compulsory—in the latter case by way of a court order made on a petition filed by a creditor (a party to whom money is owed)—but in either case the company's assets are sold, the proceeds are distributed to its creditors, and the company is dissolved. While this is the most common insolvency procedure for English companies, it is a less common, last-resort procedure for football clubs. Generally, football club insolvencies involve either administration or a company voluntary agreement.

The Insolvency Act of 1986 significantly reformed insolvency law and established, among other things, the administration process in response to a government-commissioned investigation and set of recommendations on insolvencies, commonly known as the Cork Report,[5] which found that troubled companies were too often being wound up when they were actually capable of surviving. Through the administration process, an insolvent or potentially insolvent company may be placed under the control of an insolvency practitioner—the administrator—whose primary goal is to negotiate with creditors and create a path to survival. As outlined in the Enterprise Act of 2002, the most recent of several acts that have amended the Insolvency Act of 1986, an administrator will pursue the following hierarchical purposes of administration: (1) rescuing the company, if reasonably practical; (2) achieving a better result for the company's creditors as a whole than would be likely if the company were wound up, if rescue is not reasonably practicable; or (3) realizing property in order to make a distribution to one or more secured or preferential creditors, if neither of the previous two purposes is practicable.

An administration case commences upon the filing of a petition for administration, which may be filed by the company, its directors, or any of its creditors. The court may make an administration order if (1) the company is or is likely to become unable to pay its debts and (2) the order is reasonably likely to achieve the purpose of administration. Importantly, once an administration order is made, any pending winding up petitions, with the exception of those presented under the public interest, are dismissed, and there is a moratorium, with few exceptions, on further insolvency proceedings and other legal actions. This provides the company with breathing space for the purpose of restructuring. Upon appointment, the administrator may do anything necessary for the management of the company's affairs, business, and property. This may include the sale of assets to generate cash. Within eight weeks of the date that the company entered administration, the administrator must provide creditors with a statement setting out proposals for achieving the purpose of administration, which requires a simple majority vote to be approved. If approved, the administrator is responsible for execution. The administrator has a duty to perform his or her functions as quickly and efficiently as is reasonably practicable. The process is designed to last for up to one year, although it may be extended by the consent of the creditors or by the court.

Upon entering administration, a Premier League or Football League club is served notice that it is subject to having its league membership share, commonly referred to as the "golden share," withdrawn. In practice, the league generally does not automatically withdraw membership but instead will suspend the notice of withdrawal, provided that the administrator confirms that the club will complete its fixtures for the remainder of the season and has sufficient resources to ensure that it can reasonably be expected to do so. However, a deduction of points will be imposed—nine points in the Premier League, ten points in the Football League. Under the auspices of the Football Association, the governing body of English football, the Premier League and the Football League introduced the points deductions in 2004 in order to encourage clubs to take greater financial responsibility and to prevent clubs from using the procedure as a convenient way to get rid of its outstanding debt and gain a competitive advantage. The manner in which Leicester City had achieved promotion to the Premier League at the end of the 2002–03 season after having shed significant debt through the administration process was one notable event that prompted the proposal of the penalty. In December 2004, Wrexham, while playing in League One, entered administration and became the first club to suffer the penalty, which proved decisive in its relegation to League Two at the end of the season.

When a club exits administration, the golden share is restored or transferred to new ownership, provided that certain conditions are met. Among those conditions is completion of a company voluntary arrangement (CVA). The CVA, which requires the approval of 75 percent of the creditors (by value of debt), includes a timetable for the full or partial repayment of debts; it allows the club to continue trading, while the day-to-day running of the club passes from the administrator back to the club directors. A club that fails to comply receives a further 15-point deduction.

In summer 2007, Leeds United became the first club to exit administration without a CVA and be subjected to the heavy deduction. Just a few seasons earlier, Leeds had been a force in the Premier League, and in European competition as well; yet by the end of the 2006–07 season, the club had tumbled into administration and was relegated from the Championship to League One. The club's creditors did narrowly approve a CVA, but HM Revenue and Customs challenged it. As a result, the Football League eventually allowed for a sale of the club under an "exceptional circumstances" provision within its insolvency policy and applied a 15-point deduction at the start of the 2007–08 season. In summer 2008, three more Football League clubs in administration—Bournemouth, Luton Town, and Rotherham United—were also unable to complete CVAs due to opposition from HMRC, and in each case the Football League applied points deductions at the start of the 2008–09 season.

Before Leeds, all 41 Football League clubs that had entered administration had managed to exit with a CVA. Thereafter, insolvent clubs were seeing HMRC take an increasingly hard line in negotiations over repayment of debt. This was in response to its growing frustration with the most controversial element of football insolvency policy—the football creditor rule.

THE FOOTBALL CREDITOR RULE

In order for an insolvent club to successfully exit administration with its golden share secured and without a points deduction imposed, the required CVA must be in accord with the football creditor rule. This rule, put in place by the Football Association, the Premier League, and the Football League, requires "football creditors"—e.g., the club's players (owed wages) and other clubs (owed player transfer fees)—to be paid in full prior to all other creditors. The effect of the rule has been to leave non-football creditors—e.g., HMRC, banks, and suppliers—with significantly reduced recovery, sometimes just a few pence in the pound or less. Among the many recent cases that illustrate the point are Crystal Palace and Plymouth Argyle. When Crystal Palace exited administration in 2010, football creditors were paid in full, and the unsecured creditors were paid less than 2 pence in the pound. When Plymouth Argyle exited administration in 2011, football creditors were paid in full, and the unsecured creditors were paid 0.77 pence in the pound. Such circumstances have been difficult for football executives to defend.

The Football Association (FA), the Premier League, and the Football League have generally contended that the football creditor rule protects the integrity of competition. When the Culture, Media and Sport Committee (CMSC) of the British House of Commons conducted an inquiry into football governance in 2011,[6] football executives put forth two main arguments in support of the rule. First, it was argued that the rule prevented clubs from gaining an unfair sporting advantage by signing players and then not paying for them. Second, it was argued that the rule prevented a "domino" effect of financial distress, since clubs have interrelated businesses.

Shaun Harvey, then Leeds United chief executive,[7] explained, "If Leeds defaulted in this example on a payment to Crewe, which meant Crewe had to sell their players to keep in business, that cannot be a fair and rational position for Crewe to be put into." Crewe chairman John Bowler concurred, stating that transfer fees were essential to the existence of his and many other clubs, and if not for the rule, "there could be a number of occasions where a football club might go into bankruptcy, but it would also take probably two or three other clubs with them because of the fact that the transfer money that ought to have come down to those other clubs hasn't come." In the case of Portsmouth's insolvency, for instance, the rule may have maintained Watford's solvency—Portsmouth owed

Watford money for the transfer of striker Tommy Smith, and if the debt had not been settled, Watford might also have been forced into administration.

When asked whether the absence of the rule would actually improve clubs' financial management by encouraging them to police themselves, Football League chairman Greg Clarke reasoned that clubs were not well placed to make such risk assessments of other clubs. "What that will do is stop them selling to each other because they don't have the resources or the information to make a well-informed decision on counterparty risk," he said. Clarke admitted that when he joined the Football League, he thought the football creditor rule was an "outrage," but he had since come to believe that it was the "least worst" option. "The alternative could well see Football League clubs going out of business," Clarke said.

Despite these arguments, the football creditor rule has met with widespread criticism. Former Football League chairman Lord Brian Mawhinney oversaw the introduction of the rule, but upon his retirement he wrote to all 72 clubs asking them to consider its morality:

> Talking about the moral strength of the [Football League] brand, are we all comfortable that, in financial and debt terms, we treat football clubs more favourably than we do our local communities and their businesses, other taxpayers (to whom we have a civic responsibility) or St John Ambulance? That is for you to decide.

In his 2012 judgment on the petition for an administration order in relation to Portsmouth, the presiding judge commented:

> I understand the disquiet from the creditors. The general body of taxpayers, and the ordinary consumers who do pay their energy bills, and the ordinary traders and professionals who provide services such as, from the creditor list, coach hire, catering, medical services, ground care and maintenance, must wonder why they should subsidise the club's wage bill, why it is that they are involuntarily lenders to the club of their outstanding bills and why they will only get back pence in the pound for the services they have provided.

In a 2012 *Sporting Intelligence* interview, football finance expert Dr. John Beech railed against the rule:

> The defence of the Football Creditors Rule that is habitually trotted out—that the integrity of the league must be maintained—is unreasonable in my opinion. I don't see how the existence of the rule can be justified as a means for buying and selling players on credit when the buying club is well known to be on shaky financial grounds, and the selling club can, in effect, expect the public purse to act a guarantor for payment. The rule is shameful, and reflects extremely badly on the whole football club business sector. In my view it's counter-productive as it's one of a number of factors that have contributed to the spiraling cost of transfer fees, which is hardly helpful to clubs.

The Culture, Media and Sport Committee's 2011 report strongly urged that the rule be abolished:

> The FA, Leagues and clubs all appeared defensive and uncomfortable about the Football Creditors Rule. They are right to be. The moral argument against it—that it harms the communities that football is supposed to serve—is persuasive on its own. There is, though, also a compelling systemic argument against it, namely that it positively encourages excessive financial risk-taking, in a system that already offers other inducements to so do, by offering a safety net to those who seek to benefit from such practices. The Football Creditors Rule should be abolished.

Before the CMSC had completed its inquiry, HMRC had gone to court to challenge the rule.

HER MAJESTY'S REVENUE AND CUSTOMS

Dr. Beech's studies generally show that the hierarchy of creditors seeking money from an insolvent club are, in decreasing order of the size of debts, HM Revenue and Customs, banks and corporate investors, football creditors, and suppliers. HMRC may be owed payroll taxes (PAYE—pay as you earn), national insurance contributions (NIC), and taxes on player transfer fees (VAT—value added tax). Until September 2003, HMRC enjoyed the legal status of preferred creditor, meaning it was to be paid in full prior to other creditors. The Enterprise Act of 2002 (which came into force in September 2003) removed HMRC's priority status, and it therefore began being paid *pari passu*—on an equal footing—with other unsecured creditors. In February 2010, David Conn reported that HMRC had been left with about £30 million of outstanding taxes since the law was changed.

Britain's tax authority first challenged the football creditor rule in *Inland Revenue v. Wimbledon Football Club*[8] in 2004 (HMRC was formed from the merger of the Inland Revenue and Her Majesty's Customs and Excise, which took effect in April 2005). When Wimbledon entered administration in June 2003, the club owed its unsecured creditors £24 million. In March 2004, Wimbledon's administrators agreed to a rescue plan under which Milton Keynes Dons would purchase the club's assets and assume certain of the club's liabilities and obligations. The sale was subject to a CVA, and a substantial majority of Wimbledon's creditors approved a proposal under which preferential creditors—including Inland Revenue—would be paid 30 pence in the pound and non-preferential creditors would receive nothing. Meanwhile, the sale agreement provided for football creditors to be paid in full, despite their non-preferential status. Inland Revenue objected and sought to revoke or suspend the CVA. Since the CVA would not pay Inland Revenue in full, while the sale agreement would pay football creditors in full, Inland Revenue argued that the CVA violated Section 4(4) of the Insolvency Act, which prohibited the approval of any CVA proposal under which non-preferential creditors were paid in priority to preferential creditors. The argument would not succeed. The High Court held there was no Section 4(4) violation because a third-party purchaser's own money, rather than money realized from the insolvent club's assets and business, was being used to pay the football creditors, and the law did not preclude such an agreement. Inland Revenue also lost its appeal.

In subsequent years, HMRC generally protested Football League insolvencies and the implementation of the football creditor rule by voting against CVA proposals, which were often approved anyway because other creditors were willing to accept little or no payment to allow clubs to remain in business. But its frustration was growing, and that frustration reached a boiling point when Portsmouth became insolvent. By mid-2009, Portsmouth had accumulated significant tax liabilities, and HMRC filed a petition to wind up the club in October. The following month, a payment agreement was reached and the petition was dismissed, but almost immediately the club went into arrears again. HMRC filed a new petition to wind up the club in December 2009.[9] In February 2010, Portsmouth went into administration and gained protection from the winding up petition against it. Nonetheless, HMRC warned that it was not prepared to accept anything less than full payment.

Shortly after his appointment, Portsmouth's administrator Andrew Andronikou remarked that the club was "an example of how not to conduct business in the world of football." In April 2010, Andronikou issued a report to the club's creditors.[10] The overall debt was £122.8 million. The debt to all unsecured creditors was £92.7 million. The debt to HMRC was £17.1 million. With respect to football creditors, the club owed current and former players £4.7 million in wages and image rights and owed other clubs £17.3 million in transfer fees. Though not considered football creditors, player agents were owed a stunning £9.8 million, with two agents in particular each owed in excess of £2 million (one of whom earned the amount from just one deal—the transfer of French international Lassana Diarra). David Conn ran down a list of some of the non-football creditors besides HMRC:

> [T]he list of unsecured "ordinary" creditors, who must take a hit, is a painful litany of the inexcusably unpaid. Here is the South Central ambulance service, owed £19,535.39, Portsmouth city council, £28,690 down in rates, Portsmouth Students' Union, owed £2,955. A number of schools are owed significant sums, apparently for the hire of sports facilities, including Cowplain Community School in Waterlooville, with £14,743.54 outstanding, the Priory Community Sports Centre in Southsea, owed £11,000, and King Edward School in Southampton, who will have to accept a fraction of a £41,714.01 bill the Premier League club ran up with them.

Portsmouth's creditors would approve a CVA that paid them 20 pence in the pound. In response, HMRC would challenge the CVA, ultimately unsuccessfully, in *HMRC v. Portsmouth City Football Club*.[11]

Nevertheless, HMRC was prepared to step up its efforts to take down the football creditor rule. On 18 May 2010, HMRC filed a legal writ against the Premier League over the rule. It sought a declaration that the rule was unlawful and an injunction restraining its implementation. In February 2011, the trial was postponed pending a Supreme Court decision in *Belmont Park Investments PTY v. BNY Corporate Trustee Services*,[12] in order to enable the parties to consider whether that decision affected their position. The following month, HMRC took similar action against the Football League. The Premier League and the Football League had already introduced new rules that would allow them to monitor the tax payments of its clubs, but HMRC was not satisfied. It wanted the football creditor rule eliminated.

HER MAJESTY'S REVENUE AND CUSTOMS V. THE FOOTBALL LEAGUE

The proceedings in *Her Majesty's Revenue and Customs v. The Football League*[13] were commenced by HMRC on 10 March 2011. Since the Premier League's application to dismiss the similar proceedings against it was not immediately heard, the Premier League eventually applied to intervene in the proceedings against the Football League, based on the overlap of issues, and was granted permission to do so.

"These proceedings are not concerned with whether giving priority to football creditors is socially or morally justified,"[14] wrote Mr. Justice David Richards, sitting at the High Court's Chancery Division in London. "The issue is one purely of law, whether the provisions which together accord this priority are void and of no effect on the grounds that they are contrary to insolvency law."[15] In this case, two principles of insolvency law were relevant: the anti-deprivation principle and the pari passu principle. The anti-deprivation principle renders void any provision by which a debtor is deprived of assets by reason of insolvency with the effect that the assets are not available to creditors. The pari passu principle requires the assets of an insolvent person or entity to be distributed among the creditors on an equal basis, meaning that all the creditors will receive the same percentage of their debts out of the available assets. In *Belmont*, Lord Collins explained:

> The anti-deprivation rule and the rule that it is contrary to public policy to contract out of pari passu distribution are two sub-rules

of the general principle that parties cannot contract out of the insolvency legislation. Although there is some overlap, they are aimed at different mischiefs. . . . The anti-deprivation rule is aimed at attempts to withdraw an asset on bankruptcy or liquidation or administration, thereby reducing the value of the insolvency estate to the detriment of creditors. The pari passu rule reflects the principle that statutory provisions for pro rata distribution may not be excluded by a contract which gives one creditor more than its proper share.[16]

HMRC submitted that the provisions that together gave effect to what is known generally as the football creditor rule conflicted with these two fundamental principles of insolvency law. Specifically, HMRC challenged the following provisions contained within the Football League's Articles of Association: (1) Article 4.7.4, (2) Article 77.3, and (3) Article 80.2.

Article 4.5 provides that, in each of the circumstances set out in Article 4.7, the Football League may give a member club notice to transfer its golden share at the price of 5 pence; the circumstance set out in Article 4.7.4 is "if any Member Club shall become subject to or suffer an Insolvency Event."

Articles 65 to 80 include the provisions for the financial arrangements of the Football League and for payments to member clubs. As stated therein, the Football League maintains a "pool account" into which all league income is deposited and from which all payments are made. Each of the three divisions—the Championship, League One, and League Two—is allocated a payment to be paid out to each member club as follows: television facility fees, a basic award, and a ladder payment. The basic award is £620,000 for each Championship club, £300,000 for each League One club, and £210,000 for each League Two club. The basic award is set at a level that absorbs all available funds; otherwise, the ladder payments depend on each club's league position. The Football League may make interim payments from the pool account to clubs on account, based on the sums likely to be paid out to clubs at the end of the season. The practice of the Football League is to pay the basic award to clubs in 12 equal monthly installments, notified to the clubs before the start of the season. However, Article 77.3 states that payments to a club only become a legal liability of the league if the club completes all of its fixture obligations in the relevant season. In other words, the completion of all fixtures is a condition precedent to any right to payment out of the pool account. Therefore, if a club suffers an insolvency event and, as a result, loses its golden share before the end of the season and is unable to complete its fixtures, it loses the right to payments and has to repay any interim payments it has already received.

Article 80 applies in the event that a club defaults in paying any debts due to football creditors; in such an event, the club in question is subject to Article 80.2, which states that the league shall apply any sums from the pool account that would otherwise be payable to the club directly to the football creditors.

HMRC contended that a league membership share, the right to play in the league, and the right to payments from the pool account are each "property" of the company owning the club within the meaning of the Insolvency Act. It pleaded that Article 4.7.4 is a deprivation provision, void and unenforceable as a matter of public policy, "because property of the company is purportedly removed from the company on the onset of insolvency."[17] It pleaded that Article 77.3 is a deprivation provision, void and unenforceable as a matter of public policy, "because [its] intended effect is that property of the company namely the right of the Club to payment is purportedly removed from the company on the onset of insolvency and the Club is obliged to repay all sums already paid to it by the Football League in that Season."[18] And it pleaded that Article 80.2 is void and unenforceable if it is applied in the context of insolvency "in providing that Football Creditors receive payment direct out of monies due to the Club from the Pool Account, and thus are an attempt to contract out of the provisions of the Insolvency Act 1986,"[19] adding that "[m]onies falling due to an insolvent Club should be held for the benefit of all unsecured creditors."[20]

In response, the Football League claimed that none of the challenged provisions offended either the anti-deprivation principle or the pari passu principle. As summarized by Mr. Justice Richards, the Football League (FL) argued:

> The share in the FL owned by a company in administration or liquidation has no value, and therefore neither rule can apply to its compulsory transfer. Under the terms of the FL's articles, particularly article 77, a member club has no right to the payment of any sum derived from television and other commercial contracts made by the FL unless and until it has completed all its fixture obligations

for the relevant season. If it ceases to be a member before the end of the season it is therefore not deprived of any debt or accrued right to payment. The provisions of article 80, providing for payments to football creditors, do not divert money to which a defaulting club has any entitlement under article 77, are not triggered by administration or liquidation but by default in the payment of any football creditors and are in any event outside the scope of the pari passu principle and the anti-deprivation rule by reason of authorities on "direct payments" clauses in construction contracts.[21]

It added that these provisions existed for bona fide commercial and regulatory reasons, and therefore, in accordance with the general principle of respecting the autonomy of contracting parties, they did not infringe on the anti-deprivation rule.

Mr. Justice Richards began his analysis with Article 77.3. In the view of HMRC, a right to income from the pool account accrues to each club as it plays matches during the season. In Mr. Justice Richards' words, "HMRC's case . . . is that the television revenue is earned as a result of the clubs playing their matches, some of which are televised, that the basic award is in fact paid to clubs by equal monthly instalments, and that therefore the reality is that the basic award is paid to the clubs as they earn it and, crucially, as they become entitled to it."[22] However, Mr. Justice Richards found:

> The problem for HMRC's submission is that the payments to the clubs are entirely consistent with the articles, including article 77. Unless article 77.3 is a sham, it creates the legal entitlement and obligation between the FL and its members. There can be no doubt as a matter simply of construction of article 77.3, that any legal entitlement to payments is conditional upon completion of all fixture obligations.[23]

HMRC insisted that the court should look at the substance of the matter, stressing that Article 77, particularly when read with Article 80, was "a transparent device of drafting"[24] made to prevent the anti-deprivation rule and the pari passu principle from applying to the loss of entitlement to payments from the pool account. As Mr. Justice Richards explained it:

If an individual member club has no legal entitlement to payments from the Pool Account until it has completed its fixture obligations for the relevant season, it is not deprived of an asset if, as a result of going into administration or liquidation, it cannot or is not permitted to complete the season. Likewise, if sums from the Pool Account which would have been paid to a club if it completed the season are paid instead to football creditors following an administration or liquidation occurring before the end of the season and preventing the club from completing its fixtures, there is no asset of the club to which the pari passu principle can be applied.[25]

But Mr. Justice Richards held, "Assuming in favour of HMRC that article 77 is drafted for the reasons they suggest, it does not alter the legal rights and obligations of the parties."[26] He added, "In fairness to the FL, it should be said that there are valid reasons for viewing participation in the FL's competitions as a single venture for the entire season."[27]

Next, Mr. Justice Richards moved on to Article 80.2. He framed the issue as follows:

If the anti-deprivation rule or the pari passu principle is to apply to article 80, the first requirement is to identify the asset of the member club of which it is deprived by the operation of article 80 or which is distributed on a non-pari passu basis to football creditors in priority to other unsecured creditors. If there is no such asset vested in the member club at or after the date of administration or liquidation, then the anti-deprivation rule cannot apply. Equally, if there is no such asset vested in it at or after the date of notice by an administrator to make a distribution or the date of liquidation, the pari passu principle cannot apply.[28]

HMRC submitted that the asset is the debt due from the league to the member club in respect of the basic award. If it is the case of a club that does not complete the season, then, for reasons already stated, there will be no debt due, and therefore the operation of Article 80.2 does not deprive the club of an asset or direct the distribution of an asset in a manner contrary to the pari passu principle. But it was acknowledged that, in almost all cases, insolvent clubs complete their fixture obligations, because the league permits them to do so. In order to make a judgment, it was first necessary to determine whether the requirement to apply sums in the pool account in discharge of a defaulting club's football creditors applied during the season or only at the end of the season. "The difference is critical," Mr. Justice Richards stated, "because, if it is the former, the member club is clearly not . . . deprived of an asset in the form of a debt due to it."[29] Mr. Justice Richards determined that Article 80.2 did apply during the season, so that "where there is a default in the payment of debts to football creditors during the season, the FL is obliged to pay such debts out of the Pool Account to the extent of the amount which would otherwise become due to the defaulting club at the end of the season, so far as not previously paid to the club on account."[30] As a result, "the only sum which becomes payable to a defaulting club which completes the season is the balance, if any, after the FL has paid football creditors during the season."[31] Therefore, "The defaulting club is not deprived of an asset, namely the basic award, because in these circumstances there never was a debt due to it beyond the amount of the balance, if any."[32] This holds whether or not the club goes into administration during the season. Furthermore, the Football League relied on the trigger for Article 80.2 being that a club defaults in making any payment due to a football creditor, not the commencement of an administration or liquidation. And Mr. Justice Richards observed, "The older authorities were generally clear that the anti-deprivation rule applied only to a deprivation occurring on bankruptcy or liquidation, and not on some prior event such as a breach of contract or attempted alienation of the property."[33]

Finally, Mr. Justice Richards addressed Article 4.7.4 and the question of whether the power of the Football League to require the transfer of the share of a member club that goes into administration is void by reason of the anti-deprivation rule. First, he stated:

> Assuming that the administration or liquidation occurs during a season, it follows from what I have said about articles 77 and 80 that the member club is not thereby deprived of any existing right to receive any payments from the FL. It is at most deprived of a right to continue to play in the competitions for that and future seasons.[34]

As to being deprived of a right to continue to play, he stated:

> In the absence of specific statutory provision, insolvency law does not compel a party to continue to deal with a company in administration or liquidation, nor does it prohibit a party from stipulating that all future dealings shall be on terms that not only future debts but also existing debts are paid in full. It is then for the administrator or liquidator to decide whether to accept these terms.[35]

Thus, Mr. Justice Richards made the following interpretation:

> The provisions of the articles and the Insolvency Policy, giving the FL power to permit an insolvent member club to participate in its competitions on terms that other member clubs and other specified creditors are paid in full, is no more than the exercise by the member clubs through the FL of their right to refuse to participate further with the insolvent club save on these terms.[36]

HMRC's case had failed.

Mr. Justice Richards issued his decision in *HMRC v. The Football League* on 25 May 2012. In it, he concluded:

> It follows that in most circumstances in which the relevant provisions of the FL's articles and Insolvency Policy will operate, they will not be rendered void by the anti-deprivation rule or the pari passu principle. It may be that either or both might be engaged in particular circumstances. . . . Whether that is so would have to be decided in the context of a real case if and when it ever arose. The right course in the present proceedings is to decline to make the declarations sought by HMRC.[37]

He added, "The FL should not regard the result of this case as an endorsement of its approach to football creditors. It is, as I said at the start, a decision on a challenge brought on a particular legal basis."[38] This seems to leave open the possibility of a future challenge on another legal basis.

At the same time, there is also the possibility that the government could intervene. In its latest football governance report, issued in January 2013, the Culture, Media and Sport Committee made the following recommendation: "We recommend that the Government legislate to ban the use of the Football Creditors Rule at the earliest opportunity."[39]

Chapter 8

UNION ROYALE BELGE DES SOCIÉTÉS DE FOOTBALL ASSOCIATION AND OTHERS v. BOSMAN

"IT IS FAIR TO STATE," writes European law professor Stefaan Van den Bogaert, "that *Bosman* constitutes to date the most well-known judgment in the history of the European Court of Justice." To be sure, *Bosman* revolutionized European football. In the early 1990s, the proceedings raised questions as to whether existing football rules on player transfers and foreign player match eligibility were compatible with the laws of the European Community (since replaced and succeeded by the European Union). Specifically in question were (1) rules requiring a club that wished to sign an out-of-contract player to pay a fee to the player's previous club in order to consummate the transfer and (2) rules limiting the number of foreign players who could be included in a club's team sheet for a particular match. At the time of the proceedings, such rules, established by UEFA (Union of European Football Associations) and national football associations, had essentially become standard across Europe, with only slight variation from country to country.

As David McArdle wrote in *Football Society & The Law*, "UEFA had traditionally regarded itself as immune from external regulation and entitled to run its fiefdom in whatever way it saw fit." UEFA president Jacques George made that clear when he brashly stated, "[UEFA] can make up whatever rules we want, as long as they are within Swiss laws, as we have nothing to do with the [European Community]." In other words, since UEFA was based in Switzerland, and Switzerland was not a member of the European Community, then UEFA was not beholden to European Community law. But by the late 1980s, UEFA was essentially alone in this view, and European football was, as European law professor Stephen Weatherill put it, "on a collision course with the Treaty of Rome."

EUROPEAN TRANSFER RULES AND FOREIGN PLAYER RULES

The Transfer Rules

In Belgium, the home of the events that gave rise to the *Bosman* proceedings, the 1982 statutes of the Union Royale Belge des Sociétés de Football Association (URBSFA), the Belgian football association, had established a player transfer system that can be summarized as follows. All player contracts, which could have a term from one year to a maximum of five years, were to expire on 30 June. Prior to expiration of a player's contract, specifically no later than 26 April of the year in question, the club was to offer the player a new contract; otherwise, the player would be regarded as an amateur for the purposes of the transfer system, and a new club could acquire the player by paying a transfer fee of not more than 1 million Belgian francs (approximately 25,000 euros). A player was free to reject the new contract offer, and in this event his name would be placed on a transfer list, which would be submitted to the URBSFA by 30 April. From 1 May to 31 May, a player on the transfer list could change clubs by a *transfert imposé*, a compulsory transfer, whereby a new club could acquire the player by paying a transfer fee calculated by the URBSFA. The URBSFA would calculate the fee by multiplying the player's gross income by a factor varying from 14 to 2 depending on the player's age. For instance, under the 1982 statutes, in the case of a player aged 25 or 26, the required transfer fee was ten times the player's income. The transfer fee was designed to serve as compensation for the training of the player. From 1 June to 25 June, a player could change clubs by a *transfert libre*, a free transfer, whereby a transfer fee would be negotiated freely, but the two clubs would have to reach an agreement on a fee in order for the transfer to be completed. In the event that no transfer took place, a player's club was required to offer him a new contract for one season on the same terms as had been offered in April. If the player rejected the offer, the club could suspend him; if it chose not to do so, the player would be reclassified to amateur status.

In 1993, the URBSFA established a new transfer system, but with very similar rules. While the new rules emphasized players' "freedom of contract," they nonetheless stated: "Without prejudice to the player's freedom of contract, the acquiring club shall be obliged to pay compensation to the club with which he was last registered." The transfer fee was now defined as compensation for the training and development of the player, his skill, and the cost of replacing him. Outside of Belgium, several other European football associations had similar rules in force, which in the event of a player transfer between two clubs within the association in question required the payment of a fee for training and/or development.

Each European football association is also bound to recognize UEFA and FIFA (Fédération Internationale de Football Association) regulations on the status and transfer of players. At the material time of the facts in *Bosman*, the UEFA rules on transfers between clubs from different national football associations within Europe were contained in a document titled "Principles of Cooperation between Member Associations of UEFA and Their Clubs," which was approved by the UEFA Executive Committee on 24 May 1990 and in force from 1 July 1990.

Under those rules, an out-of-contract player was free to conclude a new contract with the club of his choice. The new club was to notify the former club, which would then notify its national association, which would in turn issue an international transfer certificate. However, the former club was entitled to "compensation for . . . training and development" from the new club. In the absence of an agreement between the clubs, a board of experts set up by UEFA would determine the fee by multiplying the player's gross income in the preceding season by a factor varying from 12 to 1 depending on the player's age, up to a maximum of 5 million Swiss francs. The business relationship between the clubs with respect to the fee was to have no influence on the activity of the player, who would be free to play for his new club. If the new club did not pay the fee to the former club, the UEFA Control and Disciplinary Body could take disciplinary action.

After the events that gave rise to the *Bosman* proceedings, UEFA, in response to negotiations with the Commission of the European Communities, undertook to incorporate in every professional player's contract a clause permitting him at the expiry of his contract to enter into a new contract with the club of his choice and to play for that club immediately, and provisions to that effect came into force on 1 July 1992. From 1 August 1993, UEFA regulations on "governing the fixing of a transfer fee" established new rules that retained the principle that the business relationship between the two clubs was to exert no influence on the sporting activity of the player, who was to be free to play for the club with which he has signed the new contract, and provided that, in the event of disagreement between the clubs concerned, UEFA would determine the appropriate fee for training or development. For non-amateur players, the calculation of the fee was based on the player's gross income in the previous 12 months or on the fixed annual income guaranteed in the new contract, increased by twenty percent for players who had played at least twice in the senior national team for their country and multiplied by a factor of between 12 and 0 depending on age.

The FIFA rules on transfers were contained in regulations that had been adopted on 14 and 15 November 1953 and last amended on 29 May 1986. Under those rules, a professional player could not leave his national association so long as he was bound by his contract and by the rules of his club, league, or national association, no matter how harsh their terms. An international transfer would not be completed unless the former national association issued a transfer certificate, which acknowledged that all financial commitments, including any transfer fee, had been settled. In April 1991, FIFA adopted new Regulations Governing the Status and Transfer of Football Players. That document, as amended in December 1991 and December 1993, provided that a player could enter into a contract with a new club when the contract between him and his club had expired, had been rescinded, or was to expire within six months. Special rules were laid down for "non-amateur" players. When a non-amateur player, or a player who assumed non-amateur status within three years of his transfer, was transferred, his former club was entitled to a compensation fee for development or training, the amount of which was to be agreed upon between the two clubs. In the event of disagreement, the dispute was to be submitted to FIFA or the relevant confederation (e.g., UEFA).

The Foreign Player Rules

Going back to the 1960s, many European football associations had introduced rules that restricted the signing or fielding of foreign players.[1] In 1978, after negotiations between the Commission of the European Communities and the European football associations, UEFA undertook to eliminate restrictions on the number of players from other member states of the European Community that a club could have under contract and to set the number of such players that could participate in a match at two, though the limit would not be applicable to players who had resided in the member state in question for at least five years. UEFA would drag its feet, though, and more than a decade would pass before it would make good on its promises.

Finally, in April 1991, UEFA adopted what came to be known as the "3 + 2 rule," under which, from 1 July 1992, the number of foreign players whose names could be included on the team sheet could be restricted to not less than three per team, plus two players who had played in the country in question for at least five years uninterruptedly, including three years in junior teams. Since the rule was merely a minimum, individual associations could allow more foreign players, but in practice the associations generally used UEFA's minimum as their maximum. The rule was to apply initially to first division clubs and to extend to all non-amateur clubs by the end of the 1996–97 season. The rule also applied to matches in UEFA competitions.

European Community Concern

Within the European Community, there had long been concern with several aspects of the organization of European football, and above all with the transfer rules and foreign player rules, because these rules restricted football players' freedom of movement, which European Community law established as a fundamental right of all workers. Specifically, Article 48 of the Treaty of Rome, the founding treaty of the European Community, guaranteed the "freedom of movement for workers" and prohibited "any discrimination based on nationality between workers of the Member States in regards to employment, remuneration, and other conditions of work and employment."

From the late 1970s through the 1980s, calls for football reform grew louder. In 1989, Jim Janssen Van Raay, a Dutch member of the European Parliament, wrote an emphatic report on the matter. The Van Raay Report argued that European Community law and European Court of Justice case law extended the freedom of movement to football players and that football's transfer rules and foreign player rules were impermissible restrictions on such freedom. The report further argued that it was incumbent on the

European Commission to initiate proceedings to enforce the law and uphold the players' freedom. Although it was believed that an affected player would be unlikely to initiate proceedings out of fear that such action could end his career, a Belgian midfielder named Jean-Marc Bosman did step forward and take that risk just a year later.

UNION ROYALE BELGE DES SOCIÉTÉS DE FOOTBALL ASSOCIATION AND OTHERS V. BOSMAN

In 1986, Jean-Marc Bosman signed his first professional contract, with Belgian club Standard Liège. Two years later, Standard transferred Bosman to a smaller Belgian club, SA Royal Club Liègeois, for 3 million Belgian francs. Bosman signed a two-year contract with RC Liège, which ran until 30 June 1990. Bosman was guaranteed 75,000 Belgian francs per month; with bonuses and other payments, his average monthly earnings amounted to about 120,000 Belgian francs per month. In April 1990, RC Liège offered Bosman a new contract for one season at a basic wage of 30,000 Belgian francs per month—the minimum allowed under URBSFA rules.

Not surprisingly, Bosman rejected the offer, and as a result he was placed on the transfer list. The transfer fee for a compulsory transfer was set, in accordance with URBSFA rules, at 11,743,000 Belgian francs (near 300,000 euros). Alas, no club expressed interest in a compulsory transfer. This prompted Bosman to contact French second division club US Dunkerque. On 30 July 1990, Bosman and US Dunkerque concluded a contract that provided for wages equivalent to about 100,000 Belgian francs per month.

Three days earlier, RC Liège and US Dunkerque had agreed to terms on a temporary transfer. The two clubs agreed that RC Liège would transfer Bosman to US Dunkerque for one season in exchange for a fee of 1.2 million Belgian francs, payable upon the French Football Federation's receipt of an international transfer certificate from the URBSFA. US Dunkerque was also given an option for a permanent transfer for an additional fee of 4.8 million Belgian francs. However, both the contract between Bosman and US Dunkerque and the contract between RC Liège and US Dunkerque were subject to the condition that they would become void if the French Football Federation did not receive an international transfer certificate by 2 August. Because it had doubts as to US Dunkerque's solvency, RC Liège did not request the URBSFA to issue the transfer certificate, thus leaving both contracts to lapse. RC Liège would suspend Bosman, preventing him from playing in the 1990–91 season.

At this point, Bosman was prepared to take legal action to resolve his situation. As it happened, a few doors down from his parents' house lived a woman who was dating a young attorney who had mastered in European law. Bosman decided to knock on the woman's door to see the attorney, a Mr. Jean-Louis Dupont. After an initial look at the facts, Dupont understood that Bosman had a case. "We tried for a couple of hours to make phone calls to settle the matter in a friendly way," Dupont would later recall. "But we are talking about Belgium at the beginning of the 1990s when sport was one world and law another, and the answer we got was, 'Who is that lawyer who thinks he can ring up our club? These regulations are world regulations, what are you talking about?'" So, Bosman and Dupont would head to the courts. Ultimately, the unknown footballer and the unknown attorney would change the face of the sport.

National Proceedings

Bosman applied to the Tribunal de Première Instance, the Court of First Instance, in Liège on 8 August 1990. In addition to his main claim, he submitted an application for an interim order seeking, first, an order for RC Liège and URBSFA to pay him 100,000 Belgian francs per month until he found a new club; second, an order restraining the defendants from harming his opportunities to find a new club by seeking a transfer fee for him; and third, an order referring a question to the European Court of Justice for a preliminary ruling on the compatibility of the transfer system with European law. All three requests were granted (although RC Liège was ordered to pay Bosman 30,000 rather than 100,000 Belgian francs per month), but the Cour d'Appel, the Court of Appeal, in Liège would overturn the referral to the Court of Justice.

The interim order made it possible for Bosman to sign with French second division club Saint-Quentin in October 1990. At the end of the first season, the contract was terminated. In February 1992, Bosman agreed to a contract with another small French club, Saint-Denis de la Réunion. That contract was also later terminated. After a long search for a new club, Bosman joined Belgian third division club Royal Olympic Club de Charleroi in May 1993. According to the national court, there were clear grounds for suspicion that European clubs had boycotted Bosman. Meanwhile, the legal proceedings continued.

In the main proceedings, also brought before the Tribunal de Première Instance in Liège on 8 August 1990, Bosman claimed damages from RC Liège of 30 million Belgian francs, based, first, on breach of contract and, second, on the unlawfulness of the transfer system. The following summer, URBSFA intervened, seeking a declaration that its rules and the corresponding UEFA rules were lawful, and Bosman added UEFA as a defendant. Concurrently, Bosman brought an action against UEFA for a declaration that its transfer rules and foreign player rules were null and void on the ground of breach of Article 48 of the EC Treaty (now Article 45 of the Treaty on the Functioning of the European Union) and Articles 85 and 86 of the EC Treaty (now Articles 101 and 102 of the Treaty on the Functioning of the European Union). As previously stated, Article 48 secured the freedom of movement for workers within the European Community. Articles 85 and 86 were the main sections of European Community competition law: Article 85 prohibited anticompetitive agreements (similar to Section 1 of the Sherman Act in the United States), and Article 86 prohibited the abuse of a dominant position (similar to Section 2 of the Sherman Act).

In April 1992, Bosman submitted further applications to the Tribunal de Première Instance, in which he amended the original claim against RC Liège, brought separate proceedings against URBSFA, and developed the claims against UEFA. The action now sought an order restraining RC Liège, URBSFA, and UEFA from hindering his freedom to conclude a contract with a new employer. In addition, he sought an order for those parties individually or jointly to pay him 11,368,350 Belgian francs as compensation for the loss incurred from 1 August 1990 and 11,743,000 Belgian francs as compensation for the loss caused by the application of the transfer system from the beginning of his career until 9 November 1990, plus a provisional sum of 1 Belgian franc for the costs of the proceedings. Bosman further sought a declaration that the transfer rules and the foreign player rules of URBSFA and UEFA were not applicable to him. Finally, Bosman proposed that a preliminary ruling should be sought from the Court of Justice.

The Tribunal de Première Instance issued a judgment on 11 June 1992. It rejected UEFA's objection that proceedings against it had to be brought in Switzerland and held that it had jurisdiction to decide the case pending before it. It held that Bosman's claims against RC Liège, URBSFA, and UEFA were admissible. It held that RC Liège had acted unlawfully in causing Bosman's transfer to US Dunkerque to fail and was to compensate the resulting loss. Finally, the court made a reference to the Court of Justice for a preliminary ruling on the interpretation of Articles 48, 85, and 86 of the EC Treaty with reference to the transfer system.

In a judgment on 1 October 1993, the Cour d'Appel upheld the decision, insofar as it held that the Tribunal de Première Instance had jurisdiction and that the claims were admissible. The Cour d'Appel also agreed that the examination of the claims raised against RC Liège, URBSFA, and UEFA involved an examination of the lawfulness of the transfer system, and it therefore made its own reference to the Court of Justice for a preliminary ruling (replacing the reference by the Tribunal de Première Instance). At Bosman's suggestion, the Cour d'Appel concluded that the foreign player rules also should be examined. Bosman's claim in that respect was based on Article 18 of the Belgian Code Judiciaire, the Judicial Code, which permitted the bringing of actions "to prevent infringement of a right which is seriously threatened." Thus, the Cour d'Appel decided to stay the proceedings and referred the following questions to the Court of Justice for a preliminary ruling:

> Are Articles 48, 85, and 86 of the Treaty of Rome of 25 March 1957 to be interpreted as
>
> i. prohibiting a football club from requiring and receiving payment of a sum of money upon the engagement of one of its players who has come to the end of his contract by a new employing club;
> ii. prohibiting the national and international sporting associations or federations from including in their respective regulations provisions restricting access of foreign players from the European Community to the competitions which they organize?

European Court of Justice Proceedings

Following an advisory opinion written by Advocate General Carl Otto Lenz on 20 September 1995, the European Court of Justice rendered its judgment in *Bosman* on 15 December 1995.[2] In its judgment, the Court of Justice first had to address the issue of its jurisdiction to rule on the two questions referred by the national court. In UEFA's view, the referred questions were inadmissible and should not be answered. UEFA maintained that its regulations were not applied when Bosman's transfer from RC Liège to US Dunkerque collapsed (the national court believed that URBSFA and RC Liège had applied FIFA regulations) and if they had been applied, then the transfer would have been consummated and the proceedings would not have arisen. As such, UEFA contended that the requested interpretation of European law bore no relation to the actual facts of the main proceedings pending before the national court, and therefore the first referred question was not admissible.

As to the second referred question, UEFA considered it to be purely hypothetical, because Bosman's career was not hindered by the foreign player rules, and therefore also not admissible. The Danish, French, and Italian governments also took the position that the foreign player rules were not relevant to the main proceedings and that the second referred question was hypothetical. In their view, the dispute concerned only the admissibility of the transfer system.

In its judgment, the Court of Justice noted that it had a duty "to assist in the administration of justice in the Member States,"[3] but "not to deliver advisory opinions on general or hypothetical questions,"[4] and it had previously established that it had "no jurisdiction to give a preliminary ruling on a question submitted by a national court where it is quite obvious that the interpretation of Community law sought by that court bears no relation to the actual facts of the main action or its purpose . . . or where the problem is hypothetical."[5] In the present case, though, the Court of Justice found, "the issues in the main proceedings, taken as a whole, are not hypothetical and the national court has provided this Court with a clear statement of the surrounding facts, the rules in question and the grounds on which it believes that a decision on the questions submitted is necessary to enable it to give a judgment."[6] It determined, "even if, as URBSFA and UEFA contend, the UEFA regulations were not applied when Mr. Bosman's transfer to US Dunkerque fell through, they are still in issue in the preventative actions brought by Mr. Bosman against

URBSFA and UEFA . . . and the Court's interpretation as to the compatibility with Community law of the transfer system set up by the UEFA regulations may be useful to the national court."[7] With respect more particularly to the question of the foreign player rules, the Court of Justice observed that the national court had held the claim to be admissible based on a national procedural provision, and decided that "It is not for this Court, in the context of these proceedings, to call that assessment in question. . . . Consequently, the questions submitted by that court meet an objective need for the purpose of settling disputes properly brought before it."[8] Therefore, the Court of Justice concluded that it had jurisdiction to rule on both referred questions.

Advocate General Lenz's opinion was particularly influential on the decision to answer the second referred question. While he acknowledged that the Court of Justice "could . . . on the basis of its previous case-law, indeed reach the conclusion that the second question submitted should be rejected as inadmissible,"[9] he wrote, "I would, however, emphatically recommend the Court not to take that step." He continued, "In my opinion it is not enough to focus on the fact that the question is based on a—possibly—hypothetical factual situation. Instead the spirit and purpose of the possibility of rejecting questions submitted for a preliminary ruling should be the focus. Such an examination leads in my opinion to the conclusion that rejection of the question is possible, but neither necessary nor appropriate."[10]

Although the European Commission had long criticized the rules on foreign players, it had not brought any action for breach of the EC Treaty because the prospects of success appeared uncertain for procedural reasons. Advocate General Lenz made the case that it was "extremely unlikely"[11] that a reference such as the present one would ever again reach the Court of Justice. In the event that the Court declined to answer the question, Advocate General Lenz asserted, "regulation of this field will continue to be left to the whim of the sporting associations,"[12] which he regarded as "scarcely tolerable."[13] The Court of Justice seized the opportunity to clarify the law. In a well-regarded 1997 law review article, law professor Catherine Barnard and then law professor, now advocate general Eleanor Sharpston commented, "if the Court wants to answer a reference because it raises an interesting or important point of law, it will find a way to do so."

Once the Court of Justice had accepted jurisdiction to rule on the two questions referred by the national court, it was then necessary to address

certain arguments that had been put forward that challenged the application
of Article 48 to the rules of sporting associations. The Court of Justice had
previously ruled on the applicability of Community law in the field of sport
in two important decisions in the 1970s: *Walrave and Koch v. Union Cycliste
Internationale*[14] in 1974 and *Donà v. Mantero*[15] in 1976. *Walrave* and *Donà*
were especially significant because the EC Treaty gave no specific consideration to sport. In *Walrave,*[16] the first case involving sport to reach the Court
of Justice, the Court stated:

> Having regard to the objectives of the Community, the practice of
> sport is subject to Community law only in so far as it constitutes
> *an economic activity.* . . . [emphasis added]
>
> When such activity has the character of gainful employment or
> remunerated service it comes more particularly within the scope,
> according to the case, of Articles 48 to 51 or 59 to 66 of the Treaty.
>
> These provisions . . . prohibit any discrimination based on
> nationality in the performance of the activity to which they refer.

The Court provided the following exception: "This prohibition however
does not affect the composition of sport teams, in particular national teams,
the formation of which is a question of purely sporting interest and as such
has nothing to do with economic activity."

In *Donà,*[17] the Court, citing *Walgrave*, established that Community law
applied to the rules of sporting associations, and on the substance of the
case it stated:

> Having regard to the objectives of the Community, the practice of
> sport is subject to Community law only in so far as it constitutes
> an economic activity. . . .
>
> This applies to the activities of professional or semi-professional
> football players, which are in the nature of gainful employment or
> remunerated service.
>
> Where such players are nationals of a Member State they ben-
> efit in all the other Member States from the provisions of Com-
> munity law concerning freedom of movement of persons and of
> provision of services.

The Court provided the following exception: "However, those provisions do not prevent the adoption of rules or of a practice excluding foreign players from participation in certain matches for reasons which are not of an economic nature, which relate to the particular nature and context of such matches and are thus of sporting interest only, such as, for example, matches between national teams from different countries."[18]

Since *Walrave* and *Donà*, no substantial legal or judicial developments had occurred in the field of sport, and despite the rulings, sporting associations still maintained the attitude that sports governance should be separate from Community law. Now the URBSFA and UEFA had advanced various arguments that, in their opinion, showed that Article 48 was not applicable to the present case. URBSFA argued that only major European clubs exercised an economic activity within the meaning of the EC Treaty, whereas clubs such as RC Liège carry on an economic activity only to a negligible extent. URBSFA further argued that the transfer rules related merely to the business relationships between clubs, while Article 48 was relevant only to the employment relationships between clubs and players. UEFA argued that it was extremely difficult to distinguish between the economic and the sporting aspects of football, and that a decision by the Court concerning the situation of professional players might call in question the organization of football as a whole. Advocate General Lenz wrote, "None of those arguments is convincing."[19] The Court of Justice ultimately rejected each one.

Having confirmed that Article 48 was applicable to sport, the Court of Justice went on to consider whether the transfer rules formed an obstacle to freedom of movement. The Court, taking a broad view of freedom of movement, found that the rules did form an obstacle, even though they did not particularly discriminate on the basis of nationality.

Specifically, the Court stated, "Provisions which preclude or deter a national of a Member State from leaving his country of origin in order to exercise his right to freedom of movement therefore constitute an obstacle to that freedom even if they apply without regard to the nationality of the workers concerned."[20] It continued, "Since [the transfer rules] provide that a professional footballer may not pursue his activity with a new club established in another Member State unless it has paid his former club a transfer fee agreed upon between the two clubs or determined in accordance with the regulations of the sporting associations, the said rules constitute an obstacle to freedom of movement for workers."[21]

The Court provided the following exception: "It could only be otherwise if those rules pursued a legitimate aim compatible with the Treaty and were justified by pressing reasons of public interest. But even if that were so, application of those rules would still have to be such as to ensure achievement of the aim in question and not go beyond what is necessary for that purpose."[22]

URBSFA, UEFA, and the French and Italian governments submitted that the transfer rules were justified "by the need to maintain financial and competitive balance between clubs and to support the search for talent and the training of young players."[23] Significantly, the Court did acknowledge the unique nature of the business of football relative to other commercial activity and the notion that its rules may in certain instances require special consideration. The Court reasoned:

> In view of the considerable social importance of sporting activities and in particular football in the Community, the aims of maintaining a balance between clubs by preserving a certain degree of equality and uncertainty as to results and of encouraging the recruitment and training of young players must be accepted as legitimate.[24]

But the Court still objected to the transfer rules, holding that they did not adequately contribute to those legitimate aims.

> As regards the first of those aims,[25] Mr. Bosman has rightly pointed out that the application of the transfer rules is not an adequate means of maintaining financial and competitive balance in the world of football. Those rules neither preclude the richest clubs from securing the services of the best players nor prevent the availability of financial resources from being a decisive factor in competitive sport, thus considerably altering the balance between clubs.
>
> As regards the second aim, it must be accepted that the prospect of receiving transfer, development or training fees is indeed

likely to encourage football clubs to seek new talent and train young players.

However, because it is impossible to predict the sporting future of young players with any certainty and because only a limited number of such players go on to play professionally, those fees are by nature contingent and uncertain and are in any event unrelated to the actual cost borne by clubs of training both future professional players and those who will never play professionally. The prospect of receiving such fees cannot, therefore, be either a decisive factor in encouraging recruitment and training of young players or an adequate means of financing such activities, particularly in the case of smaller clubs.[26]

The Court submitted that competitive balance and player development could be achieved "at least as efficiently by other means which do not impede freedom of movement for workers."[27] It did not recommend an alternative system. Advocate General Lenz had suggested some form of revenue sharing or salary limits (which of course would have competition law implications).

The Court of Justice then moved on to consider whether the foreign player rules formed an obstacle to freedom of movement. Not surprisingly, it found that they did. "No deep cogitation is required to reach the conclusion that the rules on foreign players are of a discriminatory nature," Advocate General Lenz had written. "They represent an absolutely classic case of discrimination on the ground of nationality."[28] After all, Article 48 expressly provided that freedom of movement for workers entailed the abolition of any discrimination based on nationality between workers of the member states with respect to employment, remuneration, and working conditions. "The fact that those [foreign player rules] concern not the employment of such players, on which there is no restriction, but the extent to which their clubs may field them in official matches is irrelevant,"[29] the Court stated. "In so far as participation in such matches is the essential purpose of a professional player's activity, a rule which restricts that participation obviously also restricts the chances of employment of the player concerned."[30]

URBSFA, UEFA, and the French, German, and Italian governments argued that the foreign player rules were justified on noneconomic grounds, where purely sporting interest was concerned. They argued, first, that the foreign player rules served to maintain the traditional link between each club and its country, which was cited as an important factor in enabling the public to identify with its favorite team; second, that the rules were necessary to create a sufficient pool of players for the national teams; and third, that they helped to maintain competitive balance between clubs. The Court recalled the exception it had allowed in *Donà* but stressed that the foreign player rules in question "do not concern specific matches between teams representing their countries but apply to all official matches between clubs and thus to the essence of the activity of professional players."[31] In those circumstances, the foreign player rules could "not be deemed to be in accordance with Article 48 of the Treaty."[32] And the Court held, "None of the arguments put forward by the sporting associations and by the governments which have submitted observations detracts from that conclusion."[33]

In response to the first argument, it stated, "[A] football club's links with the Member State in which it is established cannot be regarded as any more inherent in its sporting activity than its links with its locality, town, region or, in the case of the United Kingdom, the territory covered by each of the four associations."[34] Moreover, "in international competitions . . . participation is limited to clubs which have achieved certain results in competition in their respective countries, without any particular significance being attached to the nationalities of their players."[35] In response to the second argument, the Court stated, "Whilst national teams must be made up of players having the nationality of the relevant country, those players need not necessarily be registered to play for clubs in that country."[36] In response to the third argument, it stated, "[Nationality] clauses are not sufficient to achieve the aim of maintaining a competitive balance, since there are no rules limiting the possibility for such clubs to recruit the best national players, thus undermining that balance to just the same extent."[37]

As to the EC Treaty's competition provisions and their application to sport, the Court decided to avoid the matter, stating, "Since both types of rule to which the national court's question refer are contrary to Article 48, it is not necessary to rule on the interpretation of Articles 85 and 86 of the Treaty."[38] Thus, the Court of Justice concluded, in answer to the questions referred to it by the national court:

1. Article 48 of the EEC Treaty precludes the application of rules laid down by sporting associations, under which a professional footballer who is a national of one Member State may not, on the expiry of his contract with a club, be employed by a club of another Member State unless the latter club has paid to the former club a transfer, training or development fee.

2. Article 48 of the EEC Treaty precludes the application of rules laid down by sporting associations under which, in matches in competitions which they organize, football clubs may field only a limited number of professional players who are nationals of other Member States.

Bosman, more than five years after his transfer from RC Liège to US Dunkerque failed, had earned a historic victory.

As a result of the decision of the Court of Justice, the foreign player restrictions would have to be eliminated and the transfer system would have to be rebuilt. Initially, some believed the decision meant that transfer fees payable on out-of-contract players between clubs in the same member state were still lawful, but it was later clarified that the decision indirectly affected national transfer fees, and any new system would cover transfers across Europe and within European countries. A new system did not immediately follow. The federations seemed unwilling to make substantial changes, which prompted the European Commission to launch an investigation. After extended and acrimonious negotiations, the European Commission reached an agreement with FIFA and UEFA in March 2001, and the new rules came into force on 1 September 2001.[39] But football was already different, even before the rules were formalized. The player market had opened up. The power had shifted to the players, and many of them, in turn, made fortunes. The game we see today can in many ways be traced back to *Bosman*.

In one of his analyses of the case, Stefaan Van den Bogaert gave Jean-Marc Bosman the following acknowledgment:

> [Bosman] exposed himself to heavy pressure from the football establishment to drop the case or at least come to a settlement out of court. He had to resist various kinds of cunning legal manoeuvers to slow down the process of the case before various courts. Had it not been for his perseverance, stubbornness and dogged

determination to defy the football system, there would simply not have been a *Bosman* case at all. It is by no means unconceivable that without Bosman, the transfer rules and nationality clauses would still exist today. Ultimately, one player thus managed to defeat the whole football establishment, a story reminiscent of David's mythical victory over Goliath. The Court's ruling in Bosman's favor clearly conveys the message that citizens' rights are taken seriously under EC law. But then again, there is also a darker side to this coin: to vindicate his rights, Bosman basically had to sacrifice his career. One career for all players' freedom at the expiry of contracts: that was the high price to be paid.

Bosman was 31 years old and playing for a fourth division club in Belgium when the Court of Justice issued its judgment. After going back through the Belgian courts, Bosman was eventually awarded 16 million Belgian francs (approximately 400,000 euros) in 1998.

Chapter 9

FEYENOORD v. UEFA

FEYENOORD, ONE OF THE THREE traditional giants of Dutch football, along with Ajax and PSV Eindhoven, is a club with a rich history and a massive, die-hard fan base known as *Het Legioen*—The Legion. Among these supporters, there are groups that have developed a reputation for violence. This can be traced back to Feyenoord's win over Tottenham in the 1974 UEFA Cup Final, when rioting Tottenham supporters clashed with Feyenoord supporters and Rotterdam police, which is described as the moment that football hooliganism was introduced to the Netherlands. In the years since, Feyenoord supporters have been involved in numerous incidents in the Netherlands and across Europe. In the 2006–07 season, the club was made to pay a heavy price for it.

On 30 November 2006, Feyenoord was set to play away to French side AS Nancy-Lorraine in the group phase of the 2006–07 UEFA Cup.[1] Earlier that month, officials of Feyenoord and Dutch police met with officials of AS Nancy and the city of Nancy in preparation for the match. As a result of the meeting, Feyenoord was allocated 1,300 tickets. Upon its request, Feyenoord was later granted an additional 250 tickets. Feyenoord sold its entire allocation through its away ticketing system, which enabled the club to identify supporters and exclude known hooligans from stadiums. But despite the ticketing system, Feyenoord soon grew concerned with the size and makeup of the traveling contingent, over which it seemed to have little control.

As Dutch football writer Ernst Bouwes explained in *When Saturday Comes*, for Feyenoord supporters the match in Nancy had become "a sort of 'sentimental journey' for those who [had] been locked out of Dutch stadiums in recent seasons." In a letter dated 27 November, Feyenoord informed AS

Nancy that it expected about 3,000 to 4,000 people to travel to Nancy without a ticket. Feyenoord further informed AS Nancy that about 400 people who could possibly be linked to the club had purchased tickets outside of the club's away ticketing system. Some supporters had driven to Nancy weeks before the match, bought tickets at the stadium without any restrictions, and then sold them in and around Rotterdam. These tickets were for sections other than those designated for the visiting supporters. Feyenoord feared there could be a significant hooligan presence in Nancy, and the match could be marred by violence or other misconduct in and around the stadium.

AS Nancy acknowledged that 300 to 350 tickets had been sold to Dutch supporters. The club had become aware of the situation about a week prior to receiving Feyenoord's letter and immediately closed the sales points at the stadium. In response to Feyenoord's letter, however, AS Nancy implemented further security measures in preparation for the match, including:

- an exclusive entrance to the stadium for Feyenoord supporters;
- pre-checking of tickets with police at all stadium entrances, with any supporter identified as belonging to Feyenoord directed towards the visitors' sections;
- isolation of the visitors' sections; and
- the addition of 100 stewards, bringing the total number of stewards to 400, and a police force of between 250 and 300 to patrol the match.

Unfortunately, this would not be enough to maintain order and security on the day.

A few hours before the match, local police had to intervene when Feyenoord supporters began fighting and smashing windows in the center of Nancy. Several bars and restaurants closed their doors in order to avoid destruction. The chief of police reasoned that it would be easier to control these supporters within the confines of the stadium, so the police forced them in that direction. Among these supporters, some had tickets, but many did not. When riots broke out in front of the stadium, the police decided to open the ticket office for those without a ticket, and usher them all into the stadium. The police were trying to subdue the riot as quickly as possible, and their decision to allow the rioting supporters into the stadium was made without consulting with Feyenoord representatives or the UEFA match delegate. These supporters were placed in sections 14 and 15, which were originally to be kept empty in order to isolate the Feyenoord supporters who had purchased their tickets through the away ticketing system in sections 16, 17, and 18.

When AS Nancy scored the first goal of the match in the 22nd minute, Feyenoord supporters in section 14 began breaking the separation wall between sections 13 and 14, and some managed to enter section 13, prompting the AS Nancy fans there to leave their seats. The police managed to push these supporters back into section 14, and the police remained in section 13 to monitor the situation. Soon after, Feyenoord supporters in section 14 started throwing seats, bottles, and other objects at the police and the AS Nancy supporters in section 13. The provocation continued through halftime and into the second half. In the second half, Feyenoord supporters in section 18—which should have been a section of "official" supporters, although the supporters in sections 14 and 15 may have had easy access to sections 16, 17, and 18—threw seats onto the field of play and at stewards. Eventually, Feyenoord supporters in section 18 tried to breach the separation wall between sections 18 and 19, and in response, in the 79th minute, the police used tear gas to disperse the crowd. Because of the effects of the tear gas on players and officials, the referee interrupted the match for about 34 minutes.

AS Nancy would go on to win the match, 3–0, and Feyenoord braced for the fallout. "We can't take responsibility for people we don't know," bemoaned Feyenoord director Onno Jacobs. "Now we will be punished for the behavior of a group of louts, whom we never invited." "We knew that a number of people with stadium bans had bought tickets not through Feyenoord, which gave me a bad feeling," said Feyenoord coach Erwin Koeman. "This is terrible—I felt so powerless."

UEFA REGULATIONS AND RULINGS

UEFA, the governing body of European football, is an association formed under the laws of Switzerland, in particular Articles 60 to 79 of the Swiss Civil Code, which provide such associations broad freedom to define their organization—a basic principle known as the "autonomy of association." UEFA's statutes and regulations are an expression of this autonomy, and they define, among other things, the association's objectives, the rights and obligations of its members, and the disciplinary measures that it may apply to its members. With respect to supporter misconduct, UEFA regulations hold member clubs strictly liable, regardless of their culpability. Specifically, Article 6 of the UEFA Disciplinary Regulations (2006 edition) provided that:

1. Member associations and clubs are responsible for the conduct of their players, officials, members, supporters and any other persons exercising a function at a match on behalf of the association or club.
2. The host association or club is responsible for order and security both inside and around the stadium before, during and after the match. It is liable for incidents of any kind, and can be rendered subject to disciplinary measures and bound to observe directives.

Under Article 14 of the UEFA Disciplinary Regulations (2006 edition), the following sanctions could be imposed on member associations and clubs:

a. warning,
b. reprimand,
c. fine,
d. annulment of the result of a match,
e. order that a match be replayed,
f. deduction of points,
g. awarding of a match by default,
h. playing of a match behind closed doors;
i. stadium closure,
j. playing of a match in a third country,
k. disqualification from competitions in progress and/or exclusion from future competitions,
l. withdrawal of a title or award,
m. withdrawal of a licence.

UEFA considers strict liability necessary to achieve its objective of maintaining order and security at its matches. UEFA has no direct disciplinary authority over supporters; its only authority is over member associations and clubs.

UEFA has two disciplinary bodies: the Control and Disciplinary Body, which consists of 10 members and has jurisdiction to rule on disciplinary issues and all other matters, and the Appeals Body, which consists of 11 members and has jurisdiction to hear appeals.[2] The members of the disciplinary bodies are independent and may not belong to any other UEFA organ or committee. In proceedings before the disciplinary bodies, UEFA disciplinary inspectors represent UEFA. The disciplinary inspectors have the authority to initiate disciplinary investigations, lodge appeals against decisions by the Control and Disciplinary Body, and support UEFA in the event that a party lodges an appeal against a decision by the Appeals Body.

On 7 December 2006, the Control and Disciplinary Body imposed on Feyenoord a fine of 200,000 Swiss francs, and ordered its next two home matches in a UEFA competition to be played behind closed doors, though the order was deferred for a probationary period of three years. The panel based its decision on the rule of strict liability, but did take into account the fact that Feyenoord was not the host club and thus had limited influence on the match organization. UEFA appealed the Control and Disciplinary Body's decision, seeking tougher sanctions. UEFA claimed that Feyenoord did not qualify to be sanctioned on probation because the club had a considerable record of supporter misconduct. UEFA further emphasized that some of Feyenoord's "official" supporters, who had purchased tickets through the club, were involved in the disturbances in Nancy. Feyenoord filed a cross-appeal, seeking acquittal. Feyenoord denied legal responsibility for the incident.

On 25 January 2007, the Appeals Body partially upheld the UEFA appeal, and as a result Feyenoord was disqualified from the 2006–07 UEFA Cup. Despite the 3–0 loss in Nancy, Feyenoord had won its final match of the group phase and advanced to the Round of 32, where it was set to face, of all clubs, Tottenham. But now Feyenoord's European campaign was stopped in its tracks. The Appeals Body's decision also included a fine of 100,000 Swiss francs and an order to settle the damages at Nancy's stadium. "What cruel irony," wrote Ernst Bouwes. "In 1974, fans of Tottenham Hotspur introduced major football violence to Holland during the second leg of the UEFA Cup final against Feyenoord. Thirty-three years later, Feyenoord find themselves banned for the rest of the European season for hooliganism at a UEFA Cup tie at Nancy while their scheduled opponents, Spurs, may receive a bye into the next round."

Feyenoord still had a final authority to which it could appeal—the Court of Arbitration for Sport.

COURT OF ARBITRATION FOR SPORT RULING

Under Article 62 paragraph 1 of the UEFA Statutes, any decision taken by a UEFA body may be disputed exclusively before the Court of Arbitration for Sport (CAS), the international arbitration body based in Lausanne, Switzerland, to the exclusion of any ordinary court or any other arbitration body. Feyenoord filed its statement of appeal on 26 January 2007, and a hearing was set for 8 February 2007. The CAS panel consisted of an arbitrator designated by Feyenoord, an arbitrator designated by UEFA, and a president designated by the CAS Appeals Arbitration Division. The panel would apply UEFA regulations primarily and Swiss law subsidiarily in resolving the dispute.

At the time, the existing jurisprudence of the CAS accepted the rule of strict liability. Five years earlier, the CAS had affirmed its application in the case of PSV Eindhoven, which was held liable for racist chanting by its fans during a UEFA Champions League match against Arsenal.[3] In its decision, the CAS concluded:

> The object of this rule is very clearly to ensure that clubs that host football matches shoulder the responsibility for their supporters' conduct, which must comply with UEFA's objectives. It should be noted that UEFA has no direct disciplinary authority over a club's supporters, but only over European football associations and clubs. The latter are responsible for conforming to the standards and spirit of the UEFA regulations. If clubs were able to extricate themselves from responsibility by claiming that they had taken all measures they could reasonably be expected to take to prevent any breach of the UEFA rules, and if supporters still managed to commit such an act, there would be no way of penalising that behavior, even though it constituted a fault in itself. UEFA's rules of conduct would therefore be nothing more than vague obligations, since they would be devoid of sanction. By penalising a club for the behavior of its supporters, it is in fact the latter who are targeted and who, as supporters, will be liable to pay the penalty imposed

by the club. This is the only way in which UEFA has any chance of achieving its objectives. Without such an indirect sanction, UEFA would literally be powerless to deal with supporters' misconduct if a club refused to take responsibility for such behaviour.

Article 6 para. 1 of the Disciplinary Regulations [DR], under which clubs assume strict liability for their supporters' actions, therefore has a preventive and deterrent effect. Its objective is not to punish the club as such, which may have done nothing wrong, but to ensure that the club assumes responsibility for offences committed by its supporters.

The strict liability provided by Article 6 para. 1 of the Disciplinary Regulations can therefore not be deemed contrary to Article 20 of the [Swiss Code of Obligations] (which provides a contract "shall be void if its subject-matter is impossible, illicit or contrary to morality"), particularly since Article 72 para. 1 of the [Swiss Civil Code] allows associations to expel their members without giving their reasons for doing so. It would therefore seem paradoxical if an association were able, through its statutes, to expel its members without having to show that they had committed some kind of violation, whilst only being allowed to sanction its members if it could prove that they had breached their obligations.

To sum up, the Panel considers, in accordance with the dominant legal opinion, that there is no reason to cast doubt over the validity of the strict liability provided for in Article 6 para. 1 of the DR.[4]

The CAS panel did not state any failure on the part of PSV Eindhoven, but it confirmed the club's liability for the incident. In the present case, Feyenoord had taken extensive measures to maintain order and security, and the club was arguing that its efforts should be enough to exonerate it from liability.

In consideration of its use of the away ticketing system and its warning to AS Nancy of the risks related to the free sale of tickets, Feyenoord submitted that it did nothing wrong and could not be blamed. On the contrary, the club said it did everything within its power to prevent disturbances. Feyenoord deflected blame to AS Nancy and the local police. It claimed that AS Nancy failed to strictly control ticket sales, contrary to Article 14.1 of the UEFA Safety and Security Regulations, and as a result it was possible for troublemakers to enter the stadium. Furthermore, it claimed that the decision of the local police not to arrest people but to let them into the stadium was contrary to Article 33.2 of the UEFA Safety and Security Regulations, which prohibited access to known or potential troublemakers, or persons under the influence of alcohol or drugs. Feyenoord also argued that the people who caused disturbances could not be considered Feyenoord supporters in the sense of Article 6 of the UEFA Disciplinary Regulations because they did not travel and enter the stadium under the guidance of Feyenoord, did not wear any Feyenoord clothing, did not buy a ticket through the Feyenoord system, and some of them were subject to stadium ban in the Netherlands. To use the strict liability rule in this case, Feyenoord contended, was way too harsh. The UEFA Appeals Body's sanction was the second heaviest sanction that could be imposed on a club, which Feyenoord called disproportionate. Feyenoord concluded that the decision of the UEFA Appeals Body should be annulled and set aside, or, alternatively, in the event that the CAS determined that a sanction should be imposed, there should be a new decision with a proportionate sanction, specifically one that would enable Feyenoord to remain in the 2006–07 UEFA Cup and play in its stadium with its supporters against Tottenham.

On 9 February 2007, the CAS panel reached a decision in *Feyenoord v. UEFA*.[5] All of Feyenoord's arguments were rejected. First, the panel observed that the term "supporter" was not defined in Article 6 of the UEFA Disciplinary Regulations. In particular, it noted that the term "is not linked to race, nationality or the place of residence of the individual, nor is it linked to a contract which an individual has concluded with a national association or a club in purchasing a ticket."[6] In the panel's view, this was clearly a "deliberate, and wise, policy,"[7] because "the only way to ensure [the responsibility of clubs for their supporters] is to leave the word 'supporters' undefined so that clubs know that the Disciplinary Regulations apply to, and they are responsible for, any individual whose behaviour would lead a reasonable and objective observer to conclude that he or she was a supporter of that club."[8]

This construction of the word "supporter" was supported by UEFA case law (*Football Federation of Bosnia and Herzegovina v. UEFA*) and by the CAS (*PSV Eindhoven v. UEFA*). As such, there was no UEFA provision that made a distinction between "official" and "unofficial" supporters—a distinction that was fundamental to Feyenoord's appeal. Besides, it appeared to the panel that both "official" and "unofficial" supporters of Feyenoord had caused trouble before and during the match in Nancy. In any case, all supporters from sections 14 to 18 were considered supporters of Feyenoord, and therefore Feyenoord was responsible for their conduct.

The panel further concluded, "The fact that Feyenoord did much to prevent disturbances such as establishing special away ticketing-systems or warning AS Nancy of the risks related to the free sale of tickets is of no help as the strict liability rule provided with Article 6 para. 1 of the Disciplinary Regulations shall apply."[9] The fact that ticket sales were not strictly controlled was considered "not relevant"[10] in the case of Feyenoord. "It may have an effect only in the sanction AS Nancy shall face according to Article 6 para. 2 of the Disciplinary Regulations,"[11] the panel wrote. "The same is applicable for the decision of the police not to arrest people but to let them in the football stadium."[12]

The CAS's jurisprudence made it clear that the sanction imposed "must not be evidently and grossly disproportionate to the offence."[13] The UEFA Appeals Body considered breaking the walls between sections in a stadium with the intent to enter an adjacent section occupied by supporters of the opposing team and throwing projectiles at individuals to be a serious offence. Furthermore, Article 18 of the UEFA Disciplinary Regulations provided that recidivism—which occurred if disciplinary measures had to be imposed within five years of a previous offence—counted as an "aggravating circumstance," and Feyenoord had 14 disciplinary cases, 12 of them supporter related, in the previous five years.

The CAS panel determined that although the sanction against Feyenoord appeared harsh—it was disqualified from an important competition, which would result in economic loss in relation to broadcasting fees and tickets—there was no evidence that the economic loss would have "anything other than a temporary economic impact on a club of Feyenoord's stature."[14] Rather, Feyenoord was able to carry out its domestic activities and was able to qualify for the European competitions of the following season. The CAS panel added that a strong stand needed to be taken against hooliganism. It stated:

> In addition, hooliganism needs to be eradicated from sport. It has nothing to do with football, and the UEFA, as other football associations, has consistently fought against this phenomenon. The

Panel is of the opinion that clubs showing constant disorder in relation to hooliganism deserve severe sanctions.

Any other sanction listed in Article 14 appears as not able to fulfil the objective of eradicating hooliganism. The match behind close door would sanction to opposite team rather than Feyenoord supporters. The disqualification means that there will not be any further act of hooliganism coming from the Appellant's supporters during this season. As such the sanction decided by the UEFA appears fit for purpose.

The same applies to the fine imposed. There is no justification for a reduction of the fine.

In view of the above, the disqualification imposed by the UEFA Appeals Body appears to the Panel as capable of fulfilling the objective of eradicating hooliganism in football. Furthermore, the Panel considers that the fine of CHF 100,000 is proportionate to the offence committed.[15]

Thus, the CAS panel confirmed the UEFA Appeals Body's decision. UEFA president Michel Platini was of course pleased:

I am very happy with the decision of CAS to uphold the UEFA Appeals Body judgement. This sends out a strong message that acts of violence by fans within the game will be heavily dealt with and punished by the relevant authorities. Recent tragic incidents have shown that we must work together to eradicate all forms of hooliganism or violence from our game.

Onno Jacobs issued the following statement on Feyenoord's official website:

We will have to accept the decision, but it is bitter that our club and real supporters are the victims of the misconduct of people we don't want anything to do with.

We have always stressed that we as a club were powerless in this matter, because the people that misbehaved got tickets through other channels. So it feels like Feyenoord has been wronged. This is a very severe punishment.

We can do nothing else but ensure that Feyenoord restores its good reputation in Europe. We hope that all supporters fully understand the importance of this and that they will assume their responsibilities in the stadiums. This club must never again be the victim of the misconduct of individuals.

As the UEFA Cup continued, Tottenham, after receiving a bye in the Round of 16, would eventually progress as far as the quarterfinals, where it was defeated by Sevilla, which would go on to win the competition for the second consecutive season. The following season, Partizan Belgrade was disqualified from the UEFA Cup for the actions of its supporters in a match against NK Zrinjski in Bosnia-Herzegovina. Since then, however, no other club has been disqualified from a major European competition for supporter misconduct. UEFA has been reluctant to apply the sanction, and Feyenoord and Partizan stand as extreme cases.

Beginning with the 2013 edition of the UEFA Disciplinary Regulations, the strict liability rule for supporter misconduct has been made considerably more specific. Article 16 now states:

1. Host associations and clubs are responsible for order and security both inside and around the stadium before, during and after the match. They are liable for incidents of any kind and may be subject to disciplinary measures and directives unless they can prove that they have not been negligent in any way in the organisation of the match.
2. However, all associations and clubs are liable for the following inappropriate behaviour on the part of their supporters and may be subject to disciplinary measures and directives even if they can prove the absence of any negligence in relation to the organization of the match:
   a. the invasion or attempted invasion of the field of play;
   b. the throwing of objects;
   c. the lighting of fireworks or any other objects;
   d. the use of laser pointers or similar electronic devices;
   e. the use of gestures, words, objects or any other means to transmit any message not fit for a sports event, particularly messages that are of a political, ideological, religious, offensive or provocative nature;
   f. acts of damage;
   g. the disruptions of national or competition anthems;

h. any other lack of order or discipline observed inside or around the stadium.[16]

The effectiveness of the rule will continue to hinge on UEFA's willingness to apply harsh sanctions in a consistent manner. But there is no consensus that UEFA should move towards a zero tolerance policy, as many observers find strict liability unreasonable, specifically in cases where clubs have made a good faith effort to maintain order and security, and submit that a more appropriate solution is to identify and eliminate the roots of hooliganism.

Chapter 10

UEFA AND FIFA v.
COMMISSION

ACROSS THE WORLD, FOOTBALL'S SOCIAL significance is well recognized. The sport's major events continually demonstrate the power to bring people together across ethnic, religious, and other divides. They continually demonstrate the power to generate a sense of belonging for millions of people. Without question, this is a societal good.

Where events have such meaning, any question of access becomes critical. Since the growth of pay television (subscription-based service) in the late 1980s and early 1990s, there has been some public concern over prominent football events, among other events, moving behind a paywall.[1] Once a pay-TV operator acquires the broadcast rights to an event, that event will generally become unavailable on free-to-air television (service available to anyone with the appropriate receiving equipment).[2] In other words, those unable or unwilling to pay the requisite subscription fee will be closed out. In the recognition that the public's fundamental right to information was at stake in such circumstances, the European Union eventually took steps to guarantee broad access to events of particular significance.

THE DIRECTIVES, THE WORLD CUP, AND THE EUROPEAN CHAMPIONSHIP

The Television Without Frontiers (TVWF) Directive,[3] adopted on 3 October 1989, established the foundation of the audiovisual policy of the European Community and subsequently the European Union. On 30 June 1997, the TVWF Directive was revised,[4] and a new Article 3a was inserted, which became known as the "list of major events" mechanism. It has since been renumbered as Article 14 of the revised and renamed Audiovisual Media Services Directive,[5] adopted 11 December 2007, and it states, in part:

> Each Member State may take measures in accordance with Community law to ensure that broadcasters under its jurisdiction do not broadcast on an exclusive basis *events which are regarded by that Member State as being of major importance for society* in such a way as to *deprive a substantial proportion of the public in that Member State of the possibility of following such events* by live coverage or deferred coverage on free television. If it does so, the Member State concerned shall draw up a list of designated events, national or non-national, which it considers to be of major importance for society [emphasis added].

In short, the European Union allows member states to prohibit the exclusive broadcasting on pay television of events they judge to be of major importance for society. If a member state chooses to draw up a list of major events, it must do so in a "clear and transparent" manner. It must then notify the European Commission, which shall verify that the measures are compatible with European Union law.

The directive does not clearly define the "major importance for society" standard but simply states that "events of major importance for society have to meet certain criteria, that is to say be outstanding events which are of interest to the general public in the European Union or in a given Member State or in an important component part of a given Member State and are organised in advance by an event organiser who is legally entitled to sell the rights pertaining to that event." It is for member states alone to determine the events of major importance for society, but the directive does specifically reference the Olympic Games, the FIFA World Cup, and the UEFA European Championship as examples of such events.

Only eight members states—Austria, Belgium, Finland, France, Germany, Ireland, Italy, and the UK—have introduced lists of major events. All eight lists include the World Cup and the European Championship. Yet two of these lists stand out: Belgium's list, which includes *all* World Cup matches, and the UK's list, which includes *all* World Cup matches and *all* European Championship matches. In contrast, the other member states have only listed matches involving their respective national teams plus some other major matches such as tournament semifinals and finals. Nevertheless, the European Commission found Belgium's list and the UK's list to be compatible with European Union law on 25 June 2007 and 16 October 2007, respectively.

The sale of broadcast rights to the World Cup and the European Championship is big business. FIFA earned approximately 1.85 billion euros in broadcast rights fees from the 2010 World Cup in South Africa (approximately 1 billion euros from the European market). UEFA earned at least 800 million euros in broadcast rights fees from EURO 2012 in Poland and Ukraine. While these are staggering figures, these two associations are aiming to *maximize* revenue, and the European Union's directive stood in the way of that goal. As a result of the measures taken by Belgium and the UK, and their approval by the European Commission, FIFA could not market any World Cup matches to pay-TV operators in Belgium or the UK, and UEFA could not market any European Championship matches to pay-TV operators in the UK. With such precedent, there would be an open path for other member states to take similar measures, should they so desire. This situation prompted FIFA and UEFA to initiate legal action.

UEFA AND FIFA V. COMMISSION

In 2008, FIFA and UEFA brought three separate actions against the European Commission before the European General Court (which hears actions taken against the institutions of the European Union). FIFA challenged the Commission's decisions to approve both Belgium's listing of all World Cup matches[6] and the UK's listing of all World Cup matches;[7] UEFA challenged the Commission's decision to approve the UK's listing of all European Championship matches.[8] FIFA's and UEFA's main claims were these:

- infringement of Article 3a of the Television Without Frontiers Directive (now Article 14 of the Audiovisual Media Services Directive);
- infringement of the freedom to provide services;
- infringement of the freedom of establishment;
- infringement of the freedom of competition; and
- infringement of the right to property.

The two associations sought to have the Commission's decisions annulled, in whole or in part, insofar as they concerned the World Cup and the European Championship. To avoid repetition and/or confusion, this chapter will focus on the UK's list and not Belgium's.

In deciding that the UK's list was compatible with European Union law, the Commission stated that it was satisfied that the events listed met at least two of the following criteria, considered to be reliable indicators of the importance of events for society:

- a special general resonance within the Member State, and not simply a significance to those who ordinarily follow the sport or activity concerned;
- a generally recognized, distinct cultural importance for the population in the Member State, in particular as a catalyst of cultural identity;
- involvement of the national team in the event concerned in the context of a competition or tournament of international importance; and
- the fact that the event has traditionally been broadcast on free television and has commanded large television audiences.

Specifically, the Commission stated that the listed events "have a special general resonance in the [United Kingdom] in their entirety, as they are particularly popular with the general public (irrespective of the nationality of the participants), not just with those who usually follow sports events"[9] (i.e., the first criterion). The Commission also observed that the listed events "have traditionally been broadcast on free television and have commanded large television audiences"[10] (i.e., the fourth criterion). In response, FIFA and UEFA argued that some, but not all, World Cup matches and European Championship matches met the two criteria applied by the Commission, meaning those matches that did not meet the criteria were not of major importance for society, and therefore the Commission's decisions were made in error and were an infringement of the directive.

FIFA argued for a division of World Cup matches into "prime" matches—including the matches involving the relevant national team, the semifinals, and the final—and "non-prime" matches—including all other matches. UEFA similarly argued for a division of European Championship matches into "gala" matches and "non-gala" matches. FIFA and UEFA accepted the inclusion of prime and gala matches in the UK's list of major events as compatible with European Union law. In other words, the associations accepted that prime and gala matches should remain on free-to-air television. But FIFA and UEFA contended that non-prime and non-gala matches were not of major importance to society in the UK, most notably because these matches had a special resonance only with football fans (failing the first criterion).

FIFA cited research finding that "the average number of non-fans who watched at least 30 consecutive minutes of all 'non-prime matches' in the 2006 World Cup represented a mere 2.8% of the total viewing audience, as compared with 14.7% of non-fans who watched at least 30 consecutive minutes of all 'prime matches,' with the figure being 18.5% for the final, 7.1% for the semi-final and 17% for matches involving the England national team."[11] UEFA cited viewing figures according to which "matches from EURO 2004 not involving a national team of the United Kingdom attracted an average of only 32% of the television viewing audience at the time of the matches, as compared with an average of 67% of television viewers who watched when a match involved a national team of the United Kingdom."[12] If non-prime and non-gala matches were not of major importance to society, it would follow that FIFA and UEFA should be able to make them available on pay television.

In its judgments, issued on 17 February 2011, the European General Court held that although the directive adopts no position on the question of whether all or some World Cup and European Championship matches should be included in a national list of events of major importance for society, there is "no valid consideration"[13] leading to the conclusion that, in principle, only prime matches or gala matches may be thus categorized and therefore included in such a list. And it characterized both the World Cup and the European Championship as "a competition which may reasonably be regarded as a single event,"[14] rather than a series of individual events divided into prime and non-prime matches or gala and non-gala matches. With respect to the World Cup, it provided the following reasoning:

> It is well known that, in the World Cup, the participation of the teams in "prime" matches, such as matches involving the relevant national team, may depend on the results of "non-prime" matches, which determine the fate of those teams. Thus "non-prime" matches determine the opponents of the relevant national

team in the subsequent stages of the competition. In addition, the results of "non-prime" matches may even determine whether or not that national team advances to the subsequent stage of the competition.[15]

It provided the same reasoning with respect to the European Championship. "It follows," the General Court stated, "that the Commission did not make any error."[16] Furthermore, the General Court found that the viewing figures for non-prime and non-gala matches cited by FIFA and UEFA actually showed that these matches had drawn large numbers of viewers, a significant proportion of whom were not usually interested in football.[17]

FIFA's and UEFA's claims alleging infringement of the freedom to provide services referred to the freedom provided by the Treaty on the Functioning of the European Union (TFEU; formerly the Treaty Establishing the European Community, or TEC), specifically Article 56 (formerly Article 49).[18] The associations submitted that the Commission's decisions placed restrictions on the freedom to provide services because it deprived pay-TV operators in other member states of the possibility of broadcasting World Cup and European Championship matches on an exclusive basis in the UK. FIFA argued, "The elimination of the possibility of acquiring such rights to broadcast in the United Kingdom on an exclusive basis removes all incentive for broadcasters from other Member States in obtaining those rights, thereby preventing them from broadcasting any World Cup match in the United Kingdom. The exclusivity is essential for broadcasters wishing to innovate or develop their services, especially in Member States other than the Member State where they are established."[19] The General Court did not dispute that the Commission's decisions had "the effect of restricting freedom to provide services in the common market."[20] However, the General Court held that those restrictions on freedom to provide services

may be justified, since they are intended to protect the right to information and to ensure wide public access to television broadcasts of events, national or non-national, of major importance for society, subject to the additional conditions that they be appropriate for attaining the objective which they pursue and not go beyond what is necessary in order to attain it.[21]

The General Court further held that the Commission's decisions were "appropriate and proportionate,"[22] again relying on the view that World Cup and the European Championship were single events. FIFA also alleged infringement of the freedom of establishment, which is provided by Article 56 of the TFEU (formerly Article 49 of the TEC),[23] submitting that the UK's list restricted "broadcasters wishing to establish themselves in the United Kingdom and wishing to offer pay television services from obtaining exclusive rights to broadcast World Cup matches."[24] But the General Court held that the "same considerations apply"[25] as with the freedom to provide services, meaning the restriction was justified as it served an overriding reason in the public interest, specifically the protection of the right to information. The freedom of expression and the public's right to information is enshrined in Article 10 of the Convention for the Protection of Human Rights and Fundamental Freedoms, signed on 4 November 1950. The General Court stated that freedom of expression "is one of the fundamental rights guaranteed by the Community legal order and is an overriding reason in the public interest which is capable of justifying such restrictions."[26]

In their claims alleging infringement of competition law, which is established by Articles 101 through 106 of the TFEU, FIFA and UEFA argued that pay-TV operators would reasonably have no interest in acquiring nonexclusive rights to the World Cup and the European Championship, and this resulted in "restrictions on competition on a number of markets, including the market for acquisition of such rights, the advertising market and the market for broadcasting sporting events by pay television channels, due to the reduction in the number of broadcasters active on those markets."[27] But the General Court observed that these consequences resulted indirectly from the restrictions on freedom to provide services introduced by the UK's measures, which, as previously stated, it found to be justified. The General Court concluded, "The effects on the number of potential competitors, which are presented as being an unavoidable consequence of those obstacles to the freedom to provide services, cannot, therefore, be considered to be contrary to the Treaty articles on competition."[28]

Finally, there was FIFA's and UEFA's claim alleging infringement of the right to property, which is a general principle of European Union law. The associations argued that the Commission's decisions to approve the UK's listing of non-prime and non-gala matches created a disproportionate restriction on their right to exploit their property rights through the grant of exclusive license to broadcast those matches. FIFA in particular noted: "The grant and acquisition of exclusive broadcast rights to broadcast sporting events are of crucial importance and are a normal commercial practice accepted as such by the Commission itself. Exclusivity significantly enhances the value of the rights and the prohibition of the exclusive grant of such rights therefore affects their very essence."[29]

However, the General Court held that, since it found that the World Cup and the European Championship were legitimately regarded as single events of major importance for society, then the listing of non-prime matches and non-gala matches could not be a disproportionate interference with FIFA's and UEFA's property rights. The General Court further held that "although the legislation in question is liable to affect the price which FIFA [and UEFA] will obtain for grant of the rights to broadcast the World Cup [and the European Championship] in the United Kingdom, it does not destroy the commercial value of those rights because, first, it does not oblige FIFA [or UEFA] to sell them on whatever conditions it can obtain and, secondly, FIFA [and UEFA] is [are] protected against collusive and abusive practices by Community and national competition law."[30] Accordingly, the Commission did not err in concluding that the United Kingdom measures were proportionate.

Thus, the General Court rejected each of FIFA's and UEFA's claims and dismissed their actions.[31] It established that any European Union member state that considers the World Cup and/or the European Championship in their entirety to be of major importance for society may prohibit the exclusive broadcast of all relevant matches on pay television in order to allow the general public to follow the events on free television. And it established that certain restrictions on the freedom to provide services, the freedom of establishment, the freedom of competition, and the right to property arising as a result of such measures may be justified by the public's fundamental right to information. On 18 July 2013, the European Court of Justice dismissed the appeals brought by FIFA and UEFA.

In 1996, the then chair of the European Parliament's Committee on Culture, Youth, Education and Media, Luciana Castellina, was quoted as saying that "watching a football match on television is a human right." It may have been hyperbole—but, in a way, this has been confirmed.

SELECTED LIST OF WORKS CONSULTED

CHAPTER 1: *FRASER V. MLS*

Case Opinions

Copperweld Corp v. Independence Tube Corp., 467 U.S. 752 (1984).

Fraser v. Major League Soccer, 97 F.Supp.2d 130 (D. Mass. 2000).

Fraser v. Major League Soccer, 284 F.3d 47 (1st Cir. 2002).

Sullivan v. NFL, 34 F.3d 1091 (1st Cir. 1994).

Books

Cozzillio, Michael J., Mark S. Levinstein, Michael R. Dimino, Sr., and Gabriel A. Feldman. *Sports Law: Cases and Materials*. Durham: Carolina Academic Press, 2007.

Dure, Beau. *Long-Range Goals: The Success Story of Major League Soccer*. Washington, D.C.: Potomac Books, 2010.

Wangerin, David. *Soccer in a Football World*. Philadelphia: Temple University Press, 2006.

Weiler, Paul C., and Gary R. Roberts. *Sports and the Law: Text, Cases, Problems*. St. Paul: Thomson West, 2004.

Law Review and Law Journal Articles

Bezbatchenko, Tim. "Bend It for Beckham: A Look at Major League Soccer and Its Single Entity Defense to Antitrust Liability After the Designated Player Rule." *University of Cincinnati Law Review* 76 (2008): 611.

Edel, Martin, et al. "Panel III: Restructuring Professional Sports Leagues." *Fordham Intellectual Property, Media and Entertainment Law Journal* 12 (2002): 413.

Edelman, Marc. "Why the "Single Entity" Defense Can Never Apply to NFL Clubs: A Primer on Property-Rights Theory in Professional Sports." *Fordham Intellectual Property, Media and Entertainment Law Journal* 18 (2008): 891.

Feldman, Gabriel. "The Puzzling Persistence of the Single Entity Argument for Sports Leagues: *American Needle* and the Supreme Court's Opportunity to Reject a Flawed Defense." *Wisconsin Law Review,* 2009, 835.

Grow, Nathaniel. "*American Needle* and the Future of the Single Entity Defense Under Section One of the Sherman Act." *American Business Law Journal* 48 (2011): 449.

———. "There's No 'I' in 'League': Professional Sports Leagues and the Single Entity Defense." *Michigan Law Review* 105 (2006): 183.

Newspapers, Magazines, and Online Resources

Golen, Jimmy. "MLS Players to Form Union After Court Defeat." *USA Today,* 8 October 2002. Accessed 1 July 2014. http://usatoday30.usatoday.com /sports/soccer/mls/2002-10-07-union_x.htm.

Kennedy, Paul. "MLS and Players Reach Agreement." *Soccer America,* 20 March 2010. Accessed 1 July 2014. http://www.socceramerica.com /article/37318/mls-and-players-reach-agreement.html.

Longman, Jeré. "U.S. Professional League Sets '96 Start with 10 Teams." *New York Times,* 7 June 1995.

Mahoney, Ridge. "MLS Goes to Federal Court." *Soccer America,* 14 November 2000. Accessed 1 July 2014. http://www.socceramerica.com /article/13425/mls-goes-to-federal-court.html.

Wasserman, Dan. "Soccer League Charges NFL Players Union with Meddling in Labor Matters." *Newark Star-Ledger,* 4 March 1997, 48.

CHAPTER 2: THE NASL AND THE NASL PLAYERS ASSOCIATION

Case Opinions

Morio v. North American Soccer League, 501 F.Supp. 633 (S.D.N.Y. 1980).

Morio v. North American Soccer League, 632 F.2d 217 (2nd Cir. 1980).

North American Soccer League, 236 NLRB 1317 (1978).

North American Soccer League, 241 NLRB 1225 (1979).

North American Soccer League v. National Labor Relations Board, 613 F.2d 1379 (5th Cir. 1980).

Books

Cozzillio, Michael J., Mark S. Levinstein, Michael R. Dimino Sr., and Gabriel A. Feldman. *Sports Law: Cases and Materials.* Durham: Carolina Academic Press, 2007.

Oriard, Michael. *Brand NFL: Making and Selling America's Favorite Sport.* Chapel Hill: University of North Carolina Press, 2007.

Wangerin, David. *Soccer in a Football World.* Philadelphia: Temple University Press, 2006.

Weiler, Paul C., and Gary R. Roberts. *Sports and the Law: Text, Cases, Problems.* St. Paul: Thomson West, 2004.

Newspapers, Magazines, and Online Resources

Associated Press. "Court Upholds Soccer Union." *New York Times,* 15 October 1980, B6.

Associated Press. "Judge Backs NASL Union." *Washington Post,* 26 March 1980, D5.

Associated Press. "Long NASL Feud Seems to Be Over." *Washington Post,* 6 December 1980, E3.

Associated Press. "NASL Ordered to Bargain with Players' Union." *Washington Post,* 4 May 1979, D8.

Associated Press. "NASL Players Consider Strike." *Washington Post,* 16 March 1979, E3.

Associated Press. "NASL Survives Strike's 1st Test." *Washington Post,* 16 April 1979, D9.

Associated Press. "NLRB Asks Contempt." *Washington Post,* 21 November 1980, D2.

Feinstein, John. "NASL Faces Court Fight on Labor." *Washington Post,* 17 December 1978, M13.

Feinstein, John. "NASL Players' Union Continues Unrecognized." *Washington Post,* 30 August 1977, D4.

Gammon, Clive. "The NASL: It's Alive but on Death Row." *Sports Illustrated,* 7 May 1984.

Huff, Donald. "Garvey Seen as Villain by Owners." *Washington Post*, 17 April 1979, D1.

———. "INS Ends Threat of Deporting." *Washington Post*, 18 April 1979, D1.

———. "NASL 'Strikebreakers' Face Possibility of Deportation." *Washington Post*, 15 April 1979, M9.

———. "Soccer's Strike Is Canceled." *Washington Post*, 19 April 1979, D1.

Lewis, Michael. "Offside Remarks: Some Lessons from a Strike 31 Years Ago." *BigAppleSoccer*, 8 March 2010. Accessed 1 July 2014. http://www h.bigapplesoccer.com/columns/lewis.php?article_id=22806.

Richmond, Peter. "NASL Indoor Fate with NLRB." *Washington Post*, 20 November 1980, D10.

Scannell, Nancy. "Labor Board Cites NASL Infractions." *Washington Post*, 6 November 1979, D3.

Shabecoff, Philip. "Soccer Strike Over, but Questions Linger." *New York Times*, 29 April 1979, S7.

Yannis, Alex. "N.A.S.L. and Players Seek Pact." *New York Times*, 9 November 1980, S7.

———. "N.A.S.L. Presses Its Demands." *New York Times*, 6 April 1984.

———. "N.F.L. Player Group Weighs Soccer Union." *New York Times*, 24 July 1977, S5.

———. "Players' Association Calls N.A.S.L. Strike." *New York Times*, 14 April 1979, 25.

———. "Players End Strike in Soccer." *New York Times*, 19 April 1979, D19.

———. "Soccer League Poses Strike Threat Today." *New York Times*, 13 April 1979, A19.

———. "Tighter Operation for the 18th Season." *New York Times*, 29 April 1984.

CHAPTER 3: *NASL V. NFL*

Case Opinions

North American Soccer League v. National Football League, 465 F.Supp. 665 (S.D.N.Y 1979).

North American Soccer League v. National Football League, 505 F.Supp. 659 (S.D.N.Y 1980).

North American Soccer League v. National Football League, 670 F.2d 1249 (2nd Cir. 1982).

Books

Cozzillio, Michael J., Mark S. Levinstein, Michael R. Dimino Sr., and Gabriel A. Feldman. *Sports Law: Cases and Materials*. Durham: Carolina Academic Press, 2007.

Harris, David. *The League: The Rise and Decline of the NFL*. New York: Bantam Books, 1986.

Wangerin, David. *Soccer in a Football World*. Philadelphia: Temple University Press, 2006.

Weiler, Paul C., and Gary R. Roberts. *Sports and the Law: Text, Cases, Problems*. St. Paul: Thomson West, 2004.

Newspapers, Magazines, and Online Resources

George, Thomas. "N.F.L. to Let Owners Have Franchises in Multiple Sports." *New York Times*, 12 March 1997.

CHAPTER 4: *CHAMPIONSWORLD V. UNITED STATES SOCCER FEDERATION*

Case Opinions

CAS 2009/A/1812 Stillitano v. United States Soccer Federation & Federation Internationale de Football Association.

CAS 2010/A/2241 Stillitano v. United States Soccer Federation & Federation Internationale de Football Association.

ChampionsWorld v. United States Soccer Federation, 487 F.Supp.2d 980 (N.D. Ill. 2007).

ChampionsWorld v. United States Soccer Federation, 726 F.Supp.2d 961 (N.D. Ill. 2010).

ChampionsWorld v. United States Soccer Federation, 890 F.Supp.2d 912 (N.D. Ill. 2012).

Law Review and Law Journal Articles

Couvillion, Joshua B. "Defending for Its Life: *Champions World LLC v. United States Soccer Federation* Denies Extending Antitrust Immunity to USSF in Regulating Professional Soccer." *Sports Lawyers Journal* 18 (2011): 325.

Newspapers, Magazines, and Online Resources

Bell, Jack. "American Tour Features Elite Teams." *New York Times*, 26 July 2013. Accessed 1 July 2014. http://www.nytimes.com/2013/07/27/sports /soccer/guinness-international-champions-cup-american-tour-features -elite-teams.html.

———. "Promoter Files Chapter 11." *New York Times*, 19 January 2005. Accessed 1 July 2014. http://www.nytimes.com/2005/01/19/sports/ soccer/19sportsbrief.ready.html.

Dreier, Fred. "International Soccer Heats up in U.S." *SportsBusiness Journal*, 11 July 2011. Accessed 1 July 2014. http://www.sportsbusinessdaily.com /Journal/Issues/2011/07/11/Events-and-Attractions/International-soccer .aspx.

———. "Judge Clears Way for Suit Against USSF, MLS." *SportsBusiness Journal*, 27 September 2010. Accessed 1 July 2014. http://www.sports businessdaily.com/Journal/Issues/2010/09/20100927/This-Weeks-Issue /Judge-Clears-Way-For-Suit-Against-USSF-MLS.aspx.

McCarthy, Kyle. "Logistics Hinder Efforts to Include MLS Teams in ICC." *FoxSports*, 4 February 2014. Accessed 1 July 2014. http://msn. foxsports.com/soccer/inside-mls/logistics-hinder-efforts-to-include -mls-teams-in-icc-020414.

CHAPTER 5: *NAMOFF V. D.C. UNITED*

Books

Cantu, Robert, and Mark Hyman. *Concussions and Our Kids*. New York: Houghton Mifflin Harcourt, 2012.

Fainaru-Wada, Mark, and Steve Fainaru. *League of Denial*. New York: Random House, 2013.

Newspapers, Magazines, and Online Resources

Associated Press. "MLS Discusses Concussion Protocol." *Los Angeles Times*, 7 January 2007. Accessed 1 July 2014. http://espn.go.com/sports/soccer /news/_/id/7436065/mls-medical-staffers-target -concussion-protocol.

Baxter, Kevin. "A Victim Takes on Concussions in Soccer." *Los Angeles Times*, 3 March 2012. Accessed 1 July 2014. http://articles.latimes.com/2012 /mar/03/sports/la-sp-soccer-concussions-20120304.

Bell, Jack. "As Concussions' Toll Lingers, an M.L.S. Career May Yield." *New York Times*, 16 March 2010. Accessed 1 July 2014. http://www.nytimes .com/2010/03/16/sports/soccer/16goal.html.

Bondy, Stefan. "Alecko Eskandarian's Career in Limbo." *The Record*, 18 March 2010. Accessed 1 July 2014. http://www.northjersey.com/sports /esky-mulls-his-future-sans-mls-1.963164.

Fleming, Richard. "Where Are They Now? Ross Paule." *ColoradoRapids*, 22 November 2013. Accessed 1 July 2014. http://www.coloradorapids.com /news/2013/11/where-are-they-now-ross-paule.

Floyd, Thomas. "Josh Gros: Reflection and Anticipation." *DCUnited*, 20 July 2009. Accessed 1 July 2014. http://www.dcunited.com/news/2009/07 /josh-gros-reflection-and-anticipation.

Goff, Steven. "Bryan Namoff Files $12 Million Lawsuit Against D.C. United, Claiming Medical Negligence Involving Career-Ending Concussion in 2009 MLS Match." *Washington Post*, 29 August 2012. Accessed 1 July 2014. http://www.washingtonpost.com/blogs/soccer-insider/post /bryan-namoff-files-12-million-lawsuit-against-dc-united-claiming -medical-negligence-involving-career-ending-concussion-in-2009-mls -match/2012/08/29/786b86c6-f1db-11e1-adc6-87dfa8eff430_blog.html.

———. "Judge Denies Motion to Dismiss Bryan Namoff Case." *Washington Post*, 10 June 2013. Accessed 1 July 2014. http://www. washingtonpost.com/blogs/soccer-insider/wp/2013/06/10/judge -denies-d-c-uniteds-motion-to-dismiss-bryan-namoff-case.

Hellman, Scott. "Wake-Up Call." *Boston Globe*, 24 April 2011. Accessed 1 July 2014. http://www.boston.com/sports/soccer/articles/2011/04/24 /after_a_concussion_revolution_star_taylor_twellman_looks_to _improve_safety_of_soccer.

McGrath, Ben. "Does Football Have a Future?" *New Yorker*, 31 January 2011. Accessed 1 July 2014. http://www.newyorker.com/reporting /2011/01/31/110131fa_fact_mcgrath.

Meyer, John. "Rapids Feeling Effects of Head Hits as Concussions Get More MLS Scrutiny." *Denver Post*, 3 June 2012. Accessed 1 July 2014. http://www.denverpost.com/ci_20770179/concussions-colorado -rapids-effects-mls-scrutiny.

O'Riordan, Kevin. "Eddie Johnson Files Concussion Lawsuit Against the Portland Timbers." *BusinessOfSoccer*, 10 February 2014. Accessed 1 July 2014. http://www.businessofsoccer.com/2014/02/10/eddie-johnson -files-concussion-lawsuit-against-the-portland-timbers.

———. "Namoff Concussion Litigation to Proceed After Judge Denies Motion to Dismiss." *BusinessOfSoccer*, 10 June 2013. Accessed 1 July 2014. http:// www.businessofsoccer.com/2013/06/10/namoff-concussion-litigation -to-proceed-after-judge-denies-motion-to-dismiss.

Schaerlaeckens, Leander. "Soccer's Concussion Problem." *ESPN*, 7 September 2011. Accessed 1 July 2014. http://espn.go.com/sports /soccer/news/_/id/6912840/soccer-big-concussion-problem-anything -being-done-protect-players.

Wahl, Grant. "Concussions Take Toll in Soccer Too." *Sports Illustrated*, 27 October 2010. Accessed 1 July 2014. http://www.si.com /more-sports/2010/10/27/soccer-concussions.

CHAPTER 6: *R V. TERRY*

Newspapers, Magazines, and Online Resources

Davies, Caroline, and Lizzy Davies. "John Terry Cleared of Racially Abusing Anton Ferdinand." *The Guardian*, 13 July 2012. Accessed 1 July 2014. http://www.theguardian.com/football/2012/jul/13/john -terry-cleared-anton-ferdinand.

Geey, Daniel. "The Issue of Racism, the FA Hearing & John Terry." *Daniel-Geey*, 24 September 2012. Accessed 1 July 2014. http://www.danielgeey .com/the-issue-of-racism-the-fa-hearing-john-terry.

Hughes, Rob. "What Chelsea Player Said May Be a Crime." *New York Times*, 22 December 2011. Accessed 1 July 2014. http://www.nytimes .com/2011/12/22/sports/soccer/22iht-terry22.html.

"John Terry Banned and Fined by FA Over Anton Ferdinand Incident." *BBC*, 27 September 2012. Accessed 1 July 2014. http://www.bbc.com/sport /0/football/19723020.

"John Terry to Be Charged Over Anton Ferdinand Race Row." *BBC*, 21 December 2011. Accessed 1 July 2014. http://www.bbc.com/news /uk-england-london-16284813.

Lyall, Sarah. "Soccer Star Acquitted in British Trial Over Racial Slur." *New York Times*, 13 July 2012. Accessed 1 July 2014. http://www.nytimes .com/2011/12/22/sports/soccer/22iht-terry22.html.

Reports

United Kingdom, House of Commons, Culture, Media and Sport Committee. *Racism in Football*. Session 2012–2013, Second Report, 19 September 2012. Accessed 1 July 2014. http://www.publications.parliament.uk/pa /cm201213/cmselect/cmcumeds/89/89.pdf .

CHAPTER 7: *HER MAJESTY'S REVENUE AND CUSTOMS V. THE FOOTBALL LEAGUE*

Case Opinions

Her Majesty's Revenue and Customs v. Portsmouth City Football Club, [2010] EWHC 2013 (Ch.).

Her Majesty's Revenue and Customs v. The Football League, [2012] EWHC 1372 (Ch.).

Inland Revenue v. Wimbledon Football Club, [2004] EWHC 1020 (Ch.).

Law Review and Law Journal Articles

Cedrone, Timothy D. "A Critical Analysis of Sport Organization Bankruptcies in the United States and England: Does Bankruptcy Law Explain the Disparity in Number of Cases?" *Seton Hall Journal of Sports and Entertainment Law* 18 (2008): 297.

Other Academic Articles

Beech, John, et al. "The Circumstances in Which English Football Clubs Become Insolvent." Centre for International Business of Sport Working Paper Series, 2008.

Szymanski, Stefan. "Insolvency and English Football." Working paper, 2012.

Newspapers, Magazines, and Online Resources

Conn, David. "Crunched Creditors Call Time on Living the Dream." *The Guardian*, 9 February 2010. Accessed 1 July 2014. http://www.the guardian.com/football/david-conn-inside-sport-blog/2010/feb/10 /portsmouth-cardiff-hmrc-winding-up.

———. "'Football Creditors Rule' Needs Change in Law to Be Made Illegal." *The Guardian*, 25 May 2012. Accessed 1 July 2014. http://www.theguardian .com/football/2012/may/25/football-creditors-rule-change-law.

———. "Portsmouth Save Their Money for Millionaires While Paupers Go Unpaid." *The Guardian*, 22 April 2010. Accessed 1 July 2014. http://www.theguardian.com/football/blog/2010/apr/22/portsmouth -football-creditors-money-millionaires.

Beech, John, ed. *Football Management*. Accessed 1 July 2014. http://football management.wordpress.com.

Gibson, Owen. "Clubs Morally Obliged to Live Within Their Means, Says League Chairman." *The Guardian*, 21 May 2010. Accessed 1 July 2014. http://www.theguardian.com/football/2010/may/21/football -league-chairman-warning-finances.

Grant, Paul. "Football Clubs Owe Tax Millions." *BBC*, 23 November 2008. Accessed 1 July 2014. http://news.bbc.co.uk/2/hi/uk_news/7741859.stm.

Lubben, Stephen J. "Soccer Case Highlights Differences Between U.S. and English Bankruptcy Law." *New York Times*, 24 July 2012. Accessed 1 July 2014. http://dealbook.nytimes.com/2012/07/24/soccer-case-highlights -differences-between-u-s-and-english-bankruptcy-law/.

Miller, Alex, and Nick Harris. "Revealed: The £39.6m in Unpaid Football Taxes (And That's Only Part of It)." *SportingIntelligence*, 25 March 2012. Accessed 1 July 2014. http://www.sportingintelligence.com/2012/03/25 /revealed-the-39-6m-in-unpaid-football-taxes-and-thats-only-part-of -it-250301.

Reports

United Kingdom, House of Commons, Culture, Media and Sport Committee. *Football Governance*. Session 2010–2012, Seventh Report, 29 July 2011. Accessed 1 July 2014. http://www.publications.parliament.uk/pa/cm201012/cmselect/cmcumeds/792/792i.pdf.

———. *Football Governance Follow-Up*. Session 2012–2013, Fourth Report, 29 January 2013. Accessed 1 July 2014. http://www.publications.parliament.uk/pa/cm201213/cmselect/cmcumeds/509/509.pdf.

CHAPTER 8: *UNION ROYALE BELGE DES SOCIÉTÉS DE FOOTBALL ASSOCIATION AND OTHERS V. BOSMAN*

Case Opinions

Case C-415/93 Union Royale Belge des Sociétés de Football Association ASBL v. Jean-Marc Bosman, Royal Club Liégeois SA v. Jean-Marc Bosman and others and Union des Associations Européennes de Football (UEFA) v. Jean-Marc Bosman [1995] ECR I-4921.

Case C-415/93 Union Royale Belge des Sociétés de Football Association ASBL v. Jean-Marc Bosman, Royal Club Liégeois SA v. Jean-Marc Bosman and others and Union des Associations Européennes de Football (UEFA) v. Jean-Marc Bosman [1995] ECR I-4921, Opinion of AG Lenz.

Books

Maduro, Miguel Poiares, and Loïc Azoula, eds. *The Past and Future of EU Law*. Portland: Hart Publishing, 2010.

McArdle, David. *From Boot Money to Bosman: Football, Society and the Law*. London: Cavendish Publishing Limited, 2000.

Law Review and Law Journal Articles

Lee, Andrew L. "The Bosman Case: Protecting Freedom of Movement in European Football." *Fordham International Law Journal* 19 (1995–1996): 1255.

CHAPTER 9: *FEYENOORD V. UEFA*

Case Opinions
CAS 2002/A/423 PSV Eindhoven v. UEFA.
CAS 2007/A/1217 Feyenoord Rotterdam v. UEFA.

Law Review and Law Journal Articles
Coenen, Peter. "True Supporters, Strict Liability, and Feyenoord." *International Sports Law Journal,* no. 1–2 (2008).

Newspapers, Magazines, and Online Resources
Bouwes, Ernst. "Unfriendly Fixture." *When Saturday Comes,* March 2007. Accessed 1 July 2014. http://www.wsc.co.uk/the-archive/99-Crowd-control -&-policing/529-unfriendly-fixture.

CHAPTER 10: *UEFA AND FIFA V. COMMISSION*

Case Opinions
Case C-201/11 P UEFA v. European Commission [2013].
Case C-204/11 P FIFA v. European Commission [2013].
Case C-205/11 P FIFA v. European Commission [2013].
Case T-55/08 UEFA v. European Commission [2011] ECR II-0271.
Case T-68/08 FIFA v. European Commission [2011] ECR II-0349.
Case T-385/07 FIFA v. European Commission [2011] ECR II-0205.

Books
Anderson, Jack, ed. *Leading Cases in Sports Law.* The Hague: T.M.C. Asser Press, 2013.

Newspapers, Magazines, and Online Resources
Geey, Daniel. "'Listing' of Major Events: UEFA and FIFA's Failed Challenge." *DanielGeey,* 1 April 2011. Accessed 1 July 2014. http://www.danielgeey .com/listing-of-major-events-uefa-and-fifas-failed-challenge.
Wilson, Bill. "Fifa Loses Free-to-Air World Cup TV Battle." *BBC,* 18 July 2013. Accessed 1 July 2014. http://www.bbc.com/news/business-23288211.

NOTES

CHAPTER 1: *FRASER V. MLS*

1. Gulati is now U.S. Soccer president; Abbott is now Major League Soccer president and deputy commissioner.

2. 15 U.S.C. § 1.

3. 15 U.S.C. § 2.

4. Under Section 1, it is not necessary to prove that the conduct in question threatens monopolization, only that it is not anticompetitive.

5. 467 U.S. 752, 768–769 (1984).

6. Ibid.

7. Ibid., 771.

8. Ibid.

9. Ibid., 772.

10. Fraser v. Major League Soccer, 284 F.3d 47, 54 (1st Cir. 2002).

11. 29 U.S.C. §§ 151–169.

12. 518 U.S. 231, 237 (1996).

13. In 2011, both NFL and NBA players dissolved their unions and filed antitrust suits against their employers—Brady v. National Football League; Anthony v. National Basketball Association; and Butler v. National Basketball Association—following expiration of their collective bargaining agreements and extended labor negotiations. These moves were designed to gain leverage in negotiations and help reach more favorable agreements.

14. Lagerwey is now Real Salt Lake general manager and senior vice president of soccer operations.

15. Agoos is now MLS technical director of competition.

16. 15 U.S.C. § 18.

17. Fraser v. Major League Soccer, 97 F.Supp.2d 130 (D. Mass. 2000).

18. Ibid., 135.

19. Ibid.

20. Ibid., 136.

21. Ibid.

22. Ibid.

23. Ibid.

24. Ibid., 137.

25. Ibid., 137–138.

26. Ibid., 138.

27. Ibid.

28. Ibid., 139.

29. Ibid.

30. Ibid.

31. Ibid.

32. Ibid., 140.

33. Ibid., 140–141.

34. Fraser v. Major League Soccer, 284 F.3d 47 (1st Cir. 2002).

35. 34 F.3d 1091 (1st Cir. 1994).

36. *Fraser*, 284 F.3d 47, 56.

37. Ibid., 57.

38. Ibid.

39. Ibid.

40. Ibid.

41. Ibid.

42. Ibid.

43. Ibid.

44. Ibid.

45. Ibid., 57–58.

46. Ibid., 58.

47. Ibid., 59.

48. Ibid.

49. Ibid.

50. Ibid., 60.

51. Ibid.

52. Ibid.

53. Ibid.
54. Ibid., 60–61.
55. Ibid., 62.
56. Ibid., 67.
57. Ibid., 68.
58. Ibid.
59. Ibid.
60. Ibid.
61. Ibid.
62. Ibid.
63. Ibid., 69–70.
64. Ibid., 70.
65. Ibid.
66. Ibid., 71.
67. Ibid.
68. Ibid.
69. Ibid.

CHAPTER 2: THE NASL AND THE NASL PLAYERS ASSOCIATION

1. 29 U.S.C. §§ 151–169.

2. The NLRB has the power to order an employer to recognize and bargain with a union in cases where the union had majority support and the employer undermined the election process.

3. North American Soccer League, 236 NLRB 1317 (1978).

4. On December 22, 2011, the NLRB adopted amendments to its election procedures that were designed to allow representation cases to be resolved more expeditiously. The amendments became effective on April 30, 2012.

5. North American Soccer League, 236 NLRB 1317, 1319.

6. Ibid., 1321.

7. Ibid.

8. Ibid.

9. Ibid., 1321–1322.

10. Today, the Major League Soccer Players Union includes players employed by Major League Soccer's three Canadian clubs, the Montreal Impact, Toronto FC, and the Vancouver Whitecaps.

11. There were 37 nondeterminative challenged ballots and six void ballots.

12. 586 F.2d 644 (9th Cir. 1978).

13. 543 F.2d 606 (8th Cir. 1976).

14. The Immigration and Naturalization Service was dissolved in 2003 and absorbed into the Department of Homeland Security.

15. North American Soccer League, 241 NLRB 1225 (1979).

16. Ibid.

17. Ibid.

18. Ibid., 1227.

19. Ibid., 1228.

20. 613 F.2d 1379 (5th Cir. 1980).

21. Ibid., 1382.

22. Ibid., 1383.

23. 501 F.Supp. 633 (S.D.N.Y. 1980).

24. Ibid., 639.

25. Ibid.

26. Ibid.

27. Ibid.

28. Ibid.

29. Ibid., 635.

30. Ibid., 639.

31. Ibid.

32. Ibid.

33. Ibid., 640.

34. Ibid.

35. Ibid.

36. Morio v. North American Soccer League, 632 F.2d 217 (2nd Cir. 1980).

CHAPTER 3: *NASL V. NFL*

1. One of Williams' more intriguing arguments was expressed in court testimony: "It's been proven time and again that it's great for Lord and Taylor to have a Neiman Marcus in the same shopping center because they both benefit. I believe the same thing holds in sports. . . . I thought it was an imprudent rule [and] that it was not in the interests of the [NFL]." In an interview with David Harris, Williams further explained: "I think [if] there is success in one sport, in one

town, [then there will be] great success in another sport. . . . I think it is good to have people get into the habit of taking their children and their families to sports events. It is part of the culture of the city . . . and . . . they all help each other."

2. North American Soccer League v. National Football League, 465 F.Supp. 665 (S.D.N.Y 1979).

3. See Bethany M. Bates, *Reconciliation After* Winter: *The Standard for Preliminary Injunctions in Federal Courts*, 111 Colum. L. Rev. 1522 (2011).

4. Ibid., 1530.

5. North American Soccer League v. National Football League, 465 F.Supp. 665, 677.

6. 15 U.S.C. § 1.

7. North American Soccer League v. National Football League, 505 F.Supp. 659, 680 (S.D.N.Y 1980).

8. Ibid.

9. Ibid., 689.

10. Ibid.

11. Ibid., 671.

12. Ibid., 672.

13. Ibid., 677.

14. Ibid., 686–687.

15. Ibid., 677.

16. Ibid.

17. Ibid., 678.

18. Ibid.

19. Ibid.

20. Ibid., 685.

21. Ibid.

22. Ibid.

23. Ibid., 689.

24. Ibid., 684.

25. Ibid., 692.

26. North American Soccer League v. National Football League, 670 F.2d 1249 (2nd Cir. 1982).

27. Ibid., 1252.

28. Ibid., 1257.

29. Ibid.

30. 352 U.S. 445 (1957).

31. North American Soccer League, 670 F.2d 1249, 1257.

32. Ibid., 1257–1258.

33. Ibid., 1258 (quoting National Society of Professional Engineers v. United States, 435 U.S. 679, 692 (1978)).

34. Ibid. (quoting Northern Pacific Railway Co. v. United States, 356 U.S. 1, 5 (1958)).

35. Ibid. (quoting Broadcast Music, Inc. v. Columbia Broadcasting System, Inc., 441 U.S. 1, 8 (1979)).

36. Ibid., 1259 (quoting National Society of Professional Engineers, 435 U.S. 679, 691).

37. Ibid.

38. Ibid., 1260 (quoting North American Soccer League, 505 F.Supp. 659, 682).

39. Ibid.

40. Ibid.

41. Ibid.

42. Ibid.

43. Ibid., 1260–1261.

44. Ibid., 1261.

45. Ibid.

46. National Football League v. North American Soccer League, 459 U.S. 1074, 1077 (1982) (Rehnquist, J., dissenting).

47. The NFL's Constitution and Bylaws can be found at http://static.nfl .com/static/content/public/static/html/careers/pdf/co_.pdf.

CHAPTER 4: *CHAMPIONSWORLD V. UNITED STATES SOCCER FEDERATION*

1. The tournament's opening match was played in Valencia, Spain.

2. Excluding the match played in Valencia.

3. In 2010, CAA did not hold the World Football Challenge, in deference to the FIFA World Cup, and instead partnered with SUM to bring Manchester United on a U.S. tour, which included participation in the MLS All-Star Game.

4. ChampionsWorld v. United States Soccer Federation, 890 F.Supp.2d 912, 919 (N.D. Ill. 2012).

5. As of this writing, ChampionsWorld's schedules of assets and liabilities can be seen at http://dcjacknut.tripod.com/cwinfo.pdf.

6. ChampionsWorld v. United States Soccer Federation, 726 F.Supp.2d 961, 964 (N.D. Ill. 2010).

7. See U.S. Soccer's categories of membership at http://www.ussoccer .com/about/federation-services/resource-center/membership.aspx.

8. CONCACAF, the continental governing body for North American, Central America, and the Caribbean, charges 2 percent of gross receipts for matches involving two foreign national teams or two foreign clubs teams, and FIFA, the world governing body, charges 2 percent of gross receipts for matches involving any two national teams.

9. See U.S. Soccer's operating procedures for the hosting of international matches and tournament at http://www.ussoccer.com/about/federation -services/international-games/operating-procedures.aspx.

10. ChampionsWorld, 890 F.Supp.2d 912, 921.

11. ChampionsWorld v. United States Soccer Federation, 487 F.Supp.2d 980 (N.D. Ill. 2007).

12. FIFA has two dispute resolution bodies, the Players' Status Committee and the Dispute Resolution Chamber. For their respective jurisdictions and procedures, see FIFA's Rules Governing the Procedures of the Players' Status Committee and the Dispute Resolution Chamber at http://www.fifa.com /mm/document/affederation/administration/50/02/92/drc_rules_efsd_2005 _all_46.pdf.

13. ChampionsWorld, 487 F.Supp.2d 980, 984.

14. Ibid., 985.

15. Ibid., 986.

16. Ibid., 985.

17. Stillitano v. United States Soccer Federation & Federation Internationale de Football Association, CAS 2009/A/1812, at 10.9.

18. ChampionsWorld v. United States Soccer Federation, 726 F.Supp.2d 961 (N.D. Ill. 2010).

19. Ibid., 966.

20. Ibid.

21. 36 U.S.C. § 220501 et seq.

22. ChampionsWorld, 726 F.Supp.2d 961, 966.

23. Ibid. (quoting Behagen v. Amateur Basketball Association, 884 F.2d 524, 529 (10th Cir. 1989)).

24. Ibid., 966.

25. Ibid., 966–967.

26. Ibid., 967.

27. See note 23.

28. 213 F.3d 198 (5th Cir. 2000).

29. 458 F.3d 1224 (11th Cir. 2006).

30. ChampionsWorld, 726 F.Supp.2d 961, 967.

31. Ibid.

32. Ibid.

33. Ibid.

34. Ibid.

35. Ibid.

36. Ibid., 968.

37. Ibid.

38. Ibid., 969.

39. Ibid.

40. Ibid.

41. Ibid.

42. Ibid.

43. Ibid.

44. Ibid.

45. Ibid.

46. Ibid., 970.

47. 15 U.S.C. § 1.

48. 15 U.S.C. § 2.

49. ChampionsWorld, 726 F.Supp.2d 961, 970.

50. Ibid.

51. 18 U.S.C. §§ 1961–1968.

52. Ibid., § 1962(c).

53. Ibid., § 1961(1).

54. ChampionsWorld v. United States Soccer Federation, 890 F.Supp.2d 912, 940 (N.D. Ill. 2012) (quoting ChampionsWorld's complaint).

55. Ibid. (quoting ChampionsWorld's complaint).

56. Ibid. (quoting ChampionsWorld's complaint).

57. ChampionsWorld, 726 F.Supp.2d 961, 972.

58. Ibid.

59. Ibid. (quoting Wooley v. Jackson Hewitt, Inc., 540 F.Supp.2d 964, 978 (N.D. Ill. 2008))

60. Ibid., 972–973.

61. Ibid., 973.

62. Stillitano v. United States Soccer Federation & Federation Internationale de Football Association, CAS 2010/A/2241.

63. ChampionsWorld v. United States Soccer Federation, 890 F.Supp.2d 912 (N.D. Ill. 2012).

64. Ibid., 927.

65. 9 U.S.C. § 201 et seq.

66. Scherk v. Alberto-Culver, 417 U.S. 506, 520 n.15 (1973).

67. 9 U.S.C. § 201 et seq.

68. ChampionsWorld, 890 F.Supp.2d 912, 926.

69. Ibid., 927.

70. Ibid.

71. Ibid.

72. Ibid.

73. Ibid.

74. Ibid.

75. Ibid.

76. Ibid.

77. Ibid.

78. 18 U.S.C. § 1341; 18 U.S.C. § 1343.

79. ChampionsWorld, 890 F.Supp.2d 912, 941 (quoting ChampionsWorld's complaint).

80. Ibid.

81. 18 U.S.C. § 1951(b)(2).

82. ChampionsWorld, 890 F.Supp.2d 912, 942.

83. Ibid.

84. Ibid.

85. Ibid., 943.

86. Ibid.

87. Ibid., 939.

88. Ibid., 940.

89. Ibid.

90. Ibid.

91. Ibid., 943 (quoting ChampionsWorld's complaint).

92. Ibid. (quoting Kinkel v. Cingular Wireless LLC, 223 Ill.2d 1, 306 Ill. Dec. 157, 857 N.E.2d 250, 263 (2006)).

93. Ibid., 944.

94. Ibid. (quoting Melena v. Anheuser-Busch, Inc., 219 Ill.2d 135, 301 Ill. Dec. 440, 847 N.E.2d 99, 109 (2006)).

95. Ibid.

96. Ibid.

97. Ibid., 945.

98. Ibid., 946.

99. See U.S. Soccer's financial statements for the fiscal years ended 31 March 2013 and 2012 at http://www.ussoccer.com/about/federation-services/resource-center/~/media/366651BD70BD435DB86FA7FDA14D49A2.ashx.

CHAPTER 5: *NAMOFF V. D.C. UNITED*

1. Complaint, 5.
2. Ibid.
3. Ibid.
4. Ibid.
5. Ibid.
6. Ibid., 6.
7. Ibid., 7.
8. Ibid.
9. Ibid.
10. Ibid., 9–10.
11. Ibid., 8
12. Ibid.
13. Ibid.
14. Ibid., 9.
15. Ibid., 11.
16. Ibid., 12–13.
17. Ibid., 14.
18. Order denying motion to dismiss, 9 (quoting USA Waste of Maryland, Inc. v. Love, 954 A.2d 1027, 1032 (D.C. 2008)).
19. Ibid.

20. Ibid., 10.

21. Ibid.

22. Ibid., 10–11.

CHAPTER 6: *R V. TERRY*

1. As of this writing, a video of the incident is still available on *The Guardian*'s website, at http://www.theguardian.com/football/video/2011/oct/24 /john-terry-anton-ferdinand-video.

2. In the UK, all criminal cases start in a magistrates' court. A magistrates' court normally handles minor criminal cases and passes more serious criminal cases to the Crown Court.

3. See http://www.judiciary.gov.uk/judgments/r-v-john-terry-judgment/.

4. Ibid., 2.

5. Ibid.

6. Ibid.

7. Ibid.

8. Ibid., 3.

9. Ibid., 5.

10. Ibid.

11. Ibid., 5–6.

12. Ibid., 6.

13. Ibid., 7.

14. Ibid.

15. Ibid.

16. Ibid.

17. Ibid., 4.

18. Ibid., 7–8.

19. Ibid., 8.

20. Ibid., 8–9.

21. Ibid., 6.

22. Ibid., 11.

23. Ibid., 14.

24. Ibid.

25. Ibid.

26. Ibid., 13.

27. Ibid., 14–15.

28. See the FA's Rules and Regulations at http://www.thefa.com/football
-rules-governance.

29. Ruling of the Full Regulatory Commission Following the Substantive
Disciplinary Hearing Held Between 24th and 27th September 2012.

30. Ibid., 9.

31. Ibid., 12.

32. Ibid., 15.

33. Ibid., 22.

34. Ibid., 32.

35. Ibid.

36. Ibid., 33.

37. Ibid.

38. Ibid., 34.

39. Ibid., 35.

40. Ibid.

41. Ibid., 36–37.

42. Ibid., 37.

CHAPTER 7: *HER MAJESTY'S REVENUE AND CUSTOMS V. THE FOOTBALL LEAGUE*

1. The Football League, founded in 1888, is the world's oldest football
league. By 1958, the league had expanded from one division to four nation-
wide divisions, known simply as the First Division, Second Division, Third
Division, and Fourth Division. In 1992, the Football League's First Division
clubs broke away to form the Premier League. Since then, the Football League
has continued to operate the country's second, third, and fourth divisions,
which have been rebranded as the Football League Championship, Football
League One, and Football League Two, respectively.

2. For a list of English football club insolvency events, see the personal
blog of football finance expert Dr. John Beech at http://footballmanagement
.wordpress.com/no-of-clubs/.

3. Stefan Szymanski, "Insolvency and English Football" (2012).

4. A fourth procedure available specifically for eight kinds of operation is
administrative receivership.

5. Formally, the Report of the Review Committee on Insolvency Law and Practice (1982).

6. See http://www.publications.parliament.uk/pa/cm201012/cmselect /cmcumeds/792/792i.pdf.

7. Harvey is now Football League chief executive.

8. [2004] EWHC 1020 (Ch.).

9. For a list of HMRC winding up petitions against football clubs, see Dr. Beech's personal blog at http://footballmanagement.wordpress.com /no-of-clubs/hmrc-winding-up-petions/.

10. See http://www.scribd.com/doc/30282572/Portsmouth-s-Report -to-Creditors.

11. [2010] EWHC 2013 (Ch.).

12. [2011] UKSC 38.

13. [2012] EWHC 1372 (Ch.).

14. Ibid., para. 3.

15. Ibid.

16. Ibid., para. 62.

17. Ibid., para. 54.

18. Ibid.

19. Ibid., para. 55.

20. Ibid.

21. Ibid., para. 110.

22. Ibid., para. 128.

23. Ibid., para. 132.

24. Ibid., para. 126.

25. Ibid., para. 136.

26. Ibid., para. 137.

27. Ibid., para. 138.

28. Ibid., para. 143.

29. Ibid., at para. 148.

30. Ibid., para. 151.

31. Ibid.

32. Ibid.

33. Ibid., para. 153.

34. Ibid., para. 162.

35. Ibid., para. 166.

36. Ibid., para. 176.

37. Ibid., para. 187.

38. Ibid., para. 189.

39. See http://www.publications.parliament.uk/pa/cm201213/cmselect /cmcumeds/509/509.pdf.

CHAPTER 8: *UNION ROYALE BELGE DES SOCIÉTÉS DE FOOTBALL ASSOCIATION AND OTHERS V. BOSMAN*

1. Nationality was defined in relation to whether the player qualified to play for a national team.

2. Case C-415/93 [1995] ECR I-4921.

3. Ibid., para. 60.

4. Ibid.

5. Ibid., para. 61.

6. Ibid., para. 62.

7. Ibid., para. 63.

8. Ibid., para. 65.

9. Lenz opinion, para. 98.

10. Ibid.

11. Ibid., para. 117.

12. Ibid.

13. Ibid.

14. Case 36/74 [1974] ECR 1405.

15. Case 13/76 [1976] ECR 1333.

16. The case concerned two Netherlands nationals, Mr. Bruno Walrave and Mr. Norbert Koch, who were acting as pacers in motor-paced cycling. In that sport, each participant cyclist has a pacer on a motorcycle in whose lee he rides. Among the races in which Mr. Walrave and Mr. Koch took part were the world championships. The Union Cycliste Internationale, the international association for cycling sport, had drawn up rules for those championships, under which from 1973 the pacemaker and the stayer had to be of the same nationality. Mr. Walrave and Mr. Koch considered that those rules were contrary to Community law. They brought an action before a court in Utrecht, which referred several questions to the Court of Justice.

17. At the material time, it was prohibited for foreign players to play in

Italian professional football. Nonetheless, a Mr. Mario Mantero, the chairman of Rovigo Calcio, a small Italian football club, commissioned a Mr. Gaetano Donà to explore football circles abroad to see if players could be found who might be prepared to play for the club. Mr. Donà thereupon put an advertisement in a Belgian sports newspaper. Mr. Mantero refused to reimburse the costs incurred thereby, however, stating that Mr. Donà had acted hastily and referring to the Italian football association's rules preventing the use of foreign players. Mr. Donà therefore brought an action before a court in Rovigo, which then asked the Court of Justice whether the rules on foreign players were compatible with Community law. Several commentators have expressed the suspicion that the main action was an artificial construction whose aim was solely to induce the Court of Justice to give a ruling on the rules on foreign players.

18. As noted by David McArdle in *From Boot Money to* Bosman, Advocate General Lenz was troubled by this exception. In paragraph 139 of his opinion, Lenz stated, "In view in particular of the fact that matches between national teams—as in the football World Cup—nowadays indeed have considerable financial significance, it is hardly still possible to assume that this is not (or not also) economic activity." Yet he was able to avoid the matter: "Since the question is not relevant for the decision in the present case, I need not discuss it further in this context."

19. Lenz opinion, para. 126.

20. Bosman, para. 96.

21. Ibid., para. 100.

22. Ibid., para. 104.

23. Ibid., para. 105.

24. Ibid., para. 106.

25. Ibid., para. 107.

26. Ibid., para. 107–109.

27. Ibid., para. 110.

28. Lenz opinion, para. 135.

29. Bosman, para. 120.

30. Ibid.

31. Ibid., para. 128.

32. Ibid., para. 129.

33. Ibid., para. 130.

34. Ibid., para. 131.

35. Ibid., para. 132.

36. Ibid., para. 133.

37. Ibid., para. 135.

38. Ibid., para. 138.

39. The most recent edition of the FIFA Regulations for the Status and Transfer of Players can be found at http://www.fifa.com/aboutfifa/organisation /footballgovernance/index.html.

CHAPTER 9: *FEYENOORD V. UEFA*

1. The UEFA Cup was rebranded as the UEFA Europa League beginning in the 2009–10 season.

2. The Appeals Body also has jurisdiction to hear particularly urgent cases referred to it directly by the chairman of the Control and Disciplinary Body.

3. CAS 2002/A/423 PSV Eindhoven v. UEFA.

4. Ibid., 10–11.

5. CAS 2007/A/1217 Feyenoord Rotterdam v. UEFA.

6. Ibid., 9.

7. Ibid.

8. Ibid.

9. Ibid., 11.

10. Ibid., 12.

11. Ibid.

12. Ibid.

13. Ibid., 13.

14. Ibid.

15. Ibid.

16. The current and previous versions of the UEFA Disciplinary Regulations are available at http://www.uefa.org/disciplinary/disciplinary-cases /regulations/index.html.

CHAPTER 10: *UEFA AND FIFA V. COMMISSION*

1. For example, in the UK, topflight domestic football disappeared from free-to-air television when the Premier League was formed and its broadcast rights were acquired by pay-TV provider Sky. From the 2015–16 season, UEFA

Champions League and UEFA Europa League football will no longer be available on free-to-air television as the broadcast rights have been acquired by Sky's pay-TV rival BT. The BBC, which is free-to-air, shares rights to the FA Cup with BT.

2. The Audiovisual Media Services Directive defines free-to-air television as "broadcasting on a channel, either public or commercial, of programmes which are accessible to the public without payment in addition to the modes of funding of broadcasting that are widely prevailing in each Member State (such as licence fee and/or the basic tier subscription fee to a cable network)."

3. Directive 89/552/EEC.

4. Directive 97/36/EC.

5. Directive 2007/65/EC.

6. Case T-385/07 FIFA v. European Commission [2011] ECR II-0205.

7. Case T-68/08 FIFA v. European Commission [2011] ECR II-0349.

8. Case T-55/08 UEFA v. European Commission [2011] ECR II-0271.

9. Ibid.

10. Ibid.

11. FIFA, para. 102.

12. UEFA, para. 111.

13. FIFA, para. 69; UEFA, para. 103.

14. FIFA, para. 70; UEFA, para. 103.

15. FIFA, para. 70.

16. FIFA, para. 118.

17. See FIFA, para. 122–130; see UEFA, para. 126–135.

18. Article 56 states: "Within the framework of the provisions set out below, restrictions on freedom to provide services within the Union shall be prohibited in respect of nationals of Member States who are established in a Member State other than that of the person for whom the services are intended."

19. FIFA, para. 148.

20. FIFA, para. 156; UEFA, para. 147.

21. FIFA, para. 158; UEFA, para. 149.

22. FIFA, para. 161; UEFA, para. 152.

23. Article 56 states: "Within the framework of the provisions set out below, restrictions on the freedom of establishment of nationals of a Member State in the territory of another Member State shall be prohibited. Such prohibition shall also apply to restrictions on the setting-up of agencies, branches

or subsidiaries by nationals of any Member State established in the territory of any Member State. Freedom of establishment shall include the right to take up and pursue activities as self-employed persons and to set up and manage undertakings, in particular companies or firms within the meaning of the second paragraph of Article 54, under the conditions laid down for its own nationals by the law of the country where such establishment is effected, subject to the provisions of the Chapter relating to capital."

24. FIFA, para. 152.

25. FIFA, para. 162.

26. FIFA, para. 47; UEFA, para. 51.

27. FIFA, para. 172; UEFA, para. 163.

28. FIFA, para. 173; UEFA, para. 164.

29. FIFA, para. 137.

30. FIFA, para. 146; UEFA, para. 183.

31. The General Court similarly dismissed FIFA's action concerning Belgium's inclusion of all World Cup matches in its list of major events.

INDEX